AF345294

The Canadian Entomologist Volume v.20

THE CANADIAN

ENTOMOLOGIST.

VOLUME XX.

EDITED BY THE

Rev. C. J. S. Bethune, M. A., D. C. L.,

PORT HOPE, ONT.

ASSISTED BY

J. Fletcher, Ottawa; E. B. Reed, J. M. Denton,
and W. E. Saunders, London.

London:

FREE PRESS PRINTING CO.

1888.

LIST OF CONTRIBUTORS TO THIS VOLUME.

ASHMEAD, W. H....................JACKSONVILLE, FLORIDA.
BATES, J. E.......................HAWKINSVILLE, FLORIDA.
BETHUNE, REV. C. J. S. (THE EDITOR)..PORT HOPE.
BEUTENMULLER, W.................NEW YORK.
BREHME, H. H.....................NEWARK, N. J.
CAULFIELD, F. B..................MONTREAL.
CLARK, HOWARD L.................PROVIDENCE, R. I.
COCKERELL, T. D. A... ....WEST CLIFF, COL.
EDWARDS, HENRY............ ...NEW YORK.
EDWARDS, W. H...................COALBURGH, WEST VA.
FLETCHER, J..... ....OTTAWA.
FRENCH, PROF. G. H.............CARBONDALE, ILL.
FYLES, REV. T. W...............SOUTH QUEBEC.
GILLETTE, C. P...................AGRICULTURAL COL., MICH.
GROTE, A. R.....................BREMEN, GERMANY.
HAGEN, DR. H. A................CAMBRIDGE, MASS.
HAMILTON, DR. JOHN.............ALLEGHENY, PA.
HOLLAND, REV. W. J.............PITTSBUGH, PA.
HOWARD, L. O....................WASHINGTON, D. C.
KIRBY, W. F...... ....LONDON, ENGLAND.
LYMAN, H. H.. ....MONTREAL.
MARSH, W. D......................AMHERST COLLEGE, MASS.
MOFFAT, J. A.... ....HAMILTON.
MORTON, MISS E. M...............NEW WINDSOR, N. Y.
PACKARD, PROF. A. S.............PROVIDENCE, R. I.
RILEY, DR. C. V..................WASHINGTON, D. C.
SCUDDER, S. H...................CAMBRIDGE, MASS.
SMITH, J. B......................WASHINGTON, D. C.
VAN DUZEE, E. P....... ....BUFFALO, N. Y.
WEBSTER, F. M...................LAFAYETTE, IND.
WHITE, J.........................EDMONTON.
WILLISTON, PROF. S. W...........NEW HAVEN, CONN.
WRIGHT, W. G....................SAN BERNARDINO, CAL.

The Canadian Entomologist.

VOL. XX. LONDON. JANUARY, 1888. No. 1

DESCRIPTION OF THE PREPARATORY STAGES OF ARGYNNIS ATLANTIS, Edw.

BY W. H. EDWARDS, COALBURGH, W. VA.

EGG.—Conoidal, truncated, higher than broad, the base somewhat rounded ; marked vertically by 14 ribs, one half of which reach the summit, the others nearly as far ; the spaces between the ribs broad, excavated and crossed by ten or twelve fine ridges ; the micropyle at top in centre of a rosette of five minute flat cells ; and about these are successive irregular rings of cells, each larger than the one next within, to the verge of top ; these are six and five sided, and some are sub-triangular, deeply excavated ; color greenish-yellow when first laid, soon turning to brown. In shape, this egg is like that of other species of this genus, but it is characterized by fewer ribs than any with which I am acquainted. Duration of this stage 16 to 18 days.

YOUNG LARVA.—Length .06 inch ; cylindrical, even ; color of dorsum yellow-green, of sides and lower parts more yellow ; marked as in other species of the genus by longitudinal rows of flattened tuberculous brown spots, there being three on either side over spiracles, each of which gives one or two long tapering hairs ; below the spiracles is another row of similar spots, smaller, and on part of the segments broken into four spots, each with its hair ; on dorsum of 2, an oval spot of same character as the others, with a row of hairs in front which are bent forward over the head, and a shorter row behind these ; this oval spot corresponds to the four upper spots of the other segments ; on the side is one spot above and another below spiracle, each with two hairs, and over the foot a smaller one, also with two hairs ; on 3 and 4 each is an additional spot below spiracle, the three, on 2, 3, 4, making a demi-row ; head obovoid, black, shining, with many long hairs. The larva hibernates directly from the egg.

After first moult, in spring Length 11 inch, color brown-green, the spines in number and position as at maturity, and as in the genus, black, as well as the tubercles from which they spring, beset with many short, divergent, black bristles, head obovoid, black, with black hairs Duration of this stage about 10 days

After second moult : Length 16 inch, color gray-black with a green tint over upper side, under side pale green, the spines black, with black bristles all the tubercles pale yellow, head as before, black To next moult about 14 days

After third moult. Length 32 inch, color gray mottled with black, a double dorsal stripe of gray, spines black, the bases of dorsal rows black on dorsal side, but yellow on outer side, of middle and lower rows dull yellow, head as before, but reddish-yellow, the back less red, more yellow. To next moult about 10 days.

After fourth moult Length 5 inch, very much as at last previous stage, the dorsal lines same, spines same. To next moult about 6 days

After fifth moult Length 74 inch, slender, color brown black, with a dorsal band of grayish-brown and not clearly defined markings elsewhere, these markings became distinct as the stage progressed

MATURE LARVA —Length 1 5 inch, slender somewhat thickened in middle, the segments well rounded, on dorsum a broad greenish-yellow band, with a black line through the middle, edged by a little green, a narrow greenish-gray band between the dorsal and middle rows of spines, and a short band between the base of each dorsal spine and the next in advance of the middle row, these gray bands are of irregular width and the edges are whitish, the spaces between the bands brown-black, the sides, from middle row to the outside of lower row, gray with a rust-red tint in the middle of this area. and below to feet a darker, or more brown shade of gray ; the spines are rather slender, swollen next base, above this tapering to a small conical top, from which proceeds a straight bristle, a few bristles about the sides, each from a tubercle, and standing at about 45° with the axis of its spine, the dorsal row are gray, the middle row gray tipped with rust-yellow, the lower row all rust color of deep shade ; feet black, pro-legs gray-brown, head sub-cordate, the vertices rounded, color dull dark brown in front, dull yellow at back, with many short black hairs From fifth moult to pupation 9 days.

Chrysalis.—Length .8 inch ; shaped as in Group 1 of the genus ; head case square, bevelled on either side about equally to the cross ridge ; mesonotum prominent, carinated, followed by a deep and narrow depression ; the wing cases very prominent at outer ends ; abdomen conical, with fine tubercles corresponding to those of the larva ; color mottled dark brown and black ; the wing cases gray-brown.   The only chrysalis I had died before imago.

I have several times in previous years had eggs of *Atlantis*, and the young larvæ from them, but always had the ill luck to lose the latter during the winter.   But, 25th Aug., 1886, I received several eggs from Miss Caroline G. Soule, then at Stowe, Vt., laid 21st and 22nd.   They hatched 3rd Sept., and the larvæ were placed in ice-house, and in October were sent to Clifton Springs, New York, to go in the "Cooler" at the Sanitarium there.   They came back to me 21st March, 1887, most of them alive, and were laid on the tender leaves of a violet plant which had been forced in anticipation of their coming.   One larva passed 1st moult 15th April, others two and three days later.   The first to pass second moult was on 25th April, two passed same 29th.   On 9th May, one passed third moult, the fourth 19th, the fifth 24th, and this larva pupated 3rd June, but died during the pupal stage.   The other larvæ had died off from time to time before 4th moult.   So that I am not able to give the length of the last stage to imago, but it is probably about 20 days, as in the allied species.   The habits of the larvæ in confinement are in all respects like those of *Cybele*.

Atlantis is found over British America from Newfoundland and Anticosti to the Pacific.   In the United States, over the mountainous parts of New England, New York and Michigan.

DESCRIPTION OF THE PREPARATORY STAGES OF ARGYNNIS EDWARDSII, Reakirt.

BY W. H. EDWARDS, COALBURGH, W. VA.

Egg.—Shaped generally like the eggs of this Group, higher than broad, about as 15 to 13, the number of ribs 30, conoidal, truncated, the middle but little narrower than the base, the upper half sloping rapidly, and convex ; about one third the ribs reach the summit, the rest end at fiom one half to two thiids distance from base , the spaces between the ribs excavated roundly, and crossed by many fine ridges , the micropyle in centie of a rosette of fine minute flat cells. outside of which are four irregular rings of excavated cells, geneially long and nairow, varying fiom sub-crescent to five sided , color gieenish-yellow Duiation of this stage 10 to 11 days, in July

YOUNG LARVA —Length o8 inch, cylindrical even, color yellow-green ; marked as in the allied species by flattened, tuberculous, brown spots in longitudinal rows, thiee iows on either side above spiracles , each of which gives one or two long, tapeiing hairs , below the spiiacles anothei row of similar smaller spots , on dorsum of 2 an oval dark patch with a row of hairs in front, tuined forwaid and a shorter row behind, head obovoid bilobed, black, shining, with many long hairs   The larva hibernates fiom the egg

After first moult, in spiing   Length 1 inch , color greenish-brown, mottled, the spines as in the genus in number and position, stout at base, tapeiing to top, with many divergent short biistles , head obovoid, black Duiation of this stage 9 days in April and May

Aftei second moult   Length .18 inch , color gray, a black mid-dorsal line , the spines black , the tubercles at base of doisal spines black, of the middle row yellow-biown, of the lower iow same and more decidedly, head as befoie, black   To next moult 7 days, in May.

After thiid moult   Length 25 inch , color gray and black, either dark gray or whitish. individuals differing , a broad, ciear gray band fills all the space between the two dorsal rows of spines, through which runs a black line, sometimes maculai, oi paitly wanting , the spines as at last previous stage, the yellow at bases daiker, head black over the front, yellowish behind   To next moult 6 days.

Aftei fourth moult   Length 46 inch . color over upper pait black with yellow white and gray bands and stripes , the dorsal band yellow-white, with moie or less of a mid line of black , between the dorsals and middle iow a gray stiipe, and from each dorsal spine a similar stiipe runs to the base of the spine next in advance on middle row ; all the spaces between the band and these stripes black , the sides gray , the lowei row of spines deep yellow at base and half way up, all others yellow at base only, remainder greenish-gray , head as before.   To next moult 7 days.

After fifth moult : Length .9 inch ; color black and gray-yellow, the dorsal band brown-gray.

MATURE LARVA.—Length 1.4 inch ; stout, the segments well rounded ; the pattern of the markings similar to that of *Atlantis;* a broad dorsal band which fills the space between the two dorsal rows of spines, in color a deep yellow, cut throughout by a black line ; between dorsals and middle row a narrow gray band, and a short band of similar color between the base of each dorsal spine and the spine next in advance on the middle row, these bands edged with whitish ; the spaces between brown-black ; below this area the sides to base are gray, mottled, with a shade of reddish-yellow, most decided in the middle part ; feet black, prolegs green-brown ; the spines as in *Atlantis;* of the two upper rows gray-green to base, a little yellow about base of those of middle row, and on 2 and 3 half up stem ; those of lower row also yellow, except the upper half ; the two dorsals on 2 are turned forward, but are not longer than the rest ; head sub-cordate, the vertices rounded ; color dull brown-black in front, dull yellow about top and behind.   From fifth moult to pupation 15 days.

CHRYSALIS.—Length .9 inch ; breadth across mesonotum, .24, across abdomen, .26 inch ; general shape of this Group of the genus, but long and slender ; head case square, bevelled on both sides to a cross ridge, which is a little arched ; the corners rounded ; mesonotum long, moderately prominent at rear and rounded, sloping to the front and rounding down to head case ; carinated, the sides convex ; abdomen conical ; the wing cases prominent ; color in shades of brown, the anterior parts dark and reddish, mottled, on mesonotum, with yellowish ; on the tongue and antennæ cases reddish-yellow streaked and specked with dark brown ; wing cases yellow-brown, with dark streaks along the nervules, and a small spot at end of cell ; the abdomen has on the front of each segment a dark brown band, somewhat broken, and serrated ; the rear part of the segments pale gray, mottled with patches of a darker shade. Duration of this stage 12 days.

This species is found in the Rocky Mountain region from Colorado to Montana, and was taken in Br. America by Captain Geddes, at Blackfoot Reserve (C. E., xv., 222).

SAPERDA FAYI, S CONCOLOR AND APHODIUS RUFIPES

BY JOHN HAMILTON, M D ALLEGHENY, PA

SAPERDA FAYI, Bland —This beautiful Saperda breeds in the small limbs of Crataegus, especially *crus-galli* and *tomentosa*, as first observed by Mr C D. Zimmermann, CAN ENT., 10, 220 ; and should it, like some of its allies, acquire a taste for cultivated fruit trees, it would be a formidable enemy, as is evidenced by the way it depredates on thorn bushes The beetles appear here the last week in May or the first week in June, according to the season, the males preceding the females three or four days They do not appear to eat and are short lived, the whole brood (except stragglers) appearing and disappearing within the space of ten or twelve days, so that should the collector be negligent, or the weather unsuitable for collecting at the time of their appearance, he may get none till the next season As soon as the females appear the males are ready to associate with them, the union lasting three or four hours. They are not much given to flying about, usually ovipositing on the same tree they inhabited as larvæ There may be several thorn trees not far apart, and one will be depredated on year after year till it is nearly destroyed, while the others will remain untouched till colonized apparently by accident The beetles are sluggish, and when approached suddenly fall to the ground and quickly endeavor to conceal themselves, not feigning death, as many insects under the same circumstances do , and when I say feigning death, I mean it literally, in opposition to an unsupported dogmatic statement which I lately saw in print somewhere, "that insects can have no knowledge of death "

Oviposition is effected probably during the night, and the process has not been witnessed, nor the eggs seen. The limbs selected for this purpose vary from one third to one and one fourth inches in diameter, and according to the thickness of the limb, the female with her powerful mandibles makes from three to six longitudinal incisions through the bark, each about three fourths of an inch long and equi-distant and parallel to one another, dividing the circumference into sections nearly equal , an egg is placed in each end of each of these slits, and as soon as hatched the larva makes a burrow beneath the outer layer of wood, perhaps one eighth inch in length at first, and uses this as a retreat whence it issues to feed on the diseased wood caused by the incision. These slits and the irritation produced by so many larvæ at work, cause an increased flow of sap to the part, and a consequent thickening of the sections between the slits, so that the injured part soon assumes a gall-like appearance. On the approach of winter, the larvæ having now attained the length of .25 inch, retire back a little further and close the opening of their burrows with borings. One of the larvæ, however, and in thick limbs two or three at each end bore obliquely till one of them reaches the centre of the limb, up which it proceeds, often two or three inches ; the others parallel this, but keep a wooden partition between the burrows. These larvæ are much larger—often twice the size—of those inhabiting the outer wood, and are the only ones that produce beetles.

The whole of the interior of the limb is now dead wood enclosed by a growth of living but unsound woody tissue, through which some openings remain. The limbs are much weakened at these places, and many of them, like the oak on which *Elaphidion villosum* depredates, would be broken off by the winter storms were the fibre not very tough and the trees very low. And here analogy leads to the conclusion that as the larvæ inhabit the portion of the limb next the tree, equally with that beyond the injured part, this is likely to be the case in the history of the Elaphidion mentioned.

Many of the larvæ in the outside wood perish during the winter, and the survivors, after feeding a while in the spring, likewise die, their mission seeming to have been merely to insure a sufficiency of dead wood to sustain the life of the favored few destined for full development.

In the spring the larvæ in the deep wood return and feed on the dead wood, which is now abundant enough for all their wants, and by autumn they are nearly full grown ; they again retire for the winter, and in the spring, after opening up communication with the outside world, feed for a short time, and when full grown measure in length about three fourths of an inch. The larvæ now return to their burrows for final transformation. Some of them bore for at least six inches, while others scarcely go from the entrance more than twice their own lengths ; the outer ends are closely packed with borings without and soft fibre within, which also fills the inner ends. The head of the larva may be either toward or away from the opening—seemingly a matter of indifference ; in the former case the beetle emerges from the place of entrance, in the latter from a round hole at right angles to the burrow, probably cut by the beetle itself, as no such hole has been detected in the many limbs I have examined containing pupæ with their heads turned from the opening. Pupation occurs after the middle of April, and the perfected beetle will be found in the limbs about the first of May, though few of them emerge till the time stated at the beginning of this paper.

The above is the result of three years careful observation of the habits of this beetle, and imperfect as the history is, the amount of time and labor expended in developing it can only be understood by those who have attempted similar things. How widely this beetle is distributed is uncertain, as till recently its habitat was unknown. The typical insects were taken in Ohio ; it is in Mr. Reinecke's Buffalo Catalogue, and occurs at Hamilton, Ontario (Moffat). Any one can readily ascertain whether it occurs in his fauna by examining the limbs of the Crataegus for the unmistakable swellings it occasions.

SAPERDA CONCOLOR Lec. appears about the same time as *S. Fayi*, and like it, is short lived, few individuals occurring after the middle of June. Its larvæ infest the canes of a small willow growing along water courses and in swampy places—*Salix longifolia*. The smaller canes are usually selected for breeding purposes, these varying from one fourth to three fourths of an inch in diameter. The beetle makes a longitudinal incision through the bark with her jaws about three fourths of an inch in length and in each end deposits an egg. Usually several incisions are made in the same cane some distance apart, which often cause its death the following year. The young larvæ follow the same course as those of *S. Fayi*, only they burrow deeper into the wood, and there are no supernumeraries, as there is no need for them, the wood of the willow dying much more quickly than that of Crataegus, and a warty, gnarly swelling occurring around each incisure.

The beetle, however, does not always select the smaller canes, sometimes choosing ones from one and one half to two inches thick, in which case the larvæ pursue a different course, for instead of boring up and down, they take a transverse direction and girdle the stem one third to one half its circumference, causing a rough annular swelling and frequently the death of the cane. Two years is the time usually required to complete the transformation, but some individuals probably pass through all the stages in a single year. The head of the pupa is toward the opening, from which the perfect insect emerges. The willow named seems to be the natural food-tree of the larvæ of *S. concolor*, and, did it confine itself to this insignificant shrub, could scarcely be classed with injurious insects; but it appears to have likewise either a natural or an acquired taste for poplar, and might become very destructive, a fact first brought to notice in Bul. No. 7, 118, U. S. Ent. Com., where the compiler writes : " Girdling the trunks of sapling poplars, by carrying a mine around the trunk, which causes a swelling often nearly twice the diameter of the tree. We have found numerous saplings of the common poplar in the woods about Providence with the unsightly swellings around the trunk." In case this taste is perpetuated, this beetle will no doubt prove a formidable enemy to this species of shade or forest tree. But in what State this Providence is, or what kind of a tree "common poplar" is, we are not informed. Here the common poplar is the *Liriodendron tulipifera*, but at that Providence it may be a tree of some other genus. This beetle seems to have an extended distribution, occurring in Texas, Michigan, Canada and New York, as well as here.

Aphodius rufipes Linn.—This fine beetle is an interesting addition to our list, and is fully described by Dr. Geo. H. Horn in his exhaustive Monograph of our Aphodiini, just published, Tr. Am. Ent. Soc. Phil., 14, 1. In Europe it is widely distributed, and, though probably indigenous here, as observed by Dr. Horn, has only recently been discovered owing to its inhabiting territory the Coleopterous fauna of which is very imperfectly known. Only three American specimens were known while Dr. Horn was writing the description, two taken at Deer Park, Garret county, Md., and one at St. Vincent's Abbey, Westmoreland county, Pa. Dr. Horn has now two specimens in his collection taken at the latter place, and I have one from Turkey Foot (now Confluence), Somerset Co., Pa., midway between there and Deer Park, which is in the extreme north-west corner of Maryland, the meridian of which to the north passes over a rugged semi-mountainous country; first over the hills bordering the Yonghiogheny thirty miles to Confluence, and thence through the Laurel Ridge Mountains forty miles to St. Vincents. How much further to the north or to the south-west from the points named it extends in a long range of country of the same general character, the future will determine. The two individuals I have examined, on comparison with my European specimens, do not differ perceptibly—a proof of the remarkable stability of species, considering the time that has elapsed since the ancestors of those of the two hemispheres parted company.

A NEW SOUTH AMERICAN GENUS OF CONOPINAE.

BY S. W. WILLISTON, NEW HAVEN, CONN.

Hitherto but a single genus *(Conops)* of this group has received general acceptance among dipterologists. A second genus, *Physocephala*, was based by Schiner on characters in themselves of but little importance, and which I did not deem sufficient to separate our species in the first paper I published * on the North American forms. A further study, however, convinced me that they were sufficiently constant to warrant their use, particularly in connection with other important ones in the neuration, which I pointed out.† I have recently had the opportunity of studying sixteen South American species of the two genera, collected by Mr. Herbert II. Smith, and I am yet more convinced of the validity of *Physocephala* as a genus.

A half dozen genera that Rondani attempted to establish (to say nothing of Lioy's fanciful productions) were based upon such confessedly trivial characters that they have no where commanded any attention by entomologists, save by Rondani's devoted follower, Mr. Bigot, who, in his last paper ‡ on this family, while rejecting *Physocephala*, accepts *Brachyglossum* Rond., based upon the comparative lengths of the proboscis. I do not think Mr. Bigot's views will receive the approbation of many dipterologists.

The only other genus which presents any claims for acceptance is *Pleurocerina* Macq., which I suspect was based upon an accidental malformation, the more so as I have seen several specimens of *Conops* and *Zodion* with a very similar projection of the front, springing from the frontal lunule, and due to some artificial cause. I am not aware that the type species, described from Tasmania, has been recognized since its original description, and I think the genus had better be held in abeyance till specimens are again examined.

The sub-family *Conopinae*, then, consists of two genera, to which I here add the third, distinguished from the closely allied *Conops* by excellent structural characters.

---

* Trans. Conn. Acad., iv., 327.
† Ibid., vi., 388.
‡ Ann. Soc. Ent. Fr., 1887, 31.

TROPIDOMYIA, gen. nov.

Face, in profile, vertical and straight, with a median sharp ridge, on the sides plane or gently concave, wholly without grooves or lateral ridges. In front view, the face shows, below, a sharp triangular notch, rising a little above the lower border of the eyes, from the apex of which the sharp carina runs to the base of the antennæ. Wings narrow ; anterior cross-vein near middle of discal cell, and opposite the termination of the auxiliary vein ; termination of second vein remote from that of the first, the interval as great as that between the terminations of the second and third veins.

The above are the most essential characters, readily distinguishing this genus from *Conops*. Other characters that may or may not be of generic value are the following : Third joint of antennæ very short, scarcely longer than wide, shorter than the first, the latter about one-third or two-fifths the length of the second. Posterior cross-vein straight, and rec-tangular to both the fourth and the fifth veins. Second segment of the abdomen in the male very slender, somewhat broader in front, nearly as long as the three following segments together ; in the female the second segment is cylindrical, but less slender than in the male, only a little longer than the third, the sixth segment as long as the three preceding together, the fifth with a large process below. Proboscis as long as the hind femora. The legs and front, and general structure otherwise, are like those of *Conops*, sens. str. ; the wings with their narrow cells present a very different appearance, however. The carinate, non-grooved structure of the face differs from that of all the other genera of Conopidae save *Stylogaster*, a species of which *(S. stylatus* Fabr., which is distinct from both the North American species) was found in the same region with the present species.

TROPIDOMYIA BIMACULATA, n. sp.

♂, ♀. Face with a silvery, or slightly yellowish, sheen, showing the black ground-color in different reflections ; a slender median black line on the carina. Vertical callosity yellowish red below, obscurely blackish and luteous, save the narrow margins, which are more yellow ; close to the eyes below, a circular opaque black spot. Antennae brownish red, the third joint red ; style short, conical, but little longer than the lateral projection. Thorax opaque black, thinly pollinose on the sides, a slender golden pollinose spot on the inner side of the humeri, humeri and scutellum red, disk of metanotum shining. Abdomen black, the second segment brownish red, sixth segment thickly whitish pollinose, fourth and fifth segments (fifth only in female?) with a narrow yellow hind margin. Legs blackish red, tibiae more red, tarsi black, a silvery spot on the outer distal part of the four anterior tibiae   Wings sub-hyaline, brownish in front, but without a distinct picture   Length 7, 8 mm.

Two males and one female, Chapada (near Cuyaba), Brazil (H H. Smith)   The yellow, intra-humeral spot and posterior abdominal margins appear to be wanting in one of the males.

THREE SPECIES OF MOTHS NEW TO OUR FAUNA.

BY HENRY EDWARDS, NEW YORK

After all, the geographical range of our fauna, as regards the distribution of insects, is but incompletely marked, and the fact that artificial lines cannot limit the habitat of a species is every day made more apparent. The Florida coast is constantly turning up species properly belonging to the fauna of the West Indies. and Texas and Arizona are as often adding Mexican forms to our list   It is, nevertheless, somewhat strange that three such conspicuous species as those hereafter noted should have only recently appeared within our limits. or at least for so long a time have escaped the watchful eyes of our numerous observers.   They may all be cited as examples of the Mexican fauna, though *Pseudosphinx Tetrio* is also found in the W. Indies, and on the continent reaches as far south as the Argentine Confederation   As the insects are probably not known to our local collectors, I have thought it advisable to append descriptions of each.

FAM SPHINGIDÆ.

Pseudosphinx Tetrio, Linn

Whole upper surface light gray, the lines and markings brownish black The basal half line is whitish, with a black dash behind it obliquely Between it and the median line are some waved brownish indistinct streaks, reaching only from the costa to the middle of the wing   There is a very prominently marked discal spot, and a sub-triangular brown patch near the apical third of the costa. Behind this is a whitish cloud, followed by a darker shade which cuts the wing directly across from about 16 mm. from the apex to about the same distance from the internal angle. This darker shade encloses, a little from the apex, a heavy black streak, and some shadings of brown. The lower wings are dusky brown, pale along costa, bluish gray at the anal angle, and there marked by a double dentate streak. Beneath both wings are brownish gray, with a submarginal dentate line, an oblique simple median line, and on the secondaries the same lines continued, the marginal one being more distinctly curved. Abdomen brownish black, the segments edged rather broadly posteriorly with whitish. A rather indistinct dorsal gray line, much widest in the male. The thorax is gray, mottled with brown, and from the middle run towards the junction of the abdomen two black lines forming an acute angle, something as in *Sph. cinerea*. Collar transversely marked with black. The shaft of the antennæ is whitish, the pectination pale brown.

Average exp. wings, male, 115 mm.; female, do., 150 mm.

Described from 6 examples in my collection, from Cuba, Brazil, Mexico and Arizona.

The claim of this species to a place in our fauna rests upon the capture of two specimens, male and female, at Tucson, Arizona, by Mr. W. S. Edwards, and one male found in N. W. Texas, and now in the collection of Prof. O. S. Westcott, Maywood, Illinois.

There is no doubt but that this is the *Sph. Hasdrubal* of Cramer = *Macrosila Hasdrubal* of Walker, and it has been so quoted by Mr. Grote in his admirable paper on Cuban Sphingidæ (Proc. Entom. Soc. Philad., 1865, p. 64), in which notice the full synonymy of the species is given. It would seem, however, that in Clemens' description of *Macrosila Hasdrubal* Cr., in Morris's " Lepidoptera of N. Amer.," p. 185, the allusion to the male must have reference to the dark form described by Butler in " Revision of the Sphingidæ," p. 610, as *Pseudosphinx obscurus*. Poey, in his description, speaking of the male, simply says that " it is smaller than the female, with the black lines more distinct." This is correct, but the under surface is not " ash gray," which I take to be the color of ashes of wood or coal, but brown gray, with the bands of a darker shade. The larva is described by Poey (Cent. Lepidopt.) and a translation or adaptation of his description is given by Clemens, loc. cit. A singular error, however, occurs with reference to the pupa. Prof. Poey is quoted by Dr. Clemens as saying, "the pupa is represented without the detached tongue-case." Now in fact, the pupa has no external tongue-case at all, such as is so noticeable in *Amphonyx Antæus*, *Protoparce Rustica*, in the other species of *Protoparce*, and to a less degree in those of *Diludia*. The pupa of *Pseud. Tetrio*, of which I possess several examples through the kindness of my friend, Wm. Schaus, Esq., jr., is as follows : Pitchy, cylindrical, tapering a little from the junction of the thorax and the head, and more abruptly from the 8th abdominal segment to the tip. It is swollen on the thorax and on the eye cases, while the head is distinctly rounded in front. The covers of the antennæ and the wing bases are slightly marked with transverse corrugations. In the earlier stages of the pupa it has a paler tint, and is marked with some black transverse bands on the upper abdominal segments, which, however, are lost in the ground color as the pupa assumes with age a darker shade. The pupa most nearly resembles that of the genus *Philampelus*. Length 65 mm.; width of head, 11 mm.; width of middle of abdomen, 16 mm.

PHILAMPELUS TYPHON, Klug.

" Cinereous, reddish beneath. Palpi red. Thorax with two dark brown abbreviated stripes. Abdomen with dark brown bands, red on the sides. Anterior wings glaucescent and testaceous mixed, with several blackish-brown sub-trigonate patches. Posterior wings red, with a denticulated band, black, varied with glaucescent, with the exterior margin brown, and the cilia white."—CLEMENS.

This grand insect, of which a specimen taken by the late H. K. Morrison is now in the collection of B. Neumoegen, Esq., is in some respects closely allied to *P. Achemon* Drury, but is larger in size, and altogether richer and darker in color, while the markings are more diffused, and in stronger contrast to the ground color of the wings. A fair figure of it is given in " N. Amer. Lepidoptera," Sphingidæ, pl. 11, by Weidemeyer, Calverley & Edwards, while that by Klug in " Neus Schmett," pl. 3, is remarkable for its accuracy and fidelity to color. Mr. Neumoegen's example was taken in N. E. Arizona.

SYNTOMEIDA EPILAIS, Walk.

Wings, thorax and abdomen bluish black, with a metallic lustre. The primaries have five white spots each, one small at base of costa, one in middle of wing near to basal third, one half way on costa, one smaller a little behind this, which is cut by the nervule, and one behind the cell also cut by the nervule. The secondaries have one rather large white central spot, almost reaching to the costa. The abdomen has two basal spots very clear white, conspicuous, and its sides have also three clear white spots, the middle one the largest. Tip of the abdomen orange-red. At the base of the coxæ are also white spots. Lower side with the markings repeated. Exp. wings, 50 mm.

Taken in Florida by Mr. C. J. Maynard. Coll. Museum Comp. Zoology, Cambridge. A figure of this beautiful species is given by Mr. Butler in Lepid. Heteroc. B. Museum, Pt. 1, plate 8, figure 5. Mr. Butler gives the locality as Honduras.

DESCRIPTION OF TWO LEPIDOPTEROUS LARVÆ.

BY WM. BEUTENMULLER, NEW YORK.

Botis magistralis, Grote.

Head pale brown, smooth, shining ; mouth parts dark brown ; cervical shield brown, divided in the middle by the color of the body, which is translucent greenish-white ; along the dorsal region two rows of shining pale brown piliferous spots, four on each segment, those on the first segment darker in color. All the spots bear a short light brown hair. Thoracic feet, abdominal and anal legs concolorous with the body. Length 30 mm. Lives singly on *Clethra alnifolia*, in a number of leaves fastened together with silken threads. Pupated July 6th. Imagos emerged July 17th and 18th.

Botis erectalis, Gr.

Head small, jet black, shining ; mouth parts whitish. In some individuals of the brood the head is marked with dirty white. First segment dirty white mottled with black. Body above ochreous, with five rows of rather large shining jet black piliferous spots on each side, placed as follows : One row on the dorsal, one on the sub-dorsal, one above, and two below the spiracles, which are black. From all the spots springs a short pale brown hair. Anal plate dirty white, spotted with black. Body beneath sordid white ; on the 4th, 5th, 10th and 11th segments two shining black spots, and two minute ones between. Thoracic feet jet black, mottled with dirty white ; abdominal legs whitish with three minute black spots outside and one inside ; between the thoracic feet are also a few minute black spots.   Length about 23 mm.

Lives socially in a web on Indian hemp *(Apocyum androsæmifolium,* L)   Sept.   Spins a thin cocoon, passing the winter in the larval state, and pupates the following spring

---

DESCRIPTION OF PREPARATORY STAGES OF DATANA MINISTRA, Drury.

BY WM. BEUTENMULLER, NEW YORK.

Egg —Pure white, ovoid, with flattened base, the apex with black dot showing impregnation.   Laid in masses, from 25 to 50 on under side of leaf.

Young Larva —Head black, shining, second segment orange brown in front, cervical shield black   Body color chestnut brown, with the stripes a little darker , anal clasps and thoracic feet jet black.   Length 3 mm.

After First Moult.—The head jet black, as is also the whole of the second segment and anal segment   Body color now much darker, as are also the stripes, these being almost obscured, except along the lateral region   Thoracic feet black   Length 12 mm.

After Second Moult.—Head black, rather small, second segment yellow except the cervical shield, black.   The thoracic feet, abdominal and anal legs, and termination of anal segment, jet black, while the stripes are very clear yellow on the chestnut brown ground.   Scattered over the body are also a few short sordid white hairs   Length 20 mm.

Until after this moult the larvæ feed upon the under side of leaf (parenchyma), and do not attack the edges until after the third moult begins.

After Third Moult —Head jet black, second segment orange, cervical shield black.   Body color reddish-brown with rather broad yellow stripes ; anal clasps, tip of legs and thoracic feet jet black ; under side striped equally with reddish-brown and bright yellow   Length 30 mm

After Fourth Moult.—Head jet black, neck yellow, cervical shield jet black, shining   Body chestnut brown, the stripes bright yellow and equidistant ; the feet and anal clasps jet black, abdominal legs yellow banded with jet black outside.   The hairs over the body are now quite long.   Length 33 mm.

MATURE LARVA.—Head jet black, sometimes chestnut-red, shining. finely punctured, neck bright yellow, cervical shield dull orange.   Body pitchy black with four sulphur-yellow equidistant longitudinal stripes on each side, all being narrower than the intervening spaces, the dorsal space being the widest ; anal plates jet black, roughly punctured.   Under side also pitchy black with three stripes.   Thoracic feet jet black, with their bases yellow ; abdominal legs bright yellow, banded with jet black outside. On the 4th, 5th, 10th and 11th segments two yellow patches. The sordid white hairs are few to each segment, though long and most numerous on the lateral region.   Length 55 mm.

PUPA.—Pitchy black, wing cases brown and very much wrinkled ; head prominent ; segments coarsely punctured about the anterior portion, smooth at the junction ; cremasters very short, four in number ; spiracles ovate, very conspicuous.   Length about 23 mm. ; width of wing cases 7 mm.

FOOD PLANTS.—Linden *(Tilia)*, cherry *(Prunus)*, pear *(Pyrus)*, quince *(Cydonia)*, walnut *(Juglans)*, hickory *(Carya)*, oak *(Quercus)*, chestnut *(Castania)*, beech *(Fagus)*, hazel *(Corylus)*, hornbeam *(Carpinus)*, birch *(Betula)*.   Found from the latter part of July to about the middle of September.   Single brooded.   Subterraneous.

PREPARATORY STAGES OF CATOCALA RELICTA, WALK.

BY HOWARD L. CLARK, PROVIDENCE, R. I.

EGG.—Shape of flattened sphere.   Diameter, 1 mil.   Color, brownish slate.   There are thirty-six vertical ribs, each alternate one only reaching the apex ; and numerous horizontal parallel striations.   The eighteen ribs which reach the apex there unite with the horizontal lines, forming an irregular network.   Duration of this period 241 to 246 days.

YOUNG LARVA.—Length, 7 mil.   Body very slender and geometrid-like, the two anterior pairs of pro-legs rudimentary.   The two posterior pairs fully developed.   Crawl with a very rapid looping movement.   Head ochreous, large and prominent, with minute black piliferous spots. Color of body light translucent green, in some cases inclining to olive.   Five longitudinal lines are faintly indicated in shades of the prevailing color. These markings and the green color becoming more pronounced in the course of a day or two.   Small black tubercles, each with a single black hair, distributed somewhat irregularly over the body.   A dark oval ventral spot on each segment.   Duration of this period five days.

After First Moult.—Length 10 mil.   Form much as before, the head perhaps a trifle less prominent.   Hairs and tubercles the same, and the anterior pro-legs still undeveloped.   Head light straw color, with three or four indistinct wavy brown vertical streaks on each lobe.   Immediately after shedding the skin, the body appears of an uniform light straw color, nearly concolorous with the head, with three narrow brownish

longitudinal lateral lines on each side.   A few hours later, after eating, the dorsum appears darker ; the spaces between the lateral lines light cream color, and the food which has been partaken of shows through in greenish patches in parts of the body.   Ventral spots as before.   Duration of this period seven days.

After Second Moult.—Length 20 mil.   Diameter 2 mil.   Head flat and rather large, of an opaque whitish color, shaded with yellowish.   The lobes are marked vertically with irregular black and brown lines, inter- lacing with horizontal lines to form a vein-like design.   Top of head marked with black.   The body is wrinkled, very slightly constricted at the third segment, is thickest at the ninth, thence diminishing suddenly posteriorly.   A dorsal excrescence indicated on the ninth segment.   Color a uniform greenish cream, with a faint rosy tint at the junctures of the segments, and thickly sprinkled with brownish atoms.   Piliferous spots very minute. The ninth segment presents the appearance of having been stippled with lamp black, and there is a less conspicuous repetition of this marking on the twelfth. Pro-legs greenish, tipped with flesh color, the two anterior pair still abortive Venter greenish with dark oval spots. A sub-stigmatical fringe of fleshy shreds as observed on larvæ of other species. Duration of this period nine days.

After Third Moult.—Length 28 mil. Body shaped and proportioned much as after the last moult. Ground color the same bluish or greenish cream, thickly sprinkled with brown dots. The same excrescence and black markings on the ninth and twelfth segments. The head is shaped as after the last moult, is opaque white with black markings much as before. Between the markings of the face and the gridiron-like marks above, is a clear white space forming a sort of crescent-shaped mark at the apex of either lobe. Piliferous spots brown, minute. Stigmata concolorous ringed with black. Legs more or less green concolorous with venter. Black ventral spots conspicuous. Towards the end of this period the stigmata appear with a black centre, and the crescent-shaped marks assume a pinkish hue. Duration of this period seven days.

After Fourth Moult.—Length 40 mil. Body rather more flattened ventrally ; the hump on the ninth segment is more pronounced and the skin is much wrinkled at the junctures of the segments. The ground color has a more distinctly greenish tinge and the numberless dots with which the body is thickly sprinkled are of a paler yellowish brown. The black markings on the ninth segment extend on to the anterior portion of the fourth pair of pro-legs. The twelfth segment also marked with black as before, and the anal pro-legs streaked with the same. Piliferous spots small and concolorous. Stigmata concolorous, ringed with black. Head very large and prominent, face measuring 4 mil. each way, a trifle broader superiorly. The gridiron markings above are suffused almost to the exclusion of the ground color, and the lateral marblings are heavier black. The mouth parts have a violet tinge. The two anterior pairs of pro-legs still lack their full development. All the legs concolorous with the venter, which is light bluish green. Duration of this period fifteen days or more.

No more moults observed.

Mature Larva.—Length 60 mil. Body same shape as before, thickest from the fifth to the tenth segment inclusive. The black markings on the ninth, tenth and twelfth segments are constant, but in some cases there are slight black stipplings on other parts of the back.   When provided with dried leaves, the larvæ drew them together, forming a very thin cocoon.

CHRYSALIS.—Length 28 mil. ; length of wing cases, 16 mil. ; depth of thorax, 8 mil.   General shape as far as the ends of the wing cases, cylindrical, rounded anteriorly and somewhat constricted dorsally at the juncture of the thorax and abdomen.   Remainder of the pupa conical, the extremity provided with eight hooks, the longest pair curving outwardly, the next longest pair the same, while the two short pairs at the base curve inwardly.   On each of the two segments, posterior to the ends of the wing cases, is a pair of ventral protuberances, which appear to be the rudiments of the posterior pro-legs of the larva.   The stigmata are plainly indicated and the abdomen is provided with a few black hairs.   Immediately after pupation the color is bright green, which, however, soon changes to a purplish brown, dusted with a whitish bloom.   Duration of this period twenty-five days.

It is probable that in their natural state the mature larvæ and pupæ attain somewhat larger proportions than those described above, as the moths which were bred expanded only from 65 to 68 mil., while the parent moth from which the eggs were obtained expanded 80 mil.   On the emergence of the larvæ they were offered leaves of white birch, which, however, they did not take to very readily.   These were afterwards changed for willow, at the suggestion of Prof. G. H. French, to whom the writer is much indebted for his kindly interest and valuable instruction in this department of entomological research.   Upon this food-plant the larvæ appeared to thrive, and some ten examples of the imagines were obtained.

The Society's Collection of Insects sent to the Colonial and Indian Exhibition in London, in 1886, came back in safety, with the exception of two cases, which were somewhat damaged.   We are anxious to replace the following species, specimens of which will be thankfully acknowledged, if sent to MR. E. BAYNES REED, London, Ont. :—*Parnassius smintheus,* var. *Hermodur ; Pieris protodice, oleracea, vernalis, virginiensis, frigida rapæ ; Colias cæsonia, eurytheme, philodice ; Terias lisa, nicippe ; Erebu odora ; Zale horrida ; Homoptera edusa, Saundersii, lunata, calycanthata, albofasciata, lunifera, benesignata, duplicata ; Ypsia undularis.*

The Canadian Entomologist.

VOL. XX.   LONDON, FEBRUARY, 1888.   No. 2

DESCRIPTION OF THE PREPARATORY STAGES OF COLIAS CAESONIA, Stoll.

BY W. H. EDWARDS, COALBURGH, W. VA.

Egg.—Fusiform, thick in middle, tapering to a small rounded summit; marked by about 18 longitudinal ribs, these being low, narrow, the spaces between flat and crossed by many fine ridges. Color yellow-green. Duration of this stage about four days.

Young Larva.—Length .08 inch; cylindrical, thickest anteriorly; on the ridges of the segments many black points, each with a short black hair; among these are black tubercles, some with long hairs, but most with white clubbed appendages, which form three longitudinal rows on either side, one appendage in the row to the segment; these rows are sub-dorsal, upper and lower lateral; color greenish-white, with a tint of brown; head rounded, a little depressed at top; on the face many rounded tubercles, each with depressed black hair; color pale yellow-brown. Duration of this stage four to five days.

After first moult: Length .14 inch; the ridges thickly beset with black points, each with black hair; among these are small tubercles of same color, mostly on middle of each ridge, with longer hairs; along base a yellowish narrow stripe, and over it, on 3 and 4 each, a rounded black process; another larva showed this stripe only near the close of the stage, and had not the black process; color yellow-green; head rounded, nearly same green as the body, the tubercles and hairs more numerous than before. To next moult four to five days.

After second moult: Length .21 inch; color yellow-green, with yellowish basal band; the processes on 3 and 4 as before, shining, black; head yellow-green, more thickly covered with small tubercles, scattered among which are others, larger. To next moult three to four days.

After third moult: Length .32 to .38 inch; color yellow-green, the band greenish-white; the two processes on 3 and 4 present; on dorsum of 2 and following segments are very small black rounded processes in cross line and equi-distant, placed on the second ring of each segment ; these are very variable in number ; one larva had four on 2, and two each on 3 and 4, no others ; another had three on 2, one on one side, two on the other, six on 3, two on 4, and these last were larger than any others ; six seems to be the full number on a segment, and they vary from that to one, present on some segments and lacking on others, with no apparent regularity ; so also the number of lateral processes differs much ; one had these on all segments except 2, 5, 9 and 13 ; as the stage progresses a yellow stain appears in the band on each segment, and at last is often orange-tinted ; head yellow-green, a little lighter than body.   To next moult about four days.

After fourth moult :   Length .6 to .74 inch ; to maturity about three days.   There was much change in the markings at third moult, but still more at fourth.   Some which had been wholly green at this moult discovered cross bands of black and yellow, one or both, and there was much variation in the extent of these bands.

MATURE LARVA.—Length 1.1 to 1.3 inch ; cylindrical, of nearly even thickness from 3 to 11; thickly covered with small black tubercles, each of which gives a short black hair ; color yellow-green, light or dark ; along base a yellow-white band with a dash of orange on each segment, and sometimes the orange is nearly continuous ; over the band on 3 and 4 each a large vitreous black rounded process, from the top of which comes a small hair, and around the base is a ring of black points ; some larvæ have additional processes of same character on the succeeding segments, but there is much variation ; occasionally all are large as on 3, usually they are much smaller ; in one example they diminished regularly from 4 to 12 ; on dorsum of one or many segments are small black processes on the second ridge, varying from six to one, and often wanting ; the same ridge is covered by a black band, sometimes present on every segment, sometimes only on the two or three anterior ones, with broken lines on dorsum or sides of the succeeding ones, frequently however wanting ; in many examples the first ridge of every segment is bright yellow, and the complete series of black and yellow bands is often present ; but others have the yellow bands broken up on middle and last segments, or lack them on these segments ; others have a yellow line instead of band ; and often there is no trace of yellow anywhere ; some larvæ therefore are wholly green, some green with yellow bands, some with black bands and no yellow, but more have both black and yellow, with variation as to extent of either ; the black bands appeared at fourth moult in examples which showed no trace of them in previous stage, and some larvæ wholly green to end of fourth stage, at the moult took on all the bands ; under side, feet and legs pale green ; head round, slightly depressed at top, with many fine black points, each with short, black hair ; color yellow-green· From fourth moult to pupation about six days.

CHRYSALIS.—Length .8 inch ; breadth across mesonotum .18, across abdomen .18 inch ; greatest depth .24 inch : shape of *Eurydice;* compressed laterally, the thorax on ventral side prominent, rising to a narrow ridge ; the abdomen tapering, conical ; the mesonotum low, rounded, with a slight carina, followed by a shallow excavation ; the head case produced to a point, a little curved up, with a regular slope on both dorsal and ventral sides, angular laterally : color bluish-green over whole dorsal side, below, the abdomen yellow-green ; the wing and head cases dusky green, on the under side a brown crescent ; on dorsum two rows of black dots from mesonotum to 12, one to each segment, and a small black spot on either side abdomen ; the whole surface except wings dotted or finely streaked whitish.

Another example gave same dimensions ; the dorsum yellow-green, ventral side of abdomen more yellow ; a brown patch on under side of head case. Duration of this stage seven to ten days.

CAESONIA is a common butterfly in the Mississippi Valley and Gulf States ; also in Southern California and to the Isthmus. I myself have never seen it on the wing, and the above descriptions are drawn from larvæ sent me during the season of 1887, by Mr. R. R. Rowley, of Curryville, western Missouri. The first lot of larvæ were received 2nd August, mostly young, and with them eggs which hatched a day or two after. On 11th Aug , there came about twenty larvæ of all stages to mature. Again, on 26th Aug., came eggs and young larvæ, and more on 8th October. The food plant was Amorpha fruticosa. In California it is Amorpha Californica, and I was able to feed the larvæ from plants of this last growing in my garden. The behavior of the larvæ is in all respects as in *Eurydice, Philodice* and other species of the genus.

A noticeable feature of these larvæ is the variation in markings, described in some degree above, the greatest change occurring at the fourth moult.

Boisduval, in Lep. de l'Amer., gives a Plate of *Caesonia*, with larva and pupa, copied from one of Abbot's unpublished sheets. This larva is roughly done, but shows the phase which has a yellow and a black stripe on each segment. The text says the larva feeds on many kinds of Trifolium and Glycine, and also Tagetes papposa.

In the latter part of the summer and in the fall the females of this species are apt to be more or less suffused with rose-pink on under side of hind wing, and about apex of fore wing, and occasionally the male shows something of this at base of hind wing, and around the margins of both wings. Mr. Rowley writes: "The females with red under the wings do not occur at all in the early summer broods. I took scores of butterflies this season in late April, all through May, June and July, and discovered not a streak on one of them. The first examples with red were taken in August. In September they were more numerous, while nearly every female of late October and November were either heavily streaked or solidly red below. I have yet to see a red under-wing of earlier date than August. The feature is surely a seasonal one."

NOTES ON THE GENUS COLIAS.

BY H. H. LYMAN, M. A., MONTREAL.

The discovery by Mr. W. H. Edwards that *Colias Hagenii* is only a form of *C. Eurytheme*, as detailed in the CANADIAN ENTOMOLOGIST for September, while very interesting in itself, serves also to show that this genus is still in a very unsatisfactory state. That a form which so closely resembles *Philodice* that nine entomologists out of ten would take it for that species, should turn out to be a variety of *Eurytheme*, emphasizes Dr. Hagen's statement "that reliable differences between these two well known forms are still a want." Mr. Edwards has also come to the conclusion that *Hagenii* is the same as the form previously named *C. Eriphyle* by him, as detailed in the November number of the CANADIAN ENTOMOLOGIST. A glance at the history of this form will be found interesting.

In 1873, Mr. G. R. Crotch collected a number of butterflies at Lake Labache, in British Columbia, among which were a number of specimens which Mr. Edwards seems to have regarded as *Colias Philodice*, as mentioned in Trans. Amer. Ent. Soc., v., p. 15. Subsequently on page 202 of the same volume, he described these specimens as a new species under the name of *C. Eriphyle*.

In the same place he said that a Colias similar to this had been taken by Mr. Mead, in Colorado, and by Dr. E. Coues. in Montana, and had been referred to by Mr. Reakirt as *Philodice*, but was, he thought, nearer to *Eriphyle* than to *Philodice*. The question now arises as to how these discoveries affect the standing of other so-called species of Colias, for it would seem that some of these forms are like children's tin soldiers set near together, in which if you knock down one, a whole row is laid low.

In But. N. A., vol I., plate 15, *C. Eurytheme* var. *Keewaydin* is excellently illustrated as a distinct species, as it was then believed to be by a number of eminent entomologists, and one figure—No. 7—depicts a greenish-yellow form with rather pale margins, which is certainly strikingly unlike the ordinary type of *Keewaydin*, but which was believed by Mr. Edwards to be merely a variety of that form. In the text, page 50, it is described as follows :

" Variety A. ♂. Upper side pale yellow with a very slight tinge of orange on disk of primaries : sometimes wholly without orange and then uniform lemon yellow ; the marginal borders also very pale (Fig. 7.) "

On page 51 the following extract from a letter of Mr. Henry Edwards is given : " I may notice that the flight of the new species is much more rapid and varied than that of *Eurytheme* ; * * * that the only variety which appears in the latter is in the case of the albino female, while the male of the new species is constantly subject to run into the lemon yellow variety, which, however, is rarely so well defined as in the specimen I send you." [Figured in plate.]

Subsequently Mr. Edwards ascertained that *Keewaydin* was only a form of *Eurytheme*, as was also *Ariadne*, which had been described as a distinct species in 1870, and he accordingly published in Part vii. of second volume of But. N. A. (pl. 21, pp. 103–116) a very full account of *Eurytheme* and its forms *Keewaydin* and *Ariadne*.

In the course of this most interesting account he said : " It (*Eurytheme*) occupies with *Philodice* the whole of the United States and much of British America, and like that species, which it resembles in every respect but in color, it is subject to great and extreme variation, there being no feature whether of size or ornamentation that is not unstable."

At the close of this notice he said (page 116): " The butterfly figured on Plate of *Keewaydin*, in vol. i., as No. 7, supposed to be a variety of that species, is regarded by Mr. Henry Edwards as distinct, and has recently been described by him as *C. Harfordii*."

C. Harfordii was described from seven males by Mr. Henry Edwards, in 1877, in Proc. Cal. Acad. Nat. Sci., and at the same time *C. Barbara* was described from two females, but subsequently he came to the conclusion that they belonged to the same species, in which opinion Mr. W. H. Edwards acquiesced.   In "Papilio," iii., p. 160 (1883) Mr. W. H. Edwards described *Colias Hagenii*, and said of it that it was close to *Eriphyle* and lay between *Phliodice* and *Eurytheme*, "the four species making a sub-group."

In CAN. ENT., xix., p. 174, Mr. Edwards said :   "*Hagenii* is known to fly throughout the Rocky Mountain region, from Colorado to British America.   *   *   *   and I think it probable the yellow form accompanies the orange over much of the territory occupied by the latter. On the plains to the east of the mountains these would have been regarded as *Philodice* by collectors.   The yellow male figured in' But. N A., vol. i., on plate of *Colias Keewaydin*, fig. 7, is *Hagenii*, a very small example."

Now if this same much abused butterfly, known as fig. 7, is both *Harfordii*, of which, as I have mentioned, *Barbara* is a variety, and also *Hagenii*, and if taken east of the mountains would be regarded as *Philodice*, and that *Hagenii* is *Eurytheme* and also *Eriphyle*, it must follow not only that *Eurytheme, Eriphyle, Hagenii, Harfordii* and *Barbara* are one and the same species, but also that it becomes extremely difficult to separate *Philodice* from the same group.   In connection with this it should be remembered that at least two well marked specimens of *Eurytheme* have been taken in this Province, one, a female, at Quebec, by the late Mr. Bowles, and another, a male, at Montreal, by Mr. C. W. Pearson, and that specimens of *Philodice* slightly suffused with orange do occasionally occur.

I am, however, not prepared to follow Dr. C. V. Riley in his suggestion that these two forms should be united.

The December number of the CANADIAN ENTOMOLOGIST contains another paper by Mr. Edwards announcing a further reduction of species in this genus by the recognition of *C. Edwardsii* as a variety of *C. Alexandra.* This reduction will, I venture to think, be followed by others, which will considerably curtail our list of species in this genus, for in view of all these discoveries it becomes impossible to believe that *Occidentalis, Chrysomelas, Emilia, Interior, Scudderii, Pelidne, Palæno, Chippewa* and *Boothii* are all distinct species.

It would of course be rash to try and indicate in what way the reduction is likely to take place, but I am inclined to believe with Dr. Hagen that *Emilia* will prove to be a variety of *Alexandra*, and that *Chippewa* will be united with *Palæno.*

There are, of course, several well-marked forms other than those above mentioned which will probably maintain their positions as distinct species, as for instance *Meadii*, unless it should prove to be a variety of *Hecla*, as Strecker has suggested ; *Christina*, which I believe to be thoroughly distinct, but I do not think that the name *Astræa* should be retained at all, as I have a ♀ supposed to be that form which I obtained from Mr. Gamble Geddes, whose specimens were determined by Mr. Edwards, and which agrees exactly with what I consider the typical orange female of *Christina; Nastes,* from which *Moina* seems to be distinct, but may probably prove to be a variety, and *Behrii*, which is certainly distinct from any other American species.

Unfortunately some of these species are only found in very remote localities, and it will, I fear, be many a long day before their life histories are worked out, if indeed, of the arctic ones, they ever can be. Let us, however, hope that the enterprising and hardy race which will result from the colonization of our mighty Northwest Territories may produce scientists who will yet push their way into the arctic regions of this continent in their search after knowledge, and succeed in wresting nature's secrets from her.

PREPARATORY STAGES OF CATOCALA DESPERATA, Guen.

BY G. H. FRENCH, CARBONDALE, ILL.

EGGS.—Diameter, .04 of an inch ; low conoidal, the edges of the base rounded ; striated, fifteen of the striæ reaching the micropyle, sixteen more that do not reach the apex, though but few of these are only half length ; shallow transverse striæ.   Color dull brownish olive.   Duration of this period 201 days.

YOUNG LARVA.—Length, .15 inch ; cylindrical, slender, shape like others of the genus, a looper from the abortion of first two pairs of prolegs.   Color of dorsum and head smoky, the head the darkest, pale between the joints ; sides a little paler than the back, with three fine dark red lines.   Towards the last of this stage the color is more of a whitish olivaceous with a slight pinkish tinge, and the head and top of joint 2 brownish.   Duration of this period 10 days.

After 1st moult.—Length, .35 inch ; shape much as before.   Color, purplish black : four white stripes tinged with the ground color, the two upper blending on joint 2, the lower situated below the stigmata ; venter pale with purple black spots in the middle of the joints ; head striped with broken whitish lines ; thoracic feet pale.   Towards the last of this stage the black stripes are separable into a paler center and a darker border line ; the pale a little lilac tinted.   Duration of this period 7 days.

After 2nd moult.—Length, .85 inch.   Colors much as before, four dark and five light stripes, the pale of the dorsum making a pale stripe, each stripe double ; the pale stripes are lilac color, but the two dark stripes on the dorsum have prominent darker patches in the dark bordering lines on the posterior part of joints 4 and 5, and some on the joints back of these, being a spreading of these lines towards the centre of the body, so that between the two there is only a fine lilac line.   Piliferous spots black, but so small as to be scarcely perceptible ; head about as during preceding stage ; venter with a prominent black patch on middle of each joint.   Duration of this period 3 days.

After 3rd moult.—Length, 1.35 inches.   Developing more into the usual Catocala larva shape, slightly flattening and fusiform.   Striped as before, but paler ; ground color, pale lilac ; the bordering lines to the stripes black, broken into dots and short bars, the central part of the stripes mottled with black, the mottling in the dark stripes heavier than in the light stripes, the one on each side near the subdorsal region with the black patches on the posterior part of joints as before, the patch on joint 5 filling the whole stripe, the next a little pale in the centre, those back of joint 6 a little darker than the anterior part of the joint in the same region; between the stripes a pale red line; piliferous spots small, orange; hairs gray. Head dull pale purplish red, marked longitudinally with yellowish white broken stripes, more yellowish towards the mouth. Lateral fringe white, well developed. Legs white, mottled with pale purplish red. Venter white, with large black patches on all the joints. Duration of this period 5 days.

After 4th moult.—Length, 1.60 inches; lateral fringe long, profuse, reaching the ends of the prolegs; head oblique and flattened slightly as in other species. Marked and colored much as before, but more of a pinkish shade. Ground color pale lilac, the stripes as before, even to the arrangement of the black spots on the dark subdorsal stripes; the dark stripes are made dark by mottlings that are mostly black dots, the light stripes are equally mottled, but the mottlings in the centre are dark reddish purple; in the paler edges—being the dividing lines of the preceding stage—is a line of purplish red dots; the dark part of the pale stripes is narrower than the dark stripes, though this dark part and the pale bordering line are altogether wider than the dark stripes. . Joint 9 is not elevated, but is black shaded on posterior part, the shading extending down the sides and into the anterior part of joint 10. Piliferous spots orange, their bases the ground color; those on joints 5 to 13 larger than on joints 2 to 4, each tipped with a short black hair. Head purplish gray, marked with dull white stripes that are made up of dots, some orange spots on the vertex with a black hair in the centre of each, these orange spots in line with the dark subdorsal stripes, the spots contiguous so as to make a short line. Lateral fringe of the same color as the body ground color. Venter white, black patches on all the joints Duration of this period 11 days.

After 5th moult.—Length, 1.90 inches. Color and markings about the same as before, a pale lilac ground color with stripes composed of black dots giving a grey appearance, the ground color of the dark stripes being a little darker than that of the light, the light and dark stripes being now nearly the same color; instead of a black patch in the dark stripe, each side of the dorsal stripe between joints 5 and 6, and 6 and 7, there is a patch of clear pale olive, without black dots ; the dark stripes on posterior part of joint 9 olive tinted, giving the joint a darker shade. Head striped longitudinally with dull lilac and white, the latter broken and irregular : the top has the lilac replaced by black, with the orange dots of the preceding stage present ; a short black stripe on each side from the clypeus. Venter white, the joints bearing legs with black patches tinted with orange, the others with orange patches. Piliferous spots the ground color, but a little rose tinted.

MATURE LARVA.—Length 2.50 inches, width of middle of body .30 inch, of head .20 inch ; depth of middle of body .25 inch, of head .15 inch. Color characters the same as at the beginning of period ; the three anterior ocelli black, the three posterior brown. Duration of this period 15 days.

CHRYSALIS.—Length from .90 to .95 inch ; lateral diameter, through joint 5, .33 to .35 inch ; dorso-ventral diameter, through the same joint, .28 to .30 inch ; the cause of the difference being a lateral expansion of the wing cases ; only a slight dorsal depression on joint 1 (referring of course to the abdominal joints) ; length of tongue and wing cases .60 to .65 inch, both extending to posterior part of joint 5 : from joint 5 taper- ing regularly to the posterior part of the terminal joint, this ending abruptly in the cremaster ; anterior part rounded, this and the tongue and wing cases moderately corrugated or wrinkled ; abdominal joints punc- tured ; the whole covered with a white or glaucous secretion. Duration of this period 28 to 30 days.

In this species, as in most I have bred, the eggs continue to hatch for several days after the first ones emerge from the shell, these later speci- mens being so much later in their pupation and in their other changes, when the hatching is not too long delayed. In some cases these belated examples are weaker than the earlier ones, and either die before reaching maturity, or produce smaller or imperfect imagines. For these reasons I have given the changes and characters of the earlier individuals. I be- lieve, however, that in the woods the delayed hatching produces the late specimens that are to be found in good condition in September and often later.

The eggs from which these observations were made were obtained October 29, 1886, by confining a dilapidated female with hickory bark and leaves, the supposed food plant. They began to hatch April 21, 1887, when the hickory leaves began to expand. This would give the egg period 201 days. They began to spin June 11, giving a larval period of 51 days. With a pupal period of 28 days, we have a period of 79 days from the egg to the imago, or 280 days from the egg to the same. It is evident from my date of obtaining the eggs that they were obtained from one of the latest specimens, and that eggs from one of the earlier moths would add one or two months to the egg period, as there is evidently only one brood in a season of any of our species of Catocalæ.

The food plant, as given before, is hickory. When ready to spin they fastened leaves together in the breeding cage, preferring seemingly the dry leaves under the fresh food. Several spun under a leaf lying on the dirt in the bottom of the box, fastening bits of sand together for the bottom of the cocoon and this to the leaf. These points would seem to imply that they do not spin on the tree, but in the dry leaves under the tree on the ground. This is further corroborated by several years ago finding a chrysalis in leaves on the ground under a hickory tree, that produced *C. Flebilis.* The cocoon, like the other species, is but slight, with the hooks of the cremaster fastened into the posterior end.

DESCRIPTION OF A NEW HEMILEUCA.

BY W. G. WRIGHT, SAN BERNARDINO, CAL.

HEMILEUCA CALIFORNICA, n. s.

Expanse, ♂, 2.40–2.50 ; ♀, 2.85–2.90. Head black. Antennæ, ♂, stem brown, pectinations black ; ♀, wholly brown. Prothorax white. Patagia white in front, overlaying longer hairs of white and black. Thorax black, with tufts of rust-red hairs behind the patagia. Abdomen black, with a few scattered white hairs toward anal end, and with white or sometimes yellow hairs in segmental spots on sides beneath ; ♂ with large anal tuft of rust-red, ♀ without tuft, but tip is hoary with short hairs of sordid white. Legs—femora with long red and black hairs, tibiæ with fewer hairs of white and black. Wings, above and beneath the same ; costa dense black to apex, base dense black, at length becoming thinner, outer margin black and like the intermediate white portion, sub-diaphanous.

When quite fresh the wings are clear white and black, and rather opaque, but with exposure speedily become sordid, yellowish and less opaque Veins all are honey color   Discal spots thin black, touching the costa, but separated from black base, and yet more widely from dark margin, at the cross vein in centre is the lunule, narrow obtusely angled, the angle clean cut and pointing toward the head   Discal spots on secondaries small, black, never with any lunule or central mark whatever Habitat, Southern California.   Types in author's museum.

This species has heretofore been run in with *H Nevadensis*, Stretch, but must be separated because of the red tufts on thorax, the white spots on abdomen beneath, the color of the nervules across the black margin, the angled lunules on primaries and absence of lunules on secondaries, in all of which the differences are persistent and without intergrades.   Indeed, there appears to be as great difference between *H. Californica* and *Nevadensis*, as between *Nevadensis* and the Eastern *Maia*

Notes on the Life History of Hemileuca Californica

This insect is quite local, being found in comparatively few places, but is fairly abundant in such localities as it frequents.   Like many other species of Lepidoptera, it is often abundant one year, and nearly wanting the next.   This present season it has been more scarce than I have ever before found it

It is first seen on the wing in the latter part of October, males and females appearing at about the same time, and it continues about three weeks   The flight is labored and clumsy, so that they often fly against sticks or twigs, yet vigorous and sustained   It flies only in the heat of the day, and by three o'clock, or at the first whiff of cool afternoon air, it hangs up for the night.   The line of flight is undulatory, with a wavy up and down motion, and slow so that it is very easily taken in the net, or it may be often caught in the hands

The insect does not feed at all, nor drink, but spends the whole time of its few days of life in the business of reproduction solely, its large body contains sufficient nutriment to sustain it a sufficient length of time to enable it to fulfil its destiny   They are rather handsome when fresh, but a clumsy flight among weeds and bushes speedily ruins all good looks   The male is gay with his showy red anal tuft, and his deeply pectinated antennæ show off beautifully as he flies slowly past with them gracefully arched in front of him   If caught when fresh, he flaps his wings stiffly together over his back, and curling his anal end round under his thorax like a caterpillar, remains rigid and immovable ; but if he be old and worn, he is likely to struggle continuously for liberty. The female has similar habits.

Copulation takes place as soon as the female emerges, often, and perhaps usually, before her wings are developed sufficiently to enable her to fly. The emergence is from the ground, and as she climbs up some grass stem or weed, shaking out and developing her wings, her presence becomes known to the males, who cluster around, on the wing and on foot, fluttering up blunderingly and with clumsy efforts to touch her with their antennæ. And here occurs a most singular thing. that in many instances, as soon as the male actually touches the female with his antennæ, he becomes alarmed and instantly flies off in precipitate flight, dismayed and demoralized, and does not return. But there are plenty of others left, and they crowd around, and it is not long before the right one arrives and speedily becomes attached, when in a little while all the other males fly away and leave the pair in peace.

The next business for the female is to lay her eggs. She flutters about the willow twigs a few feet above the ground, and selecting a suitable twig a line or two in diameter, catches hold with her claws, and hanging suspended, bends her ovipositor up to the twig and deftly places the eggs in a solid ring all round the twig. She commonly begins to oviposit in the afternoon, and continues hanging in the same place all night, placing eggs occasionally as they mature. When thus engaged in ovipositing, if she be annoyed or roughly interfered with, she flaps her wings violently back like those of a butterfly, and remains sullenly immovable. The males, becoming weary with their heavy flight, frequently stop to rest by hanging on a twig or leaf, looking very much like a female ovipositing. He, also, if picked off in the fingers, suddenly flaps his wings back forcibly, making no effort to escape, except that probably he will exude upon the captor a drop or a fine stream of vile fluid, which seems to be his chief weapon of offence and defence. When at rest, or ovipositing, the wings lie down over the body the same as do the wings of most moths, but when caught they throw the wings back and curl the abdomen around under the thorax, without further effort in self-defence.

The eggs hatch in the spring as soon as the leaves have grown sufficiently to afford them food ; they are gregarious when young, but become solitary toward maturity. They feed chiefly upon white willow, *Salix lasiolepis* and *S. lasiandra,* or the smooth-barked willow, like the Eastern golden willow, and also upon the cottonwood, *Populus Fremonti.* I have also found their eggs upon Artemisia, " Roman wormwood," but I do not think that plant can be a normal food-plant. The larvæ are yellowish, very much like those of *Vanessa Antiopa,* but are larger and lacking the red dorsal tufts of the latter ; are spiny, and apt to be annoying if they fall upon a person's neck as he goes among the trees where they live, wherefore they are locally known as " the poisonous caterpillar." At maturity they come down the stem of the willow, and pupate in the ground or among the rubbish. Such as I have had to pupate in confinement, do so without making any sort of cocoon, but with chrysalis naked, like that of a butterfly.

STRAY NOTES ON MYRMELEONIDÆ, PART 4.

BY DR. H. A. HAGEN, CAMBRIDGE, MASS.

(Continued from vol. xix., page 217.)

Gen. nov., BRACHYNEMURUS.

Tibiæ calcarate ; spurs as long as the two basal joints, or a little shorter ; antennæ longer than head and thorax, stout, cylindrical, a little thicker to tip, which is bluntly pointed, but not clavate : palpi about equal, last joint of labials (except in *B. longipalpis)* with the basal two thirds inflated, fusiform ; abdomen long, slender, about half longer than the wings (male) ; or as long as the wings (female) ; male appendages very short, less than half the length of last segment, stout, cylindrical, very hairy and spinous ; a very small ventral triangular plate below and between them. Female superior parts split, with numerous very strong spines ; a short flat appendage each side of the ventral part. Wings long, bluntly pointed, hind wings narrower ; costal space with two series of areoles, or with one series, and the apical transversals forked.

1. *Brachynemurus longicaudus* Br.

Burm. II., 994, 8 : Ramb., 386, 2. pl. 12. f. 3; Walk., 329, 46; Hag. Syn. N. A., 227. 4.

Body luteo-fuscous, hairy, very slender: head very small; antennæ longer than head and thorax, strong. thicker to tip, brown, somewhat reddish before the apical part ; vertex elevated, with a split in the middle anteriorly, luteous, with a transversal blackish band; another larger transversal blackish band, in which the antennæ are inserted, is notched below ; face luteous, with a faint black longitudinal line.   Palpi short, feeble, pale luteous : maxillary cylindrical, apical joint brown ; labial not longer, paler, last joint fusiform, its basal half brown ; prothorax slender fuscous, variegated with gray, two pale gray spots near the front border, and some laterally ; mesothorax and metathorax fuscous, with yellowish marks ; abdomen very slender, a little less long than twice the length of hind wing. hairy, fuscous. basal half above with a yellowish band, a little enlarged on the articulation, and divided by a median fine black line ; segments 2 to 5 of equal length, 7 a little shorter ; appendages blackish, fuscous, with long black spines and hairs ; compressed, about one fourth the length of the last segment, straight, after the basal half narrowed ; a short triangular yellow plate below ; legs pale, densely sprinkled with black. with long bristles ; tip of tibiæ, third joint of tarsi on tip, fourth joint entirely, and tip of last joint black ; spurs light brown, of the fore legs nearly as long as the two basal joints : wings narrow, hyaline, venation close, two series of areoles in the costal space of front wings ; transversals in the costal space of hind wings furcate in the apical half; veins brown, interrupted with white ; pterostigma small, white ; front wings rarely sprinkled with fuscous, with three obsolete dots along the submediana.   Male.

Length of body, ♂ 38 to 45, ♀ 27 m.m.; expanse al., 44–48 m.m.

Hab. Georgia, Burmeister's type with label in his handwriting, from Savannha, collect. Winthem ; two males from Millin, Scriven Co., Ga., July, 1876, coll. by Morrison ; two males from Florida, Cedar Keys, June 4, and Crescent City, by Hubbard ; one male Amer. merid., out of the late Dr. Schneider's coll. (perhaps this locality is erroneous).

Burmeister, l. c., quotes a female : "Abdomine alis æquali ; fusco hirsutiusculo ; length 25 m.m." When Winthem's collection came in my hands, this female was wanting. Formerly I had this species determined in my publications as *M. abdominalis* Say ; I believe now this species to be different.

Mr Taschenberg (Zeitschr. Giebel vol 52, p 213) describes the types of Burmeister in the Halle Museum of *M irroratus*, from S Carolina, Zimmermann   The two females belong evidently to *M longicaudus* Though I have no female of this species before me, the identity is proved by Taschenberg's description and by the mention of the three obsolete dots along the submediana of the front wings   There can be no doubt that these females are the types of *M irroratus*, as in the Halle coll, and in Burm. Hdl, No 11 but I repeat that the male described by me has on the pin the label "*irroratus* Burm" in his handwriting   As the name *irroratus* is pre-occupied, no change is needed

2. *Brachynemurus nebulosus* Ramb

Myrmeleon nebulosus Ramb, 387 4, Walk, 330, 48

Very slender, villous, head small, blackish, face dull yellowish, with a fine transversal line before labrum and a longitudinal line, black, below the antennæ an incurvate black line, vertex elevated, not cut sharply in front, more rounded, grayish-fuscous, as well as the occiput, with some blackish not well defined spots; antennæ as long as head and thorax, strong, cylindrical rather enlarged to tips, rufo-fuscous, articulations faint yellowish palpi dull yellowish, the labials about as long as the maxillary, last joint longer, cylindrical, its basal half a little thicker and darker, Prothorax narrow, blackish, with three ill defined yellowish bands, beginning on the front margin, the median very short, split, the two others running together before the wings, meso- and meta-thorax blackish each above with a yellow geminate spot and some marks near the wings, on each side above the legs some yellow stripes. Abdomen of the male very slender much longer than the wings, villous, blackish, basal half above with a pale longitudinal band, interrupted on tip of segments apical half black with a pale basal dot, and sometimes another one in the middle, appendages about half the length of last segment, with long black hairs, compressed the base enlarged to reach the dorsum, below and between them a very short and small triangular whitish plate. Abdomen of the female as long as the wings, compressed on the more enlarged apical third, colored as the male, genital parts in the last segment above yellow, split, surrounded with strong black bristles, below two short thick black appendages   Legs short, pale yellow, much sprinkled with black, with white and black hairs, tip of tibiæ and of all joints of tarsi (the fourth entirely) black, spurs brown, as long as the two basal joints claws brown, as long as the spurs.   Wings narrow, with fringes on hind margin, which is very little emarginate before tip ; hyaline ; venation pale interrupted with brown ; base of numerous forks and around many transversals brown ; front wings with many large rusty-brown round spots along the mediana and submediana ; apical half of costal space with two series of areoles ; hind wings similarly spotted, but without the large rusty-brown spots.

Length of body, male, 38 to 45 m.m.; female, 28 to 31 m.m.; exp. al., 40 to 50 m.m.

Habit., Millin, Scriven Co., Georgia ; July, Morrison.   I have before me two males and three females ; it is a very pretty species and doubtless Rambur's *M. nebulosus.*

I had accepted this species to be *M. contaminatus* Burm.. which is, with a short diagnose, only mentioned by his *M. irroratus.*   Mr. Taschenberg describes a female, which is not labeled, out of Burmeister's collection.   This female belongs doubtless to *M. conspersa* Rbr.; he calls the spurs of the anterior legs shorter than the first joint of tarsi, but these are probably spines.   If this is really the type of Burmeister, and I have no doubt of it, the name has to be dropped, as it belongs to *M. conspersa.*

3.   *Brachynemurus versutus* Walk.

Myrmeleon versutus Walk., 331, 51 ; Hag. Syn. Neur. N. Amer., p. 238, No. 8.

Black, very slender, faintly villous ; head narrow ; front shining, yellow, above a broad black band, notched in middle below, narrowly yellow around the eyes and around the base of antennæ ; a black longitudinal line from the middle of the notch to the epistom, where it is enlarged and united with a larger transversal black band (which is sometimes divided into four spots) on the epistom ; labrum black shining with yellow side-margins ; vertex elevated, rounded, black, with a transversal yellow band, interrupted in middle, and a posterior one, representing a larger yellow spot on each side, and a smaller middle one, a little before them ; antennæ of male much longer than head and thorax, about 10 m.m.; of female shorter, about as long as head and thorax, 7 m.m. ; long, filiform, a little thicker to the tip, bluntly pointed ; those of female a little more enlarged on tip ; blackish-brown, the two basal joints shining black ; palpi yellow, apical joint of the maxillary black shining, and the two foregoing black externally , labials scarcely longer, last joint shining black, except at extreme base, long, a little inflated, but the apical half thinner. Prothorax yellow, as broad as long, a little narrower in front, with two broad black stripes, each of which includes a yellow dot in front, and another behind them , meso- and meta-thorax yellow with two interrupted black longitudinal bands and some spots , sides below the wings black with yellow stripes and dots   Abdomen of male very slender, much longer than wings, 40 m m , blackish-brown, shortly villous, three basal segments dull yellowish above, with a fine dorsal median black line, the other segments black, with a fine yellow dorsal line ; appendages testaceous, more yellowish at base and tip, with long black hairs and bristles, long, but shorter than the segment before last, straight ; between them below a very short triangular yellow plate ; abdomen of female as long as wings. stouter, enlarged and compressed to the tip , same coloration, genitals yellow , upper part inflated, with many strong black spines , below two very short cylindrical yellow appendages   Legs yellow, largely sprinkled with black, with numerous hairs , tip of tibiæ and of all joints of tarsi black , spurs brown, as long as the two basal joints , claws brown   Wings hyaline, thickly and almost equally covered with small brown dots, which are all at the base of the small forks. and on base and tip of the transversals , veins brown interrupted with white , pterostigma larger, bright yellow , apical half of costal space with forked veins , wings around and on the veins hairy

Length of body, male, 42 to 46 m m , female, 28 m m , exp al , 55 to 60 m m .

Hab , San Luis, Mexico , September and October, Dr Palmer , three males and six females.   I think there is no doubt that this is the species described by Walker after one male

NOTE ON LATE PAPERS ON THE NOCTUIDÆ

BY A R. GROTE, A. M.

My last paper in the Proceedings of the Am. Philosophical Society, Philadelphia, contains a number of typographical errors, the most serious of which I corrected subsequently by an " errata ' in a later volume, not being able to see the proofs. This paper reviewed the main and first two groups, leaving the Fasciatæ *(Catocalinæ* Pack.) and the Deltoids unrevised. I would recognise five very unequal groups both in structural value and extent. Adopting Packard's nomenclature so far as he went (this author excluded the Deltoids at the time), we may call these groups subfamilies, but in Europe my *Thyatiridæ* and the *Brephidæ* are taken out of the *Noctuidæ* as distinct families. We have thus the following classification, which can only be changed by throwing all five together as subfamilies, which does not alter the matter in reality. The larvæ of the *Thyatiridæ* are, however, almost Notodontiform.

> (1). Family THYATIRIDÆ.
> (2). Family NOCTUIDÆ.
>   (a) Sub-family *Noctuinæ.*
>   (b) Sub-family *Catocalinæ.*
>   (c) Sub-family *Deltoidinæ.*
> (3). Family BREPHIDÆ.

The groups I have recognised and named may be regarded as tribal with the ending *ini,* as *Hadenini, Orthosiini, Heliothini, Stiriini, Scolecocampini,* etc. The Deltoids contain two such tribes, viz , *Herminiini* and *Hypenini.* My object has been to bring the classificatory terms to correspond with those in Coleoptera as used by Leconte.

In my last descriptional paper in CAN. ENT., the genus and species (8) *Phiprosopus callitrichoides,* is omitted accidentally on page 132, vol. xv. My work is now to bring our genera into closer agreement with European genera by comparison of types, as I say on page 131 of the same volume, to which I direct the attention of students.

CORRESPONDENCE.

CALLIMORPHA.

Dear Sir : I am sure that Mr. Lyman's article on Callimorpha, with its excellent plate, has given an impetus to the study of this genus. It will be no question with the Derivatists that these forms are all descended from a single species. The test by breeding from the egg must now decide whether these forms have each an independent cycle of its own or are interdependent still. The test for *species* remains to be applied to them. As yet we can only compliment Mr. Lyman's tact in sorting the moths. I had the opportunity of examining a lot of *Clymene*, taken in the vicinity of Buffalo, and I came to the conclusion that it was possible that the yellow and white forms are yet interchangeable. All the white forms show traces of yellow on costa or body parts. I also possessed an example of var. *albanchora* m. (corresponding to Lyman's fig. 5), which very nearly resembled *interrupto-marginata* as to the brown markings, but on a white ground. I believe it is Dr. Packard who first drew attention to the interesting fact that our Callimorphas are buff and white, corresponding to the prevailing colors of our *Arctiinæ*, whereas the European species is gaudily tinted, agreeing with the brighter European representation of the sub-family of which it is a member. Like *Datana* and *Hemileuca*, *Callimorpha* is an example of a generic group in which the species or forms are more nearly related than usual, and is thus one of those assemblages which I have called *Progeneric.*

A. R. GROTE.

NOTES.

MR. ALFRED WAILLY, Tudor Villa, Norbiton, Surrey, England, is anxious to obtain specimens of the wild Silk-worms of all parts of the world for exhibition in the Department of Sericulture at the Paris International Exhibition of 1889. In order to make the exhibition as complete as possible, he wishes to obtain specimens of live cocoons, in large quantities or small, with names of food-plants for each species, whenever possible, and also specimens of the moths; any specimens sent will be purchased or exchanged, as desired. Small samples (in strong tin or wooden boxes) of live cocoons and specimens of moths, can now be very rapidly and safely sent by Sample or Parcels Post; to avoid the risk of emergence during transit, cocoons should be sent before the end of March. The production of mulberry silk has been so deficient of late years, it is most important that efforts should be made to utilise as many as possible of the wild Silkworms, many of which produce silk of great strength and beauty.

PROFESSOR SAMUEL PIERPONT LANGLEY, LL. D., has been appointed Secretary of the Smithsonian Institution at Washington, to succeed the late Professor Spencer F. Baird.

CHANGE OF ADDRESS.—Mr. C. H. T. Townsend, from Constantine, Mich., to War Department, Adjutant General's Office, Washington, D. C.

The Canadian Entomologist.

VOL. XX.   LONDON, MARCH, 1888.   No. 3

DESCRIPTION OF THE PREPARATORY STAGES OF PAPHIA TROGLODYTA, Fabr. (GLYCERIUM, Edw., But. N. A., Vol. 1, Pl. 46; ANDRIA, Scud.)

BY W. H. EDWARDS, COALBURGH, WEST VA.

Egg.—Nearly spherical, a little higher than broad, somewhat flattened at base and slightly depressed at top; surface smooth; crossed near the top—at about one fifth distance from top to base—by two to four parallel rows of raised points, about 22 in the full circle; these seem to be placed in vertical lines; in some examples the rows are nearer together than in others, and there is often irregularity in the number or position of the points, some of the series wanting, or misplaced, in this last case lying between the rows. Color pale green. Duration of this stage four to five days.

Young Larva.—Length, at 12 hours from egg, .09 inch; cylindrical, tapering from 2 to 13 on dorsum and sides, the end of 13 rounded; color brown-green; the cross-ridges on each segment studded with small white rounded tubercles, from the top of each coming a short, fine, white hair; there are also four rows on either side of large white tubercles, one to the segment, three above spiracles, a sub-dorsal, mid-lateral, lower lateral, and one below spiracles; each with a short stiff hair; each of the basal row has a half circle of small tubercles, but larger than those over dorsum on its lower side; under side, feet and legs nearly as above, a shade more green; segments 5, 6, 11, 12 are crossed by two or three rows of tubercles; head a little broader than 2, rounded at top, the outline that of a horse-shoe, the front somewhat flattened; color yellowish; across the forehead a broad stripe of brown, within which are two little patches of the yellow ground, one on each lobe, and the stripe bends at right angle and narrowing passes down each cheek; in a curve about the top in front six small tubercles, and near the suture two others which with the second and fifth of the curved row make a cross row of four. Duration of this stage three to five days.

After First Moult.—Length at 12 hours .18 inch ; shape as before ; color gray-green, the dorsum of 12, 13 discolored brown or blackish, and a sub-dorsal patch of same hue on 8 and 10 ; thickly covered with fine tubercles as at first stage ; the rows of larger tubercles as before, ivory white, bell-shaped, the hair or process from top brown or black ; the basal tubercles large, each with its crescent of smaller ones on lower side ; head higher than broad. narrowing at upper part, depressed at suture ; color of the upper front greenish, over mandibles yellow-white, at the back gray-green ; on each vertex a low duplex black process, the outer part larger and higher than the other, each with a black short bristle at top ; at back, on either side the suture, a duplex small yellow process and others down the side of face at back ; over the front minute tubercles as at first stage, and in addition three large conical white tubercles on either lobe, each three in triangle with base above, so arranged that four tubercles cross the forehead in line. To next moult four to five days.

After Second Moult.—Length at 12 hours .25 inch ; shape as before ; tuberculated as before ; color gray-brown, discolored on posterior segments as before ; head shaped as before ; the processes on vertex larger, triplex, shining black, two being in line across front, the outer one larger, the third lying behind and between the others ; the back and the front face armed as before. To next moult five days.

After Third Moult.—Length at 24 hours .34 inch ; shape, armature and color as before ; there is much variation in the extent of the black ; on one example 6 and 11 were quite black dorsally, on sides of 8, 9, 10 black patches, on sides of 3, 4, 5 paler black ; another was pale black on 12, 13, a very little of same on 5 and 6, and the sides of 8, 9, 10 pale black ; head as at last previous stage, the front greenish-black, the vertex processes black : of the four cones across front the outside ones were black, the others white, with brown rings at base. To next moult four and five days.

After Fourth Moult.—Length at 24 hours .7 inch ; after five days was fully grown.

Mature Larva.—Length 1.3 inch ; stout anteriorly, thickest at 3, 4, tapering on dorsum and sides to 13; the end of 13 rounded and the dorsum much curved ; color gray-green, segment 2 darker green ; usually marked by patches of black on dorsum or sides of segments after 6, but some examples have little, or it is pale colored, and others have none at all ; entire upper surface studded with low rounded tubercles varying in size, but always small, placed on the cross-ridges ; these are whiter than the ground color and from each proceeds a very short, straight white hair ; under side, feet and legs a shade lighter than the upper, 5, 6, 11, 12 crossed by tubercles ; head sub-ovate, depressed at top, the height to the breadth as 8 to 7 ; color gray-green, thickly covered with tubercles like those on body, small and large ; among these are larger ones, three on either lobe in triangle, so disposed as to make a row of four across forehead ; these are white, with a brown rim about base, or the inner pair are white, the others black ; on each vertex a triplex process as described at fourth stage, black ; along the back and sides white processes, of which a duplex or bifid one, taller than elsewhere, stands on either side suture ; ocelli black. From fourth moult to pupation ten days. Mr. French, But. East. U. S., p. 228, gives the length of mature larva as 1.55 inch, and probably wild examples are larger than my bred ones.

CHRYSALIS.—Length .65 inch ; breadth across mesonotum .38 inch, across abdomen .4 inch ; shape much as in Danais *Archippus*, the last segments retracted in same way, so that the abdomen is greatly shortened, and the shape that of a dome ; the head case short, narrow at top and bevelled to a sharp, slightly incurved ridge ; the sides sloping ; mesonotum prominent, carinated, rising posteriorly to a rounded point, the slope to top of head regular, and at about 45° ; the depression behind shallow and broad ; the dorsal edges of wing cases prominent, the sides excavated ; color light green granulated with whitish ; the edges of wing cases and top of head case whitish. Duration of this stage nine to twelve days.

Some stages of the larva of this species were figured in Butterflies of N. A., vol. 1, 1871, under the name of *Glycerium*. The drawings were made expressly for me by the late Dr. H. K. Hayhurst, then at Sedalia, Mo. They are before me as I write. The same drawings were used by Prof. Riley, before my Plate appeared, in his paper on *P. Glycerium*, Second Ent. Report, Mo., 1870, and his wood cuts were reproduced in Prof. French's Butterflies of the Eastern U. S., p. 228, 1886. These are the only published illustrations of the life history of any species of Paphia so far as I know, and whatever defects there may be in the figures of the larvæ are common to all three of the works mentioned. The principal figure is that of the mature larva, and in But. N. A. a fair general view of the stage is given. But the peculiar armature of the body and head is not represented, and therefore this figure has very little value. Another figure shows the beginning of the case, and a third the completed case, and this last is best of the three   The pupa is better than the larva, but does not give the pretty green hue of nature.   I intend to give a more satisfactory Plate of all the stages in Vol. 3

By the kind aid of Prof Rowley, of Curryville, Mo , I was able to follow the history from the egg, in 1887   Mr Rowley not only sent eggs at different times, beginning with 15th May, and larvæ of all stages of growth and pupæ so late as August 1, but kept me supplied with the food plant, Croton capitatum   The eggs are laid on Croton monanthygnum also, and these are the only plants known to Mr Rowley   They are laid usually singly on the under side of the leaf   The young larva, soon after emerging constructs for itself a perch on which it rests, after the manner of a Limenitis   It is at the tip of the leaf, made by eating away alongside the mid-rib, and using this rib as the base, covering with silk and lengthening by chewed bits of leaf bound and held by the silk   One perch in first stage measured .28 in length, and on it the larva rested with the anterior segments arched, only the pro-legs furnishing the support   But if there be two larvæ on one leaf, the second perch may be made anywhere at the side   After the first moult the perch was lengthened and made heavier by binding it with larger pellets, so that it looked like a string of knobs, and the greatest length I observed was 4 inch   The young larva bears much resemblance in body and head to young *Limenitis Disippus* but is more like that larva at second stage than the first, and the head with its many tubercles and processes on vertices and at back still more resembles either second or third stage of *Disippus* than the first

After the second moult, the perch is deserted, and a case is made by covering the upper surface of the leaf with silk, and bringing the edges together   The larva lies at first quite concealed, and eats the base of the leaf   Here the next moult takes place, and the larva then builds a new case, and goes outside to feed, after the habit of the nearly mature *Papilio Troilus*   By the time the fourth moult approaches, the larva is as long as the case, and the head will be exposed at one end and tail at the other, the rounded case being a pretty good fit, rather loose   When in suspension, the attitude is almost circular, and both ends meet and touch   The pupa is often found, Mr Rowley tells me, attached to a branch of the food plant   There are at least two broods of the imago, and it is the latter which hibernates. Mr. Rowley calls my attention to a decided seasonal dimorphism in the two broods of the females.

Prof. French gives the localities as the Western States, from Illinois and Nebraska to Texas, the presence of the butterfly no doubt being determined by the presence of the food plant.

SOME OBSERVATIONS MADE IN 1887 ON DANAIS ARCHIPPUS, Fabr.

BY WM. D. MARSH, AMHERST COLLEGE, MASS.

Mr. Scudder, in his " Butterflies," p. 136, says of this species : " It is the longest lived of our butterflies. It leaves its winter quarters later in the season than other hibernating butterflies, and continues upon the wing until July and August, laying eggs all the time, so that the insect may be found in all its earlier stages most of the summer. . . . . Whether or not there is a second brood in New England is doubtful ; but the earliest butterflies which have not hibernated may be found in July, so that while the earlier stages are passed rapidly, the perfect insect often lives a full year, mingling on the wing with its own progeny, and witnessing the decay and renewed growth of the plant which nourished it : for the milk-weed dies early, and is not sufficiently grown to support the caterpillars when the first butterflies appear in the spring."

I understand that Mr. Scudder still holds substantially these views of the habits of *Archippus* in New England, and at any rate has published nothing to the contrary.

Early in the summer of 1887, Mr. W. H. Edwards wrote me with the request that I would make a study of *Archippus*. As my college term did not close till June 25th, all my observations before that date were made at Amherst ; from June 25th to August 12th, at Randolph, Vt., a hill-town, 37 miles N. W. from White River Junction.

1. Hibernated *Archippus* were observed at Amherst, May 15 and May 21, and recognised as such by their faded and ragged condition. I searched for eggs, but found none. I may say here that at no time after

this, either in Mass. or Vt., did I see an imago that could have been a hibernator.

2. A fresh ♀ was taken at Randolph, July 4th, and another perfectly fresh was seen the same day. This would be the first generation in descent from the hibernator. On 20th July, a larva two thirds grown was taken, raised to pupa, and sent to Mr. Edwards, Aug. 1st. On August 11th, 2 ♂ 1 ♀, perfectly fresh, were taken, plainly of same generation as was the larva of July 20—the pupal period being then but 9 or 10 days. These imagos were in the second generation from the hibernators.

3. On 5th Aug., found a fresh egg at Amherst, where the season would be a week or ten days in advance of Randolph ; on 17th and 18th

Aug., two larvæ, evidently by their size of the same generation as the egg of 5th. Continued to find larvæ all through September, the last one on 30th, in all 34 larvæ.

4. From 30th Sept. to 15th Oct., butterflies from pupæ bred from said larvæ emerge. And besides, many pupæ were found in the fields, and the imagos came from them. These butterflies were then the third generation from the hibernators, and individuals were seen on the wing into November. Giving the above facts in a table, thus :

1. May 15th, hibernating female seen, Amherst.
2. July 1st to 7th, imagos of 1st brood from hibernator, Randolph.
3. Aug. 11th to 19th,   "   2nd   "   "   "   Amherst.
4. Oct. 1st to Nov. 4th, "   3rd   "   "   "   Amherst.

I communicated these facts to Mr. Edwards as they were noticed. I cannot see wherein the behavior of *Archippus* is different from that of any other hibernating butterfly.   Nor have I found any evidence of exceptionally long life, or of the old hibernating females being about all summer, laying eggs with their progeny.   And of course they do not witness the decay of the food plant, for the milk-weed does not die early, but lasts till frost in October, and will stand pretty severe frost.   On 28th Sept., I wrote Mr. Edwards : "We have had two pretty heavy frosts within a week, but the *Archippus* larvæ and more than half the milk-weeds are fresh and vigorous."   On 30th Sept., I wrote.: "Found the 34th larva this morning.   Frosts have not been severe enough to kill larvæ.   Most of the 34 have been on young milk-weeds, after the first mowing.   Now the fields have been mowed the second time, and this explains why the late brood of the larva and imago may be scarce in some parts of N. England."

On 26th Oct., I wrote : "I now have four pupæ, of which one should give imago to-morrow, and three will wait a week.   The pupal period in October, the pupæ being kept in a cool room, is about three weeks.   In September, it was of about 15 days duration.   Larvæ taken 2nd Sept., pupated 9th to 12th Sept., and the imagos came out 25th to 30th Sept."

I wrote 29th Oct. : "The one pupa has given imago."   On 4th Nov., I wrote : "Another imago out this morning, a fine female.   I have two pupæ left, and send you them by this mail."

It is plain to be seen why imagos are rare in the fall, and therefore more rare in spring, for there must be more or less loss of them in the winter.   In New England quite generally the fields are mowed the second time, and that very late.   Thus, while on Sept. 9th were taken nine larvæ in a field near my house from a group of milk-weeds, before larvæ of the same generation could have completed their stages, all the food plants were cut down.   So myriads of larvæ must be annually destroyed in New England.

I saw wild *Archippus* flying on the 5th of Oct., again on 13th, in both cases after some frosts, as I have before mentioned. Of course these late flying ones are the hibernators, and liable to be caught any day at that season by cold that would compel them to seek hiding places or else become torpid out of doors.

DESCRIPTIONS OF SOME NEW GENERA AND SPECIES OF CANADIAN PROCTOTRUPIDÆ.

BY WM. H. ASHMEAD, JACKSONVILLE, FLORIDA.

The following paper is devoted to the description of new genera and species of parasitic Hymenoptera belonging to the family Proctotrupidæ, collected at Ottawa, Canada, by my esteemed friend, Mr. W. Hague Harrington, to whose liberality I am deeply indebted for sending me these and many other interesting forms in this family now in my collection.

Sub-family CERAPHRONINÆ.

The following table will be found useful to separate some forms closely allied to the genus *Megaspilus* Westwood.

    Eyes hairy.
    Metathorax spined . . . .*Megaspilodes* Ashm.
    Metathorax not spined.
    Wingless, or with rudimentary wings. 2
    Winged ; a large semi-circular stigma and a stigmal vein.
    Mesothorax with three grooves ; ♂ antennæ filiform, ♀ flagel-
         late. . . . .*Megaspilus* Westw.
2. ♀ antennæ sub-clavate ; ♂ unknown. . . . .*Eumegaspilus*, n. g.
    Mesothorax with only a median groove. . . . . *Megaspilidea*, n. g.
             Megaspilodes Ashm.

The writer has recently characterized this genus elsewhere. It is at once distinguished from *Megaspilus* Westw. by having a blunt spine, or a bi-forked spine, in the middle of the metathorax. Two species pertain to it, viz., *Megaspilodes armatus* Say, and *M. fuscipennis* Ashm.

Megaspilus Westwood.

(1) *Megaspilus Harringtoni*, n. sp.

Male and female. Length .07 to .10 inch. Black ; head and thorax finely reticulately sculptured ; abdomen polished black. Antennæ 11-jointed, the scape and pedicel dull honey-yellow, the flagellum brown-black. Legs dull honey-yellow, the posterior femora obfuscated, the anterior and middle coxæ honey-yellow at apex, while the large posterior coxæ are black. Wings sub-hyaline, heavily pubescent, the large stigma and stigmal vein brown. The male differs from the female only in its smaller size, and is readily distinguished by its long, filiform antennæ, the scape of which at apex and the flagellum, brown ; the joints of the latter are about four times as long as thick.

Described from two specimens, male and female.

Eumegaspilus, n. g.

This genus is distinguished from *Megaspilus* Westwood in being entirely wingless or then with rudimentary wings, and by the shape of the flagellum, which is sub-clavate. In *Megaspilus* it is flagellate, i. e., tapers gradually to a point at apex.

(2) *Eumegaspilus Canadensis*, n. sp.

Female. Length .09 inch. Polished black ; the head and thorax only showing a delicate, reticulated sculpture under a high power lens. On the head are a few large punctures, particularly on the vertex, two small foveæ or depressions on each side of front ocellus ; occiput prominently margined ; eyes pubescent. The antennæ are 11-jointed, wholly brown-black ; flagellum sub-clavate. the first funiclar joint longer than the pedicel, the others sub-equal but gradually widened, the terminal joint being the longest and thickest. Mesothorax with three grooves. Legs, including coxæ, of a uniform brownish-yellow. Abdomen highly polished with a depression near the base.

Described from one specimen.

(3) *Eumegaspilus Ottawensis*, n. sp.

This species is much like that just described, but it is more slender and more highly polished ; the head is impunctured, while the scape at base, the pedicel, the 2nd, 3rd and 4th flagellar joints, and the legs, including the coxæ, are honey-yellow. The rudimentary wings are linear and reach not quite to the middle of the abdomen.

Described from one specimen.

Megaspilidea, n. g.

This genus is at once distinguished from the others by having but one groove on the mesothorax—the median one, the parapsidal grooves not being present ; also by the difference in the flagellar joints.

(4) *Megaspilidea minuta*, n. sp.

Female. Length .04 inch. Head and thorax shining black, microscopically, reticulately sculptured. Eyes large oval, pubescent. Antennæ 11-jointed, scape ob-clavate, more than half the length of the flagellum ; flagellum sub-clavate, first joint hardly half the length of pedicel, others short, gradually widened toward tips, terminal joint very large and as long as the three preceding joints combined ; scape yellowish at base and beneath, flagellum brown-black.   Legs, including coxæ, brownish-yellow. Abdomen highly polished, smooth, excepting a few longitudinal lines near the base ; the color above is black, excepting a large orange-colored blotch across the base ; beneath, it is wholly brownish-yellow.

Described from two specimens.

Sub-family SCELIONINÆ.

Acolus Forster.

(5) *Acolus Canadensis*, n. sp.

Female.   Length less than .03 inch.   Black, shining, sparsely pubescent.   Antennæ black, excepting the scape at base ; the first and second funiclar joints are about as long as thick, third and fourth smaller and not as long as wide, club very large, joints not well separated.   Scutellum sub-lunate.   The legs, excepting the honey-yellow knees, are dark red. Abdomen broadly oval, the second segment occupying most of its surface, first segment with a transverse depression occupying nearly its whole width, striated and with a fringe of white hairs at base.

Described from one specimen.

(6) *Acolus borealis*, n. sp.

Female.   Length .03 to .04 inch.   Differs from *A. Canadensis* only in being relatively more robust, and in being distinctly, finely, confluently punctate ; the lower part of face and the abdomen alone being smooth and shining.   The antennæ are dark reddish brown.   Legs uniformly red, while the abdomen is striated at base.

Described from four specimens.

Prosacantha Nees.

(7) *Prosacantha brachyptera*, n. sp.

♀ .   Length .03 inch.   Black, shining.   Thorax sub-opaque, microscopically punctate ; metathorax with an acute spine on its disk.   Antennæ brown-black.   Legs red.   Abdomen broadly oval, black, excepting the first segment, which is red and striated.   Wings short, narrow, somewhat spatulate, not ciliated ; the marginal vein long, black, the stigmal short, post-marginal vein wanting.

Described from three specimens.

This species comes nearest to *P. minutissima* Ashm., from which it is, however, readily distinguished by the narrow, non-ciliated wings, and the color of the first abdominal segment.

Pentacantha, n. g.

This genus is closely related to *Prosacantha* Nees and *Trisacantha* Ashm.; but is at once separated from them by having five spines on the metathorax, three short ones on the disk and one long one on each side ; and besides, there is a short, smooth, blunt horn at the base of first segment, partly prolonged over the metathorax. Its other characters are exactly as in *Prosacantha*. The blunt horn issuing from the base of first segment would seem to indicate a relationship with *Inostemma* Haliday, but that genus is in another sub-family.

(8) *Pentacantha Canadensis*, n. sp.

Female. Length .08 inch. Polished black ; thorax opaque. Head smooth, except some lines back of eyes and on occiput. Antennæ 12-jointed, brown ; first funiclar joint twice as long as the pedicel; second two thirds the length of first ; third about as long as wide ; fourth shorter than wide ; club large, six-jointed. Thorax and scutellum rather coarsely rugose ; no parapsidal grooves. Legs, including anterior coxæ, honey-yellow, middle of femora and tibiæ obfuscated. Abdomen polished black, the third segment longest and widest ; first and second segments, and the third excepting on its disk, longitudinally striated. Wings dusky-hyaline, venation as in *Prosacantha*, veins rufo-piceous.

Described from one specimen.

Sub-family PLATYGASTERINÆ.

Metaclisis Forster.

(9) *Metaclisis erythropus*, n. sp.

Female. Length .08 inch. Black. Head opaque, coarsely rugose on vertex and back of eyes. Antennæ 10-jointed, the terminal joints of funicle enlarged into an irregularly rounded club ; club six-jointed, fili-form   Thorax shining, finely reticulated or scaly ; parapsidal grooves distinct, converging and meeting at the base of the scutellum. Legs red. Abdomen polished black. Wings dusky hyaline.

Described from one specimen.

Ectadius Forster.

(10) *Ectadius Canadensis*, n. sp.

Female. Length .12 inch. Polished black. The head is delicately transversely striated on vertex back of the ocelli and on the lower portion of the face. Antennæ reddish brown. Legs red, tarsi paler, yellowish. The thorax has two distinct parapsidal grooves and is delicately microscopically punctate. Metathorax, metapleuræ and base of abdomen densely pubescent. Abdomen polished black and prolonged into a long point posteriorly, being more than twice the length of the head and thorax combined. Wings hyaline.

Described from one specimen.

Sactogaster Forster.

(11) *Sactogaster Howardii*, n. sp.

Female. Length .07 inch Polished black, impunctured. Antennæ and legs dark red, the posterior femora obfuscated, tarsi paler. The scutellum is convexly high, striated and ends in a spine. The tail is nearly twice the length of the inflated venter. Metathorax and metapleuræ wrinkled. Wings hyaline. Hab.—Washington, D. C.

This species is described from one specimen taken by myself last summer, on the outskirts of Washington. It is dedicated to my friend, Mr. L. O. Howard, of the U. S. Dept. of Agriculture. Its much larger size, striated scutellum and longer tail will at once distinguish it from *S. anomaliventris*, described from Florida. In that species the scutellum is smooth, while the tail is not as long as the inflated venter.

Sub-family DIAPRINÆ.

Aneurhynchus Westwood.

(12) *Aneurhynchus mellipes*, n. sp.

Female. Length .10 inch. Black, shining, sparsely pubescent. Antennæ 12-jointed, red, stout, clavate ; the scape is greatly thickened, a little shorter than half the length of the flagellum ; pedicel thicker, but not half as long as the first funiclar joint ; second shorter than the first, and the third shorter than the second ; from thence the joints are shorter than wide and well separated. Parapsidal grooves distinct. Legs, including the coxæ, honey-yellow. Abdomen polished black, petiole rugose. Wings sub-hyaline, pubescent ; the submarginal vein ends in a callosity and a short stigmal vein, but it does not reach the costal margin ; the sub-marginal vein is very pale.

Described from one specimen.

Paramesius Westwood.

(13) *Paramesius clavipes*, n. sp.

Female. Length .08 inch. Polished black, covered with some long, sparse hairs on head, thorax and surrounding apex of abdomen ; the metathorax, metapleuræ and abdominal petiole densely pubescent. Antennæ 13-jointed, red, gradually incrassated toward tips ; first funiclar joint very slightly shorter than pedicel, following joints to fifth, sub-equal, from thence moniliform, slightly pedicellated, the terminal joint more than twice the length of the preceding joint, fusiform. Thorax without grooves, somewhat flat, sides compressed ; collar red at sides. The abdomen is pointed ovate, a deep depression above near base, while the ovipositor is exserted between two short valves, probably unnaturally so. Legs red, the femora strongly clavate, the tarsi very long, the anterior and middle pairs being longer than their tibiæ. Wings sub-hyaline, the marginal vein but slightly developed, not longer than the very short stigmal vein.

Described from one specimen.

Loxotropa Forster.

(14) *Loxotropa pcsomachoides*, n. sp.

Female. Length .04 to .05 inch. A small, highly polished, black, apterous species, sparsely covered with some long hairs. The antennæ and legs dark red. Antennæ 12-jointed, moniliform, the four terminal joints being much widened and slightly pedicellated, the last joint of which is large, fusiform.

Described from six specimens.

(15) *Loxotropa Harringtoni*, n. sp.

Female. Length .04 inch. Black, polished, covered with some long, sparse hairs. The collar at sides, metathorax and abdominal petiole well covered with dense, white pubescence. Antennæ 12-jointed, dark red, the four terminal joints abruptly larger than the preceding, and the species may be readily known by this character, and by the last funiclar joint being a little longer and more slender than the preceding one. The legs, including all coxæ, red. Abdomen clavate, the ovipositor slightly exserted. Wings dusky-hyaline, heavily pubescent and ciliate ; the marginal vein hardly developed, thickened.

Described from one specimen.

(16) *Loxotropa armata*, n. sp.

Female. Length .07 inch. This species is very closely related to

L. Harringtoni, agreeing with it in color, wing characters, etc , but it is much larger, the antennæ much more incrassated toward apex, the terminal joint being very large and thick, and as long as the three preceding joints combined , these four terminal joints, which constitute the club, are as usual slightly pedicellate. Another character which will readily distinguish it from all other species is a short conical spine in the centre of the metathorax.

Described from one specimen

(17) *Loxotropa abrupta* Thompson

This European species must now be added to our fauna. Mr Harrington having taken a specimen in Canada which I am unable to separate from types from Europe in my collection

Monelata Forster

(18) *Monelata hirticollis*, n sp.

Stature and size of *M melluollis* Ashm , but differs in being entirely black , the collar, metathorax and petiole densely pubescent , antennæ dark red, the very large terminal joint nearly black, while the legs are reddish-yellow. Wings hyaline, ciliate.

Described from one specimen

Sub-family BELYTINÆ

Zygota Forster.

(19) *Zygota Americana*, n. sp.

Female. Length 14 inch. Polished black, covered with a fulvous pubescence. Antennæ 15-jointed, filiform-moniliform ; first funiclar joint twice longer than the pedicel, other joints almost round, sub-pedicellate Parapsidal grooves of mesonotum broad, distinct. Scutellum with a deep depression at base. Metathorax carinated. Legs, including all coxæ, honey-yellow , first tarsal joint of anterior legs long, deeply emarginate at base. Abdomen ovate, black, a lateral streak on the apex of sixth segment red , venter densely pubescent , petiole twice as long as wide, fluted. Wings fusco-hyaline, pubescent ; veins brown, the marginal cell not quite closed

Male Length .12 inch This may be distinguished from the female principally by the antennæ They are 14-jointed, long, filiform, pubescent, pedicel rounded, the first funiclar joint about five times as long as thick, excised at base, the following joints about four times as long as thick.   There is a tooth beneath anterior femora, near the base ; while the anterior tibiæ are peculiarly twisted, the twisted part ending in a spine, besides the apical tibial spine.   Otherwise as in the female.

Described from one male and one female specimen.

AN INTERESTING NEW CHALCID FROM CANADA.

BY WM. H. ASHMEAD, JACKSONVILLE, FLA.

Among a small collection of parasitic Hymenoptera sent me by Mr. James Fletcher, the Dominion Entomologist, for names, I found an interesting Chalcid belonging to that remarkable Pteromalid genus *Caratomus* Dalman, no species of which has as yet been described as occurring in our fauna ; and as the present species seems to be distinct from the European species, *Caratomus megacephalus* Dalm., I believe it to be undescribed, and submit herewith the following description :

Caratomus leucophthalmus, n. sp.

Male.   Length .10 inch.   Robust, blue-black, confluently, granulately punctate.   The head is very large, its breadth being nearly twice the width of the thorax when measured from eye to eye ; its front is deeply, broadly emarginated, and there is a deep emargination or broad groove extending from the eye obliquely towards the mouth, the upper edge of which forms an acute tubercle, while the lower edge forms an acute ridge The eyes are satiny white, finely pubescent.   The antennæ are 13-jointed, clavate ; scape, the long pedicel, and first and second funiclar joints brownish-yellow, the following joints brown.   The legs are red, excepting the trochanters, extreme tips of femora and tibiæ and the anterior tibiæ, which are wholly brownish-yellow.   The abdomen is oval, with a dull bronzy tinge ; petiole short, yellow.   The wings are hyaline with a large fuscous blotch across the middle ; veins thick, rufo-piceous ; the submarginal vein is distant from costal edge and nearly three times as long as the marginal vein ; the stigmal vein is about as long as the marginal, curved ; while the post-marginal is distinctly longer than the stigmal vein.

Described from one male specimen taken on a window at Ottawa, in 1885, by Mr. James Fletcher.

MOTHS NEW TO OUR FAUNA

BY JOHN B SMITH, WASHINGTON, D C

Mr Hy Edwards, on p 12 of vol xx of the CAN ENT, records three species of moths as additions to our fauna—two of them *Sphingidæ*, viz , *Pseudosphinx tetrio* and *Philampelus typhon* Mr Edwards is undoubtedly correct in the record of localities, and in calling attention to their capture within our faunal limits , but, with all due respect, I do not think that these species should be added to our faunal list *Erebus odora* has been found in Canada, yet it would be an absurdity to cite it as a Canadian insect. The mere fact that an insect well known and abundant in one faunal region is occasionally found in another, does not authorize its addition to the latter fauna unless it breeds in or regularly migrates to it. *Sphinx tetrio* is a very common species which we have from Mexico, South America and the islands of the Carribean Sea. It is essentially a tropical and sub-tropical insect, and does not come into the temperate fauna except accidentally. It is undoubtedly true that political boundaries cannot limit faunal regions, and yet the southern boundary of the United States very nearly accords with the faunal line separating the temperate from the sub-tropical fauna Species occurring near this faunal border, especially species of strong flight like the *Sphingidæ*, will often cross the line , but this does not make them members of both sides The rule should be that only insects which breed within the faunal limits should be considered as forming parts of it Ordinarily the presumption is that an insect breeds where found This presumption fails where the insect is known to breed in a different fauna, and then positive proof should be required of its right. On this view I must dissent from Mr. Edwards's idea that these particular species should be added to our fauna In a monograph of the *Sphingidæ* now ready for the press, I have excluded these species, and in addition *Diludia brontes* and *D leucophæata*—both species possibly occasional visitants to our fauna, but really members of the next, or sub-tropical

Southern Florida has a peculiar fauna, and one that perhaps should not be classed within the temperate limit It really in many respects should be classed with the West Indian fauna, but on this point I make only the suggestion. It seems to me that Mr. W. H Edwards, in the Rhopalocera, has followed the wiser plan of separately calling attention to species occasionally found in but not really belonging to our fauna

DESCRIPTION OF THE PREPARATORY STAGES OF DATANA DREXELII, Hy. Edw.

BY WM. BEUTENMULLER, NEW YORK.

Egg.—Similar to *D. ministra;* cannot be distinguished from it. Laid in masses on the under side of leaf.

Young Larva, after First and Second Moults.—Cannot be distinguished from *D. ministra.*

After Third Moult.—Little change except in size. The stripes are now confluent about the anal segments. Length 30 m.m.

After Fourth Moult.—Head jet black, cervical shield now chestnut brown instead of black; otherwise as in *D. ministra.* Length 40 m.m.

Mature Larva.—Head jet black, shining, slightly punctured; cervical shield and neck wholly golden yellow. Body black, with four equidistant stripes of citron yellow on each side, and three on the under side. Abdominal legs and bases of thoracic feet orange. The stripes all become conjoined at the posterior extremity. The anal plates jet black, *very shiny and nearly smooth, and not roughly punctured,* as in *D. ministra.* The hairs over the body are sordid white. Length 55 m.m.

Pupa.—Cannot be distinguished from *D. ministra.*

Food Plants.—Huckleberry *(Vaccinium),* and Witch Hazel *(Hamamelis).* Single brooded.

STRAY NOTES ON MYRMELEONIDÆ, PART 4.

BY DR. H. A. HAGEN, CAMBRIDGE, MASS.

(Continued from vol. xix., page 38.)

4. *Brachynemurus abdominalis.*

 Myrm. abdominalis Say, Godm. West. Quart. Rep. ii., 163—Edit. LeConte, I., 173.

 M. juvencus Hag., Syn. N. Am. Neur., 234, 21 (var. with longer spurs).

Yellowish, slender, faintly villous; face yellow; between the antennæ and a little above, a longitudinal median line, connected with a transversal one on the epistom, all black; palpi equal, pale, the apical joint of maxillary and this of labial, which is very little thickened in the basal half, somewhat brownish; antennæ longer than head and prothorax, in the male fuscous annulated with luteous, especially before the tip, which is clavate ; shorter, more clavate in female ; the two basal joints brown, shining : vertex elevated, rounded, yellowish with two blackish dots ; prothorax little longer than broad, yellowish, with two dorsal black lines, ending on the anterior transversal sulcus ; sometimes a darker spot in front of the lines ; on each side and nearly below a black band connected with the lateral one of the thorax ; two black maculose bands including yellow spots on the thorax ; mesothorax before wings black, with yellow spots ; abdomen of male much longer than wings, faintly villous yellow, with a fine black median line, apical part blackish, yellow on articulation and some lateral marks ; appendages less than half the length of last seg- ment, cylindrical, yellowish, brown at base, densely clothed with black hairs ; below and between them a small triangular yellow plate ; abdomen of female as long as wings ; coloration similar, but the dorsal yellow band divided by a black line reaches the apex ; genital parts yellow, the superior part split, with many black spines ; below two short yellow appendages. Wings hyaline with a faint yellowish tint ; veins pale interrupted with brown, which covers in front wings most of base of the small forks and the base and apex of the transversals ; therefore the wing is faintly sprinkled, more densely along the mediana and submediana ; hind wing similar but less and more faintly sprinkled ; pterostigma white, larger in the female ; wing around and on the venation faintly villous ; apical half of costal space with forked veins. Legs short, pale, sprinkled with black, with black hairs ; tip of tibiæ and of joints of tarsi black, fourth joint entirely black ; spurs as long as three basal joints, or at least longer than two, brown. Length of body, male, 30 to 37 m.m.; female, 28 to 30 m.m. Exp. al., 36 to 54 m.m.

Habit., New Jersey, Uhler ; Pennsylvania ; Georgia, Morrison ; Wash- ington, O. Sacken ; Rock Island, Ill., Walsh ; Utah, Lake City, O. Sacken, August 1, and Packard, August 13 ; Colorado, Golden City, Boulder, July 3, Packard ; Texas, Dallas, Boll ; Waco, Belfrage, June, July, Sept., Oct.; San Antonio, A. Agassiz ; Carrizo Spring ; New Mexico, Zuni, Hayden's Exped., July ; Umatilla, Washington Territory, S. Henshaw, June 28 ; California, Vulcane Mts., Stinking River, H. Edwards.

The size of the specimens is rather variable in the same locality ; there are before me now more than 50 of both sexes, but I have seen more. The species seems very common in Texas, Colorado and New Mexico.

There is not much variation. Texas specimens have on the front part of the prothorax two brownish spots, and younger specimens are more bright in colors ; a number of specimens have the spurs longer, equal to the three basal joints, though others of the same locality have spurs two joints long. *M. juvencus* Hag. is *Myrm. abdominalis* Say.

5. *Brachynemurus peregrinus.*
Myrmeleon peregrinus Hag., Syn. N. Am. Neur., 234, 20.

Face yellow, with a short black band above, surrounding the antennæ below ; sending a faint black median line on the upper part of the face, not reaching the clypeus ; mouth yellow ; palpi yellow, the maxillary with the last joint cylindrical fuscous ; labials a little longer, last joint shining black, extreme base and tip yellowish, seen from above strongly fusiform with a kind of ocellus-like transparent median spot ; seen from beside the joint is less bulky, the third apical part strongly narrowed, conical. Antennæ longer than head and thorax, strong, clavate, black, scabrous, dull, the two basal joints below shining brown ; the base and apex of the antennæ sometimes pale brown, and very faintly annulated ; vertex elevated, rounded, yellow ; black in front with three not well defined yellow dots and two black transversal bands, the last one interrupted in the middle, and arcuated ; prothorax scarcely longer than broad, yellow on the dorsum, with four longitudinal black lines, and beneath on each side with a black stripe ; the pattern of the dorsum and its many variations is better to be understood in describing it as black, divided by a narrow yellow line and each part divided again by a yellow line not reaching the front ; broken in the middle and forming two elongate spots, of which the inferior ones may disappear ; mesothorax black with yellow dots near the prothorax ; after this yellow with three black forks ; metathorax yellow with a black cross ; sides of thorax black with some yellow bent stripes. Abdomen faintly villous ; above yellow with three longitudinal black bands, the median much finer on the male, which has the three last segments black ; venter fuscous ; abdomen of male much longer than wings ; appendages light brown with very long black hairs and bristles, very short, blunt pyramidal, divergent ; between them and below a small plate of the shape of a leaf, which can be folded in the aperture between the appendages ; abdomen of female as long as the wings, dilated and compressed to the apex ; genitals light brown, the superiors split, below with a transversal row of very strong black spines ; below two short cylindrical appendages, brown with black hairs, they are retractible into the abdomen, and so often not visible Legs yellow, sprinkled with black, and with black hairs, hind femurs sometimes fuscous in middle, tip of tibiæ and of the joints of tarsi blackish, spurs brown, as long as the two basal joints Wings long, broad, hyaline, pterostigma yellowish, veins fuscous interrupted by pale yellowish, transversals along the median and submedian pointed with fuscous, the points above the submediana are larger and more numerous, forming nearly a serrated black line, also the gradate veins going from the end of the submediana upwards and outwards to the tip of wing form often a brown line, more or less visible. the smaller forks along the hind margin dark, costal space of front wings only with a few forked transversals before the pterostigma, hind wings a little shorter, narrower, nearly hyaline.

Length of body, male, 42 to 51 m m, female, 30 to 36 m m Exp. al, 60 to 75 m.m.

Hab, Washington Terr, Ainsworth July 20, very common, opposite Umatilla, June 27, Oregon, Umatilla, June 24–25 all these coll by S. Henshaw, 1882 California. Fort Tejon, by Xanthus de Vesey, San Francisco, 1865 Nevada, Humboldt Station, July 29, O. Sacken Colorado, Pueblo New Mexico (formerly W. Texas). Pecos River, July 7, and Matamoras, Mexico, Exped of Capt. Pope

There are 40 specimens before me of both sexes In the small town Ainsworth, in the middle of a sandy desert, the windows of the office in the little inn where we had to stay the night, were literally covered with specimens This species belongs to the west of the Rocky Mts. The specimens from Mexico—Matamoras—are smaller than the others, but not different.

THE BUTTERFLIES OF NORTH AMERICA by W. H. Edwards Part IV of the Third Series has recently been issued It contains the usual three magnificent plates, the first represents both sexes and several varieties of *Colias Chrysomelas*, the second the upper and under surfaces of both sexes of the lovely *Argynnis Nausicaa*, and the third fully illustrates all the stages of *Cœnonympha Galactinus*, form *California* The letterpress contains much interesting matter on the life histories. in addition to the descriptions of the species

The Canadian Entomologist.

VOL. XX.   LONDON, APRIL, 1888.   No. 4

NATURAL HISTORY NOTES ON COLEOPTERA.—No. 4.

BY JOHN HAMILTON, M. D., ALLEGHENY, PA.

Bembidium undulatum, Sturm. There are now about thirty-eight species of Carabidæ recognized as indigenous to North America and Europe, and some of them also to Asia. The most of these are arctic or very northern, this being one of the few that occur in temperate America, but how far northward it inhabits is unknown, as I know only of its occurrence here, though in Europe and Asia it is found in sub-arctic regions. Here it is taken abundantly in July and August under decaying vegetation in moist alluvial places subject to occasional inundation. It is a Notaphus, .20 inch long, shining, elytra obscurely rufo-piceous, paler at apex with oblique pale mark, punctures of striæ obsolete behind middle and surface undulated. Identical with European specimens, and also verified by Dr. Horn.

Bembidium assimile Gyll. (*frontale* Lec.) is found here with the preceding, but much more abundantly ; I have it from Florida, and it seems to occur generally eastward from the Mississippi, and also in Kansas. In Europe and Asia it has the same distribution as *undulatum.* On comparison with European specimens no point of difference has been discovered.

Platynus pusillus Lec. Having recently examined and compared a number of *Anchomenus oblongus* Fab. from Sweden with the same number of the foregoing from Massachusetts, I conclude that Dr. Horn would have been entirely justifiable in pronouncing the species identical (Tr. Am. Ent. Soc., ix., 142), where he writes, "the only striking difference between the two being in the slightly wider thorax of our species." This difference, when a number of each is examined, is observed to be merely individual, and were I to write of the thorax, on the basis of a numerical estimate of what is before me, the statement in the above quotation would be reversed. The species has a wide distribution on this continent—Vermont, Massachusetts, New York, Canada to Kansas. In the Eastern

 .isphere it extends across Europe, and in Asia, throughout Western
:ria.

Harpalus caliginosus Fab. The stridulation of this common beetle is
referred to in Ent. Amer., ii., 239, as not recorded previously and as a
discovery of Dr. Horn, and also that stridulation takes place only when
the beetle is at liberty, and can not be made to do so when handled.
This species and *H. pennsylvanicus* DeG. feed on ragweed *(Ambrosia
artemisiæfolia)* when it is in bloom—here, in July, and both are exces-
sively abundant. Let the entomologist visit on a calm, sultry evening,
before sunset, some stubble field bordered by woods, when this weed is in
flower, and he will often witness a lively and by no means quiet scene ;
hundreds of the former and thousands of the latter will be seen mounted
on the weeds, each actively and intently employed in collecting the pollen
from the flowers, or licking some delectable morsel from the leaves and
occasionally evidencing its delight in a sonorous manner—a sudden
squeak—somewhat like the noise made by a steel pen scratching rough
paper ; and so intent are they on the business in hand as to be captured
before observing the approach of an enemy.

Stridulation is effected in both by the beetles rubbing the large costæ
of the wings against the elytra, these costæ being coarsely transversely
rugose from the base to near the apex. Stridulation is readily produced
after death by pressing intermittently on the elytra, provided the costæ
are in a position to be brought in proper contact with them.

H. compar and *H. longicollis* are catalogued as varieties of *H. pennsylvanicus*, but curiously enough, though abundant, they do not seem to
have the same tastes, as I have never taken a single specimen of either
on ragweed, though carefully sought for. I strongly suspect they are
really three distinct species, notwithstanding the near approach in form of
some individuals, and certainly nothing is gained by the collector by
classifying them as varieties.

Graphoderes fasciatocollis Harr. was considered to be the same as the
European *G. cinereus*, till separated by Dr. Sharp in his learned Monograph of the Dytiscidæ, p. 693 ; this separation is pronounced "unwar-
ranted" by Dr. Horn, Tr. Am. Ent. Soc., x., 280. Two primary points
of difference are given by Dr. Sharp ; the first, that the male of *fasciatocollis* has " twenty-three " small pallettes on the anterior tarsus and twelve
on the middle, while that of *cinereus* has "about twenty-eight" on the
anterior and fourteen on the middle one ; the second, that in the former

the punctuation of the elytra is dissimilar in the sexes, being in the fen.
fine and deep at the sides and somewhat dense at the base, while those
the latter are alike in both sexes. Recently I examined several specimens
of *cinereus* from Prussia and compared them with American forms, with
the result of confirming Dr. Horn's opinion. Four males have each from
thirty to thirty-three small pallettes on the anterior tarsus, and four have
twenty-eight—all with fourteen on the middle; one has twenty-five on the
anterior and twelve on the middle, with two rudimentary; one has twenty-
three on the anterior and twelve on the middle, with doubtful traces of two
others. As the pallettes decrease in number they increase in size and
distinctness, but do not equal those in my single American male. The
sculpture of the elytra in the sexes (seven females seen) might be termed
uniform, though the punctuation is more pronounced in two or three
females; the anterior black band of the thorax does not " always attain
the front margin," but exhibits the same variableness as exists among
American individuals. With the above I have compared one male and
three females of *fasciatocollis* from Massachusetts and one female taken
here; the male has twenty-three small pallettes on the anterior and twelve
on the middle tarsus, all larger than in the European forms. Whether
this number is constant, or variable as in the foreigners, would be desirable to know, that is, in a number taken together, for Dr. Horn has
demonstrated the variableness when from distant localities. The three
Massachusetts' females have the elytra sculptured like the male and could
not be distinguished in this respect from their European sisters; but the
female taken here is much coarser sculptured and punctured than ever
Dr. Sharp's description requires. Both the points insisted on by the
learned Doctor for separate species are shown by the above to be untenable.

Philhydrus fimbriatus Mels., one of the most common of the Hydro-
philidæ, inhabits in great abundance all wet places, especially where there
is mud—swamps, ponds, springy places, springs on hill and mountain
sides, etc. It is variable in sculpture, size and color. The intention here
is to bring to notice a dwarf race that inhabits the little rivulets that flow
down hill and mountain sides from springs. While the normal form is
piceous black with pale thoracic and elytral margins, and about .20 inch
in length, this might be termed gray with paler margins, and in length is
not over .15 inch. In summer these spring runs are often dry for long
periods, and the beetles then crawl under stones and rubbish where there

is a little moisture; these long droughts and the comparative scarcity of food undoubtedly have dwarfed them, and living in clear water clinging to stones has called into exercise a potential element that seems to inhere in many insects of accommodating their colours to their surroundings. The black colour of the mud-inhabiting race would make them too conspicuous, so they have changed it to sober gray to correspond with the general colour of the stones and bottom of the brook.

Oxyporus 5-maculatus Lec. Seven other species of this genus occur here more or less abundantly from the middle of August onward, all living on various species of living mushrooms; but *5-maculatus* appears to be rare, as I have only taken it three times—two at a time, and like the others, feeding on mushrooms, but in June, and on rocky, mountainous places. It differs remarkably from the other species by having the sides of the thorax posteriorly so compressed as to elevate the disk at the middle of each side at base into a flattened tubercle in such a way as to make the expression, "thorax posteriorly concave," not inappropriate.

Dendrocharis flavicornis Guer. A specimen of this curious insect, now in the cabinet of Dr. Horn, was recently taken near St. Augustine, Florida, by Mr. Charles W. Johnson, who dug it out of a tree. This is the only native specimen in any of our collections so far as known. See figure and description, Tr. Am. Ent. Soc., xiii., 12.

Meristhus. If the definition of this genus in the Classification, " Front tarsal grooves wanting," is correct, the two species under it in the Catalogue should be placed under *Lacon*, as they have these grooves deep. I suspected a misprint of " tarsal " for tibial, but a careful examination shows the existence of these grooves quite evidently in some specimens of *cristatus*, though obsoletely so in others. There seems to be little need of the genus anyhow.

Dicerca prolongata Lec. and *D. divaricata* Say. A single character that will in all cases separate these species infallibly is something not yet in print. The prolongation and degree of divarication of the elytra are the same in both; a typical specimen of the former kindly sent me by Mr. Ulke, collected in Dakota, has the tips of the elytrons as widely separated as in *divaricata*, while on the other hand I have a specimen of the latter with the tips very prolonged and contiguous to near the end (*D. dubia* Mels.) The depth and distinctness of the thoracic channel is not a character to be depended on; my type of *prolongata* has a very deep and uninterrupted channel, but I have a specimen of the other taken here approaching it closely, and from this are all degrees of variation to the slightest noticeable depression. No character can be derived from the spurs of the middle tibiæ of the males, for when a large number of *divaricata* are examined, this will be seen to vary from a mere tubercle to a formidable spur with long teeth on the distal edge. Colour, as a character, is not worthy of consideration. I have a specimen of *prolongata* from Canada with the upper side polished black with a purple reflection and the under coppery black. A point given me by Mr. Ulke (a character given by Dr. LeConte) is more permanent than any of those mentioned above, viz., tips of the elytrons with the angles rounded—*prolongata ;* tips of the elytrons with the sutural angles terminating in a small spine—*divaricata*. This is the most constant character noticed, but by itself fails in individual cases under observation. I do not question the distinctness of the species. *Prolongata* breeds, so far as known, in conifers, and inhabits high altitudes and latitudes, while *divaricata* is more southern, being abundant in parts of Canada and all the States east of the Mississippi, breeding in diseased or dead deciduous trees, as beech, maple, apple, cherry, etc.

Dicerca obscura Fab. For a set of typical specimens of the real *obscura* as defined by Dr. LeConte, I am indebted to Mr. Ulke, who takes it quite commonly at Washington, D. C., on persimmon *(Diospyros Virginiana)*. There is a tendency among collectors to confuse this with Dr. Leconte's *lurida* Fab., as defined in his Monograph, and to give the latter either name according to fancy. My observations, however, are that there are sufficient differences to keep them apart, at least as races, and to the collector this is the same as if they are separate species. In an examination of about one hundred and twenty specimens of *lurida* taken here or received from other places, I find that the thorax is in every case wider near the middle than at base, and that behind the middle the sides converge more or less to the base in a line varying from nearly straight to deeply sinuous. In *lurida* the reverse occurs, the widest part of the thorax is the base, and the convergence, though not great, is directed anteriorly, and from the middle to apex is more pronounced. The directions of Dr. LeConte in his Monograph, if strictly followed, are quite sufficient to effect a separation. *Lurida* breeds in dead and diseased hickory, and is very abundant, but I have never seen a specimen of *obscura* taken here.

Dicerca spreta Gory appears to be rare and I have it not, though *asperata* Lap. & Gor. has been sent me for it by good collectors. Errors are mostly difficult to eradicate, and this one is not likely to be got rid of soon, at least not till the genus is monographed anew. The trouble is about this way. Dr. LeConte in his Monograph (Tr. Am. Phil. Soc., xi., 198) fully and clearly described a *spreta* and an *asperata*, which, of course, went so into all collections; but fourteen years afterwards Mr. G. R. Crotch (Proc. Acad. Nat. Sci., 1873, p. 85) states that the names given by Dr. LeConte should be reversed, but in his Catalogue misplaces the species, though giving the synonyms. In Mr. Henshaw's Catalogue the same order is followed, but the synonyms dropped, and now nothing points to an error in Dr. LeConte's Monograph. The error was corrected in few of the older collections, and is transmitted from them by tradition, while the latest catalogue indicates no error to one not conversant with the whole literature of the subject.

Aphodius rufipes Lin. is mentioned at page 9. Mr. Blanchard, of Mass., writes that he has a specimen collected in the mountains of North Carolina. These mountains are the Alleghany, the same as at St. Vincent's and at Deer Park. Thus, this recent discovery is already traced in a direct line over this continuously rugged country more than 400 miles.

Stenosphenus notatus Oliv. breeds in the limbs of dead hickory; it becomes a pupa the latter part of the second year and the imago is perfected before winter, but remains in the wood till the April or May following. *Neoclytus capraea* Say, which breeds in ash and often renders worthless logs cut before June, follows the same course. A manufacturer who uses this timber showed me a log in his shop in December that must have contained hundreds. When split in any direction the beetles crawled out of the opened burrows and appeared quite active.

Saperda concolor, mentioned page 8, Mr. Blanchard informs me, breeds in a low willow and in *Populus tremuloides*—in Massachusetts, the " Common Poplar," but here and everywhere west of the Alleghanies, the " Quaking Asp." How many other trees are " Common Poplar ? "

Chrysomela præcelsis Rogers, when found, is in abundance, but its habitat is limited. It feeds on the leaves of Convolvuleæ *(Ipomœa pandurata* and *Calystegia sepium)* growing on the banks of rivers and moist alluvial ground, but not on the same plants when away from water. Its season of abundance is about the middle of June.

Apion herculaneum Smith occurs plentifully about the last of May on the cymes of the maple-leaved arrow-wood (*Viburnum acerifolia*) just as they are going out of bloom. The fruit of this does not ripen till October, and some larva lives in the fleshy substance in which the thin, flat coriaceous seed is immersed, which is probably that of this *Apion*, though not yet so proven. This is one of the largest species of the genus, and when beaten into the umbrella behaves and looks so much like the worthless *Anthonomus quadrigibbus*, that till the past season it was always rejected.

DESCRIPTION OF THE PREPARATORY STAGES OF ARGYNNIS HESPERIS, Edw.

BY W. H. EDWARDS, COALBURGH, W. VA.

Egg.—Conoidal, round-topped, nearly as broad at base as high, the top depressed ; marked by about 19 thin, elevated, vertical ribs, one half running from base to summit, the others but four fifths or more the distance ; the spaces between crossed by many low horizontal ridges ; the micropyle surrounded by two or three circles of very fine depressions, outside of which are rows of very large four or five-sided depressed cells ; color yellow-green. Duration of this stage about ten days.

Young Larva.—Length .06 inch ; cylindrical, thickest in middle ; color yellow-green ; marked as in the allied species by rows of flattened tuberculous brown spots, each of which gives one or two long, tapering hairs ; on dorsum of 2 a dark oval patch with a row of hairs in front, turned forward, and a shorter row behind ; head obovoid, black, with many long hairs. The larva hibernates directly from the egg.

After First Moult : Length .1 inch ; color green, mottled with brown over dorsum ; the under side pale green ; the spines in number and position as at maturity, and as in the genus, small at base, tapering little, wholly black, beset with many short black bristles ; head obovoid, black, with black hairs. Duration of this stage eight days, in April and May.

After Second Moult : Length .15 inch ; color brown and gray ; a double indistinct gray dorsal stripe, and a similar one between dorsal and upper lateral spines ; the spines black ; those of the middle row have the bases on outer side pale yellow, of the lower row the bases are wholly pale yellow ; head as before. Duration of this stage eight days, in May.

After Third Moult : Length .28 inch ; color black and dark gray, the sides mottled ; the double dorsal stripe more definite than before ; the spines as before ; head same also. To next moult four days, in May.

After Fourth Moult : Length .44 inch ; color black and gray ; the dorsal stripe now solid, dark gray ; the spines black to bases except those of lower row, and on 3 and 4 of middle row, all which have yolk-yellow at base and half way up the stems ; all bristles black ; head brown-black over the front with many black hairs, long and short, the back brownish-yellow. To next moult eight days, in May.

After Fifth Moult : Length .7 inch ; in about eight days was fully grown.

MATURE LARVA.—Length 1.2 to 1.4 inch ; slender, somewhat thickened in middle, the segments well rounded ; color wholly velvet-black or brown-black (no gray dorsal stripe as before last moult) ; three rows of spines on either side, as in the genus, all of them yellow nearly to tip, the rest black ; feet black, pro-legs brown-yellow ; head sub-cordate, the vertices rounded, dull brown in front, dull yellow at back. From fifth moult to pupation 14 days.

CHRYSALIS.—Length .9 inch ; breadth across mesonotum .26, across abdomen .23 inch ; like *Atlantis* in shape, but stouter ; color dark brown over head and wing cases ; so also on the front of each abdominal segment, in serrations, the rest yellow-brown. Duration of this stage ten days, in June

HESPERIS flies in Colorado, Utah and Montana. Mr. Bruce writes me of its habits thus : " *Hesperis* is by far the most abundant species of the genus along the canons and water courses of the eastern or front range of the Rocky Mtns., in Colorado, at from 6,500 to 8,000 feet elevation. It is very active and restless, and difficult of capture except when on flowers. They are very partial to the bloom of Clematis, and I have frequently taken several at one sweep of the net on this plant ; later in the season, on the tall Sunflower. The wild Bergamot and Horse-mint are much frequented by them. They are also fond of alighting on the ground in damp places, especially, late in the summer, when they are worn. I have taken them in Clear Creek and Platte canons from June 16th till end of August. *Hesperis* is a very pugnacious insect, and will circle round and boldly flap the Lycaenas and Theclas off the blossoms. I was amused one day, on the South Platte, with watching a male *Hesperis* endeavoring to drive a Zygaenid moth *(Anatolmis Grotei)* off the blossoms of a large species of Senecio. The moth, which is a sluggish creature at all times, would not fly, but slowly backed round the corymbose head of flowers, occasionally lifting its front legs in feeble protest *Hesperis* followed it, flapping its wings and clawing at it like a cat, till the persecuted moth at last escaped by slipping over the petals, and hanging on the under side   It is probably owing to this restless and quarrelsome disposition that individuals are so soon worn and broken   They vary much in size and in the color of the spots on under side, some being of a deep buff, others a dead white, and others with a trace of frosted silver. I have taken *Hesperis* just below the timber line, but it is not common at such elevations, nor below 6,500 feet in Colorado."

Mr Bruce sent me eggs of this species from Denver, Colorado, which I received 9th July, 1886, and a second lot three days later.   The eggs hatched at ten days, and after eating the shells, the larvæ went into lethargy   I sent them soon after to Clifton Springs, N Y , to go in a cold room there, and they were returned 21st March, 1887, nearly all alive But they came unexpectedly, and a month too soon, and before I could force a plant of violet for them nearly all had died.   Of the few survivors, one passed 1st moult 20th April, the second 3rd May, the third 11th May, the fourth 15th, the fifth 23rd.   This larva pupated 6th June, and the imago came out 16th June   Another pupated 11th June, but died before imago.   The habits of the larvæ in confinement are similar to those of *Atlantis*   The butterfly is figured in Vol 1, Butterflies of N America

SOME NEW NOCTUIDÆ

BY G. H. FRENCH, CARBONDALE, ILL

Cucullia Hartmanni, n sp.

Expanse 1 75 inches, length of body 75 inch   General color of fore wings pale gray, so suffused in places with dark gray as to give the wings a moderately dark gray cast, but not so dark as *C intermedia,* Spey Lines black, basal half line only indicated on the costa   T. a line double, the inner part almost imperceptible , strongly dentate, from its origin projecting obliquely outward to a strong tooth on the fold in the discal cell, with a short tooth on the fold between the costal and subcostal veins, from discal tooth it recedes to median vein a little nearer the body than its inception on the costa, from this it extends out in another tooth nearly twice as far out as the discal tooth. the point resting on the submedian fold, almost reaching the inflection of the t. p line, the points of both lines nearly obsolete in a white patch at this place that fades out into the general color, about the middle of the space from the median vein to submedian fold a brownish black spur is sent out parallel with the median vein. terminating above the middle of the white patch ; the line reaches the posterior margin by another inflexion on submedian vein, and another outward tooth below the vein   A fine line extends along the submedian fold to the white patch   Median shade distinct above the cell, outwardly oblique.   Stigmata only indicated by a slight brown discoloration, except below the reniform is an arc on the median vein as though part of the annulus.   T p line obsolete except on costa and below second median venule, the angle next to the white patch filled with a black shading, from this a slightly double curved line extends to end of first submedian venule. Veins finely black, in s t space a tendency to black interspaceal lines. Terminal line black, broken, a few inward inflexions   Fringe gray, brown tinted, a paler central line, cut with white at the end of veins to this line.

Hind wings sordid white, veins dark, a broad smoky black border that is narrow at the anal angle.   Fringe pale with a dark sub-basal line

Palpi porrect, third joint slender, dark brown, sides of first and second, brown mixed with white, white beneath   Eyes naked, without lashes   Head gray, a space between the antennæ with a black annulus Collar gray with three narrow black lines, first space suffused with pale brown, tips of posterior scales white   Pategia clear pale gray, apparently a narrow terminal line. Thorax gray, one specimen shows indication of a very slight posterior tuft, but not more so than some *Agrotis*   Abdomen whitish, slight dorsal dark gray tufts on joints 1 to 3, usually a dorsal dark line, suffusion of pale brown on joints 4 to 7   Beneath whitish with a slight yellowish tinge, legs gray, tarsi dark, tibiæ unarmed

Described from three specimens taken at Hockley, Harris Co, Texas, by my friend, Leopold Hartmann, to whom I have dedicated the species, his number, 105, white label

This is near *C serraticornis*, Lintn, but differs in the antennæ being simple, and several points in coloration.

Hadena Evelina, n sp.

Expanse 1.50 to 1.70 inches, length .80 inch. General color of fore wings dark gray, washed with wine color over subterminal space, between and beyond the stigmata, and between median and submedian veins between t. a. and t. p. lines, the gray having a slight purplish reflection over the rest of wing. Markings black, of a brownish cast, perhaps more properly vandyke brown. Lines moderately distinct, double, the enclosed space a little pale ; inner part only of basal half line distinct ; t. a. line slightly oblique, straight in its general course : outward teeth on subcostal, median and submedian veins, the last two the most prominent ; t. p. line only moderately outward curved beyond the cell, dentate ; claviform extending one third across the median space, the t. a. and t. p. lines connected through this by an umber shade bar ; s. t. line sometimes continuous, ochreous, dentate, the inner teeth interspaceal, these more prominent ; five of them continued nearly across the s. t. space by umber dashes, these connected with black interspaceal dashes that extend across the terminal space to the outer margin. In others only the interspaceal light points are present, with mere traces in places of the line ; stigmata concolorous, annulate with broken ochraceous, with mere traces of a black annulus ; orbicular large, nearly circular, slightly oblique. A basal dash below half line. Fringe gray, a fine pale basal line, next to the terminal black lunulate line at the end of the wing.

Hind wings smoky white, a little more soiled terminally ; a black terminal line ; fringe concolorous, pale at the base.

Eyes naked ; antennæ of male serrate, female simple ; head, palpi and thorax concolorous with fore wings ; a central black line on the collar, a black line also on pategia ; dorsal tufts on thorax and abdomen prominent, concolorous. Abdomen darker than hind wings. Beneath, body pale purplish gray ; tibiæ unarmed.

Described from three males and one female taken by Mr. C. F. McGlashan at Truckee, California ; his number, 93. I have also a faded specimen from Shasta Co., Cal., taken by Mr. James Behrens.

In color and lack of strong outward inflection of the s. t. line, forming the usual M, this species belongs with *H. Arctica,* Bd., and its western ally, *H. Occidens,* Grote. The shade bar between the t. a. and t. p. lines relates it to *H. Bridghamii,* G.-R., placing it between *H. Arctica* and *H. Bridghamii.*

STRAY NOTES ON MYRMELEONIDÆ, PART 4.

BY DR. H. A. HAGEN, CAMBRIDGE, MASS.

(Continued from vol. xx., page 60.)

6. *Brachynemurus nigrilabris* Hagen. N. sp.

Very similar to *B. peregrinus*. Face yellow, above with a large black band, which is rounded below and reaches nearly the clypeus ; this band is going between and around the antennæ and connected above with the black part covering the whole anterior half of the vertex ; posterior half yellow with a broad black longitudinal band, dilated angularly in middle ; the angle sometimes protracted on each side in fine line, which does not reach the eyes ; labrum shining black ; palpi yellow, last joint of the maxillary cylindrical black ; labials a little longer, last joint shining black, fusiform, sharply pointed, less inflated than in *B. peregrinus*. Antennæ longer than head and prothorax, fuscous, the apex nearly luteous ; of the male, 8.5 m. m. long ; of the female shorter, 7 m. m. long, visibly more clavate. Prothorax a little longer than broad, rounded, before yellow, with two approximate black bands, reaching the front margin, connected below with a shorter black external band, which reaches only the transversal furrow ; a black line below the side margin ; mesothorax black with two yellow dots in front, and two on each side near the wing ; on the disc two yellow triangles in opposite position ; hind middle portion yellow, with the anterior margin and two longitudinal bands black ; metathorax similar, a black dot in the yellow triangles ; sides of the thorax black with a few yellow stripes. Abdomen faintly villous, brownish, below fuscous, articulations pale ; of male much longer than wings, three last segments blackish ; appendages very short, pale brownish, hairy, cylindrical, blunt ; between them and below a short pyramidal part ; abdomen of female as long as wings, similar, articulations pale, last segment pale, on each side a dark spot : genitals pale, superior part split, with a row of strong black spines ; below two short pale cylindrical appendages. Legs yellow, with black spines, femurs with a black band externally on the two hind pairs, with a black spot on tip of fore legs ; tibia internally with a black line, those of fore legs variegated with brown ; tip of tarsal joints faintly black ; spurs brown, as long as the two basal joints. Wings hyaline, pterostigma white ; venation brown interrupted with pale ; subcosta and mediana black interrupted with yellowish : only a few costals before the pterostigma forked.

Length of body, male, 45 to 55 m.m. ; female, 33 m m. ; exp. al., 56 to 60 m.m.

Hab., New Mexico, Aug., 1872. Mr. Yarrow ; Colorado, Manitou ; Wyoming, Bridger Basin, Mr. Garman ; Salt Lake City, Sept , 1877, Mr. Austin ; Farmington, July 23; Ogden, Aug. 2, O. Sacken ; Dakota, Custer Co., Garman.   Four males and three females in alcohol, and four females dry.

7.   *Brachynemurus blandus.*

Myrmeleon blandus Hag., Syn. N. Am. Neur., 235, 22.

Small, yellow, marked with black.   Face pale yellowish, with a superior trifid black spot ; it is united with the vertex by a narrowed part going upward between the antennæ; on each side below the pale ring around the antennæ it reaches nearly the eyes ; the inferior margin bisinuated, sending a fine black median line to the clypeus ; labrum yellow ; palpi pale, maxillary with last joint cylindrical, brownish : labials scarcely longer, last joint fusiform, very pointed, brown except on base. Antennæ clavate, strong, about as long as head and thorax, a little shorter in the female, where they are larger clavate, brown, luteous on clava, visibly annulated with yellow, principally on the basal half ; the two basal joints black.   Vertex elevated, cut straight in front, black ; above yellow with two large approximate black spots, a little dilated externally.   Prothorax as long as broad, yellow, with two black bands, which have anteriorly an external yellow incision ; the outer part of the black band reaches not the transversal furrow ; beneath on each side of the prothorax a black stripe ; mesothorax and metathorax black marked with yellow similar to *B. nigri-labris;* sides below the wings black, with some yellow stripes. Abdomen clothed with white hairs, yellow above, trilineated with black ; beneath black ; of the male longer than the wings, slender : appendages half the length of last segment, pale with long dark hairs ; cylindrical, obtuse on tip, which is bent up a little ; between them beneath a small short triangular plate ; of the female as long as the wings ; genitals pale, the upper part split with a transversal row of black spines ; below two short pale cylindrical appendages.   Legs yellow, sprinkled with black, with black hairs ; tip of all joints of tarsi black ; spurs brown, as long as the two basal joints.   Wings hyaline, hairy around and on the venation, which is black, interrupted by pale yellowish ; pterostigma large, pale yellow.

Length of body, male, 33 m.m.; female, 26 m.m.; exp. al., 40 m.m.

Habit.—The type, a female in bad condition from New Mexico (formerly Western Texas), Pecos River, May 14, from Capt. Pope's Expedition ; a female from Idaho, Snake River, by Cyrus Thomas, 1872; a male from Bridger Basin, Wyoming, by Mr. Garman ; Nevada, H. Edwards. I have never seen more than these four specimens, which are all alike.

The words of my description, Syn., p. 235, " vertex with two transverse black lines, the hind one interrupted," are to understand that the first line is formed by the front edge of the vertex, the second by the spots described.

ON THE DIAGNOSES OF N. AM. PHYCITIDÆ, BY E. L. RAGONOT.

BY A. R. GROTE, BREMEN, GERMANY.

I have received from the author a copy of this pamphlet in which a large number of North American species and genera are somewhat briefly described in anticipation of the publication of a general Monograph. That M. Ragonot is in a situation to materially increase our general knowledge of the group cannot be doubted.   He has long collected types and specimens, and has studied the characters of the Old World genera. I have deprecated the description of *Phycidæ* without giving the full structural characters, and in so far as this has been done do I agree with M. Ragonot's introductory remarks.   But I by no means consider that American authors should wait upon M. Ragonot to name their material, nor that what Dr. Staudinger chooses to do is binding upon them in the matter.   I object to any hasty descriptions in this group, without denuding the wings and studying the head and mouth parts under the microscope.   When this is done and a full description given, the term " haphazard " will no longer apply.   For the element of certainty in a generic reference in these moths is only relative.   I objected to Prof. Riley's descriptions, not because I differed as to the generic references, but because the species were described without structural characters being given, and from the obscure nature of the ornamentation and the great general resemblance among the *Phycidæ*, one can hardly determine a species from a description of the colour and markings alone.

We must wait upon the "Monograph' for the reasons which induce M. Ragonot to call the Family *Phycitidæ* and the typical genus *Phycita*, and not as I have given it, *Phycidæ* and *Phycis* Haw. I have, however, not yet seen a copy of Haworth. I regard the *Phycidæ* or *Phyciinæ* as a sub-family of the *Pyralidæ;* and M. Ragonot's *Anerastinæ* as merely a tribal division of the sub-family. I am not then agreed with M. Ragonot's divisional terms.

I have had no occasion to study M. Ragonot's types. As the generic term *Ciris* (p. 17) is long ago used by me for *C. Wilsonii*, I propose for *discigerella* the name *Ragonotia* after its learned discoverer.

A NOTE UPON AUTHOR'S TYPES.

BY A. R. GROTE.

It has occurred to me to say a few words upon the subject of author's types. It sometimes happens that a specimen is labelled "type," which is not the true type, i. e., the one (or ones) from which the original description was drawn up and which *accords with that description*. This is the criterion for types, that they do not contradict the original description. The late Mr. Morrison sent me at one time a "type" of Harris's *Agrotis tessellata*. Upon my wonder at his having such a specimen, I found it was merely a compared example, but it should not have been labelled "type." To my certain knowledge, Mr. Morrison on occasion labelled as types subsequent material (vide genus *Agrotis*). Only the material at hand and compared when the original description is drawn up, should be labelled as "type." On this head I would say a word as to Walker's types. Only when the evidence is complete and satisfactory should an earlier name of Walker's replace a designation in use. What I call incomplete evidence may be recently offered by Mr. Hulst in proposing to change *Selenia Kentaria*. Dr. Packard it seems had figures drawn from what are supposed to be Walker's types. There is no evidence that these are in every instance the proper types. The cases where more than one species was included by Mr. Walker are not solitary. Dr. Packard interpreted this figure as applying to another form of *Selenia*. Mr. Hulst interprets it differently, and drops a settled name without a question. In whatever way the matter is finally settled, Mr. Hulst would appear to have acted without sufficient evidence, Having studied the original collection in 1868, during Mr. Walker's lifetime, I am justified in saying that care must be taken that subsequently added specimens are not taken for types. Restitutions should be left to Mr. Butler and the British Museum authorities. The original description must be studied, and facilities other than Mr. Hulst's are needed to make such changes.

ON THE GEOGRAPHICAL DISTRIBUTION OF CITHERONIA.

BY A. R. GROTE, A. M.

I wish to draw particular attention to this genus and its allies. I have, in 1865, drawn a parallel between the group and the Hawk Moths, from the young stages and the peculiar pupation, and in my pamphlet on " the Hawk Moths of North America," I have discussed the probabilities of their relationship. But I here wish to point out that the group is American ; that in America we may expect to find old types among that portion of the fauna which is indigenous, pre-tertiary, and to this *Citheronia* belongs. Further than this, the *Ceratocampinæ*, which are tropical continental, or South American rather than North American, but comparatively equally spread to-day, seem to belong to the Eastern portion of the New World. That is, east of the Rocky Mountains, the Cordilleras, the Andes ; east of the great rocky back-bone of the continent running from north to south. If this is so, it will further illustrate my remarks on the " Geographical Distribution of North American Lepidoptera," which has recently appeared in the pages of the CANADIAN ENTOMOLOGIST. The sub-family, which I separate from the *Saturninæ* or *Attacinæ*, contains two series of genera cr tribes based on larval structare—*Citheronia*, *Anisota* and *Dryocampa (rubicunda* and var. *alba)* standing together, as opposed to *Eacles imperialis* and allies. This sub-family, remarkable for its *form* and habit of pupation, its thick wings, velvety-scaled, its short, sub-simple antennæ, stands lower than the *Attacinæ* or true Emperor Moths, and seems to borrow some characters from the *Cossinæ*. But the larvæ are very different ; they approach somewhat *Bombyx mori*, which is the most Sphinx-like larva of all the Spinners, yet spins a cocoon, which *Citheronia* does not. That this group is American and has a comparatively defined range, between the mountains and the Atlantic, are matters of no little interest in the study of the distribution and the origin of our North American moths. In the Annals of the New York Lyceum, colored figures are given by the late Mr. C. T. Robinson and myself of

Citheronia regalis Fabr., *C. sepulcralis* G. & R., and *C. Mexicana* G. &
R.   The Pine Citheronia, *C. sepulcralis* G. & R., is found from Massachusetts to Florida, but I have not heard of its being taken farther north,
or in Canada.   It seems to be a rare moth, having been taken by Abbot,
who seems not to have known its transformations.   It was unknown to
science until we described it from material found by the late Mr. James
O. Treat, of Massachusetts.

NEW WORK ON JAPANESE BUTTERFLIES.

The task of preparing and illustrating a work upon the Butterflies of
Japan, after the model of Mr. Distant's RHOPALOCERA MALAYANA, has
been undertaken by Mr. H. Pryer, of Yokohama, who with persistent
enthusiasm for the past seventeen years has been engaged in collecting
the Lepidoptera of the Empire, and studying their habits.   The work,
entitled RHOPALOCERA NIHONICA, will appear in three parts, 4to.   It is
printed upon Japanese " untearable paper," made of a curious combina-
tion of the fibres of rice straw and silk.   The text is in English and
Japanese.   The plates are drawn upon stone and printed in colours by
native lithographers under Mr. Pryer's own supervision, and are truly
excellent.   The first part, bearing the imprint of the " Japan Mail "
office, is before us.   The writer during a recent stay in Yokohama had the
privilege of examining a portion of the MS. of the Second Part and the
proofs of the Plates which are intended to accompany it.   It may be
worthy of note that the letter-press of Parts II. and III. will greatly exceed
in volume that of Part I.

The Japanese islands, stretching from Shumshu, the northernmost of
the Kuriles, in Lat. 50° 40′ N. to the Riu-kiu group in Lat. 24° N., possesss
every variety of climate from the semi-arctic to the tropical.   The islands
of the great central group, Yesso, Nippon, Shikoku, and Kiushiu, are
traversed by lofty mountain ranges, and dotted with volcanic peaks, some
of which rise from 9,000–10,000 ft., and one of them to 12,450 ft. above
sea-level.   Upon the summits of these mountains perennial winter reigns,
while at their feet a semi-tropical vegetation blooms and flourishes.   In
addition to the wide diversity in climates which prevails in the islands and
the contiguity of colder and warmer climates due to the mountainous
character of the country, there are more subtle influences at work depend-
ing for their operation upon the rainfall and the aerial currents.   The

atmosphere is characterized in spring and early summer by an excessive humidity, surpassing that of the British Islands, while at other periods of the year there is a well marked "dry season" The result of these various facts. taken in connection with the additional fact that at a remote geological period the islands doubtless were connected with the Asiatic and North American mainland, has been the development of a fauna marked by a wonderfully composite character, and revealing to an unusual extent the phenomena of varietal change, and in the case of the insect tribes, seasonal dimorphism. To these phenomena Mr Pryer has paid especial attention. with the result of ascertaining that not a few of the so-called species erected by recent entomologists, into whose hands Japanese collections have happened to fall, must be relegated to the great and evergrowing mass of synonymical species This is especially true of the genera *Papilio*, *Pieris* and *Terias*, in which seasonal dimorphism reveals itself most strikingly The course pursued by Mr Pryer in massing a large number of forms of the species originally described by Linnaeus as *Terias Hecabe* under the name *Terias Multiformis* Pryer, is open to criticism on the ground that the labour of the elder nomenclator should have been respected and his name retained, while the names of later writers should have been adduced as synonyms Nevertheless the fact seems to be established beyond reasonable doubt that the species lumped by Mr Pryer under the newly coined name *Multiformis*, are all mere local or seasonal variations of *Hecabe* L It was the privilege of the writer to spend many days in Mr. Pryer's laboratory, and he can testify to the painstaking care which he has taken to avoid error in his deductions The most surprising result of breeding is, however, one which is not alluded to in Part I of the RHOPALOCERA NIHONICA, since it was only definitely confirmed during the past summer, viz, the discovery that *Terias Bethesba* of Janson is a dimorphic form of *Terias Laeta* of Boisduval The entire difference in form of the two has naturally led students unhesitatingly to accept them as widely different species Careful breeding has established their practical identity

As the first attempt at a comprehensive and accurate survey of a part of the beautiful insect fauna of 'Dai-Nippon," the new work will no doubt be hailed with pleasure by all entomologists who raise their eyes beyond the narrow confines of their own immediate neighborhoods, and seek to ascertain the truth as to the whole of Nature

W J HOLLAND, Pittsburgh. Pa

CORRESPONDENCE

CALLIMORPHA

Ed Can Ent—*Dear Sir* In reference to my former note on *Calli-morpha* I would state that in my "Check List" the white forms were referred to *Lecontei* as varieties I was totally unacquainted with what may be a more Northern form, viz., *confusa* Lyman Mr Lyman's excellent plate and paper must be commended, but I must *insist* that neither Mr Lyman (nor Mr Smith for that matter) have done more than separate the forms in the perfect state , and in this Mr. Lyman seems to have shown great tact and is the more correct, having made no fresh synonyms The yellow species commence the series in my Check List, in which *vestalis* and *fulvicosta* are distinguished as different forms or varieties. and I have only to add to my former communication respecting the interchange of yellow and white in this Subfamily, that it notoriously occurs in the sexes of *Leucarctia acraea* The American species of *Callimorpha* are probably not long separated from an original type—they form to-day a pro-genus, like *Datana* In such cases where the naturalist attempts to still further separate the species or races as Mr Smith has done, the work of all previous describers should be studied and certainty attained as to what forms have been already named and what remain without a designation In all this work there is nothing really original When some one *breeds* all these forms, as Mr Edwards does the doubtful Butterflies, there will be a real scientific addition to our present imperfect knowledge

A R GROTE

Dear Sir Dr Harris, in his well known work on Injurious Insects, states that the caterpillars of the Callimorphas conceal themselves in the day time under leaves and stones According to my experience, the larvæ of *Lecontei* and *confusa* may be found on the food plants at all hours of the day About ten or twelve years ago. *Lecontei* was rather abundant on certain parts of Montreal Mountain, and I observed quite a number of the larvæ, from some of which I reared the moths. I unfortunately neglected to take a description of the larva, nor did I ascertain what the food plant was When the Mountain was opened as a public park, a carriage drive was cut right through the *Lecontei* ground, and since that time it has become very scarce, and I have so far failed to re-discover the laiva, however, as I have elsewhere stated, I feel confident that careful breeding will prove *Lecontei, confusa* and *contigua* to be good species In his paper on Callimorpha (CAN. ENT , vol xix , p 237), Mr Smith is in error in stating that I "assumed the distinctness of *Lecontei* and *militaris.*" I gave *militaris* as a variety of *Lecontei* and assumed the distinctness of *Lecontei* and *confusa*, which is a very different thing, and should have aided rather than misled him I have found hibernated specimens of *Lecontei* and *confusa* easy to rear, the latter in confinement feeding freely on almost any kind of leaf. Might not these hibernating Arctians be reared by placing them on ice, as Mr. Edwards has done so successfully with the diurnals ?

F. B CAULFIELD, Montreal

Dear Sir In reference to Dr. Hagen's recent notice of Calverley's illustrations of Sphingidæ, I would say that the plates are neither "unknown " nor "forgotten," but simply "unpublished." References to their existence may be found in my printed papers. To certain of the figures I furnished the types Dr Hagen makes some remarks as to the quality of the illustrations It is perhaps not remarkable that he does not notice that many figures are copies from Cramer and Drury, and that the plate of *Papilio Calverleyi* is the same as published in Proc. Ent. Soc Phil , on different paper. Copies of Calverley's Sphingidae were sent to a few principal libraries, hence it is not extraordinary that Dr. Hagen should have found one at Harvard The work owes its inception perhaps to the zeal of the late Mr. Stephen Calverley, who was a correspondent of Doubleday. The names of its two original authors are remembered in *Limenitis Weidemeyerii* and *Papilio Calverleyi*, as well as *Deilephila Calverleyi* from Cuba The text should have been written by myself, as at one time at least intended, but the plates were finished at such irregular periods and over so many years (1860 to about 1869) that they were never placed complete in my hands for the purpose

A R GROTE.

ERRATUM —On page 57 (March No.), line 11 from the bottom, for "vol xix." read "vol. xx "

Mailed April 10th Delayed by accidental loss of proofs in transmission.

TO OUR FRIENDS.

It has been deteimined by the Council of the Entomological Society of Ontario to make their collection a representative one of Canadian Entomology, and thus enable it to be of permanent use for iefeience and comparison

This is the more desirable as owing to the Collection having been exhibited in England and the United States on various International occasions, many specimens have lost their color and freshness

Mr J Alston Moffatt, of Hamilton, Ont , has kindly consented to revise and re-arrange the Collection.

Printed lists will be published from time to time of *desiderata* required to fill up and replace the various sections

We appeal to our members and friends to help the Society in this useful work, and to send what specimens they can procure of the insects requiied

Insects used by the Society in this way will be labelled in the Collection with the name and addiess of the donor

The following list of Lepidoptera has been prepared, showing what are the moie immediate wants in this class

It is not expected that all these will be obtained fiom present Collections, but members might bear in mind what is wanted, and endeavor to make special captures during the next and following seasons

All specimens should be secuiely packed and sent by express at the cost of the Society, directed to Mr. W E. SAUNDERS London, Ont.

April, 1888

LEPIDOPTERA—LIST A.

Papilio
    marcellus, *Cram*
    cresphontes, *Ci im.*
Phyciodes
    nycteis, *Walker*
    tharos, *Cram*
    tharos *var* marcia
        Edw
Limenitis
    ursula, *Fab*
    arthemis *var* proserpina,
        Edw
Debis
    Portlandia, *Fab.*
Neonympha
    canthus, *Bd -Lec*

Chionobas
    jutta, *Hub.*
Satyrus
    nephele, *Kirby*
Thecla
    calanus, *Hub*
    Ontario, *Edw*
    hyperici, *Boisd & Lec*
    Edwardsii, *Saunders*
    falacer, *Godt*
    niphon, *Boisd et Lec*
    strigosa, *Harr*
    humuli, *Harr*
    titus, *Fab.*
Feniseca
    tarquinius, *Fab*

Lycaena
    comyntas, *Godt*
    neglecta, *Edwards.*
    violacea, *Edw*
Carterocephalus
    maudan, *Edw.*
Ancyloxypha
    numitor, *Fab.*
Pamphila
    zabulon *var.* pocahontas,
        Scud.
    cernes, *Bd -Lec*
Pyrgus
    centaureæ, *Ramb*
Nisoniades
    persius, *Scudder*

Nisoniades
  brizo, *Boisd et Lec.*
  juvenalis, *Smith*
Amphion
  nessus, *Cram*
Thyreus
  Abbotii, *Swains.*
Philampelus
  pandorus, *Hubn*
  achemon, *Drury.*
Ampelophaga
  versicolor, *Harr.*
Paonias
  myops, *Abb & Sm.*
Sphinx
  kalmiae, *Smith*
Ellema
  bombycoides, *Wall*
Alypia
  MacCullochii, *Kirb*
Scepsis
  fulvicollis, *Hubn.*
Lycomorpha
  pholus, *Drury.*
Clemensia
  albata, *Pack*
Hypoprepia
  fucosa, *Hubn.*
  fucosa, *var* miniata, *Kirby*
Crocota
  ferruginosa *Walk*
  quinaria, *Gr*
  Treatii, *Grote*
  rubicundaria, *Hubn.*
Utetheisa
  bella, *Linn.*
Callimorpha
  clymene, *Esp*
Platarctia
  parthenos, *Harr*
Arctia
  nais, *Drur*
  decorata, *Saunders*
  celia, *Saunders*
  virguncula, *Kirb.*
  arge. *Drury,*
Phragmatobia
  rubricosa, *Harris.*
Euchates
  egle, *Drur*
Halesidota
  tesselaris, *Sm. Ab.*
  caryae, *Harris.*
Euclea
  quercita, *H S.*
  ferruginea, *Pack.*

Parorgyia
  Clintonii, *G & R*
  parallela, *Pack*
Limacodes
  biguttatus, *Pack*
Empretia
  stimulea, *Clem.*
Phobetron
  pithecium, *Abb. & Sm.*
Tortricidia
  testacea, *Pack.*
Ichthyura
  inversa, *Pack*
  albosigma, *Fitch.*
Datana
  ministra, *Drury.*
Nadata
  gibbosa, *Walker*
Prionia
  bilineata, *Pack.*
Actias
  luna, *Linn*
Platypteryx
  genicula, *Grote.*
  arcuata, *Walk*
Dryopteris
  rosea, *Walk*
Eacles
  imperialis, *Drury.*
Anisota
  stigma, *Fabr*
  senatoria, *A & S.*
  virginiensis, *Drury*
Dryocampa
  rubicunda, *Fab*
Clisiocampa
  disstria, *Hubn*
Microcoelia
  diphteroides, *Guen*
  obliterata, *Grote.*
Bryophila
  lepidula, *Gr*
Chytonix
  palliatricula, *Guen.*
Dipthera
  fallax, *H S*
Coelodasys
  unicornis, *A & S*
Hepialus
  thule, *Strk*
Apatela
  dissecta, *G. & R.*
  grisea, *Walk.*
Agrotis
  Normaniana, *Grote*
Mamestra,
  distincta, *Grote.*

Hadena
  mactata, *Guen*
  fractilinea, *Grote.*
Oligia
  versicolor, *Gr*
Anytus
  sculptus, *Gr.*
Oncocnemis
  occata, *Grote.*
Prodenia
  flavimedia, *Harvey.*
Gortyna,
  sera, *G & R.*
  nictitans, *Borkh*
  immanis, *Guen*
  cataphracta, *Grote*
  nebris, *Guen*
  rutila, *Guen*
Achatodes
  zeae, *Harr.*
Arzama
  obliquata, *G & R*
Heliophila
  pallens, *Linn*
  Harveyi, *Grote*
  phragmitidicola, *Grote.*
  lapidaria, *Grote*
  adonea, *Grote*
  commoides, *Guen*
  unipuncta, *Haw.*
  pseudargyria, *Guen*
Ufeus
  satyricus, *Grote*
Caradrina
  multifera, *Walk*
Pyrophila
  pyramidoides, *Guen.*
Taeniocampa
  furfurata, *Gr*
Parastichtis
  gentilis, *Grote*
Ipimorpha
  pleonectusa, *Grote*
Nolaphana
  malana, *Fitch*
Aletia
  argillacea, *Hubn*
Marasmalus
  histrio *Grote*
Calpe
  Canadensis, *Beth*
Plusia
  contexta, *Grote*
  Putnami, *Grote*
  biloba, *Steph*
  viridisignata, *Grote*
  mortuorum, *Guen*

Plusia
    ampla, *Walk*
Lygranthœcia
    rivulosa, *Guen.*
Anthœcia
    arcifera, *Guen*
    Spraguei, *Gr*
Anarta
    cordigera, *Thunb.*
Tarache
    candefacta, *Hubn*
    erastrioides, *Guen.*
Eustrotia
    albidula, *Guen*
    muscosula, *Guen*
Celiptera
    frustulum, *Guen*
Phoberia
    atomaris, *Hubn.*
Remigia
    latipes, *Guen*
Parthenos
    nubilis, *Hubn*
Catocala
    unijuga, *Walk.*
    faustina, *Strecker.*
    semirelicta, *Grote*
    briseis, *Edw.*
    parta, *Guen*
    coccinata, *Grote*
    ultronia, *Hubn*
    concumbens, *Walk.*
    amatrix, *Hubn*
    cara, *Guen.*
    ilia, *Cram*
    neogama, *Abb & Sm*
    subnata, *Grote*
    Meskei, *Grote*
    antinympha, *Hubn*
    palaeogama, *var pha-*
      langa.
    palaeogama, *Guen*
    habilis, *Grote*
    Clintonii, *Grote.*
    fratercula, *G & R.*
    polygama. *Guen*
    crataegi. *Saund*
    amica, *Hubn*
    ilia, *var uxor, Guen*
    innubens, *Guen*
    cerogama, *Guen.*
    serena, *Edw*
    similis, *Edw*
    grynea, *Cram.*
Panapoda
    rufimargo, *Hubn*

Erebus
    odora, *Linn*
Homoptera
    lunata, *Drury*
    Saundersii, *Beth.*
    calycanthata, *Abb & Sm.*
    albofasciata, *Beth.*
    edusa. *Drury,*
    duplicata. *Beth*
    benesignata, *Harris.*
Ypsia
    undularis, *Drury*
    umbripennis, *Grote.*
Zale
    horrida, *Hubn*
Spargaloma
    sexpunctata, *Grote*
Pangrapta
    decoralis, *Hubn*
Pseudaglossa
    lubricalis, *Geyer.*
Epizeuxis
    aemula, *Hubn.*
    americalis. *Guen*
Megachyta
    lituralis, *Hubn.*
Litognatha
    nubilifascia, *Grote.*
Chytolita
    morbidalis, *Guen*
Pityolita
    pedipilalis, *Guen*
Zanclognatha
    laevigata, *Grote*
    ochreipennis, *Grote*
    cruralis, *Guen*
    marcidilinea, *Grote.*
Philometra
    longilabris *Grote*
    serraticornis, *Grote*
Palthis
    augulalis, *Hubn.*
    asopialis, *Guen*
Renia
    Belfragei, *Grote.*
Bleptina
    caradrinalis, *Guen.*
Hypena
    baltimoralis, *Guen.*
    scutellaris *Gr*
    manalis, *Walk*
    abalienalis, *Walk*
    achatinalis, *Zell.*
    profecta, *Gr*
    deceptalis, *Walk*
    perangulalis *Harv*
    vellifera, *Gr*

Hypena
    evanidalis, *Rob*
    scabra, *Fabr.*
Choerodes
    clemitaria, *A & S*
    transversata, *Drury*
Metanema
    quercivoraria, *Guen.*
Ennomos
    alniaria, *Linn*
Eudalimia
    subsignaria, *Hubn*
Endropia
    obtusaria, *Hubn*
    effectaria, *Walk.*
    bilinearia, *Pack*
    armataria, *H S*
Therina
    fervidaria, *Hubn*
    endropiaria, *G. & R*
    bibularia, *G. & R*
Metrocampa
    margaritata, *Linn.*
Anagoga
    pulveraria, *Linn*
Sicya
    macularia, *Harris.*
Plagodis
    rosaria, *G & R.*
    phlogosaria, *Guen.*
    alcoolaria, *Guen.*
Hyperetis
    amicaria, *H. S.*
Aplodes
    mimosaria, *Guen*
Synchlora
    rubivora, *Riley.*
Annemoria
    unitaria, *Pack*
Nemoria
    subcroceata, *Walk*
Eucrostis
    chloroleucaria, *Guen.*
Acidalia
    nivosata, *Guen*
    quadrilineata, *Pack.*
Eudeilinia
    herminiata, *Guen*
Aspilates
    Lintneriana, *Pack*
Nematocampa
    filamentaria, *H-S.*
Thamnonoma
    subcessaria, *Walk.*
    argillacearia, *Pack*
Eufitchia
    ribearia, *Fitch*

Caripeta
  angustiorata, *Walk.*
Hibernia
  tiliaria, *Harris.*
Anisopteryx
  vernata, *Peck.*
  pometaria, *Harr.*
Cymatophora
  humaria, *Guen.*
Tephrosia
  canadaria, *Guen.*
  anticaria, *Walk.*
Eubyja
  quernaria, *A. & S.*
Rheumaptera
  ruficillata, *Guen.*
  basaliata, *Walk.*
  lacustrata, *Guen.*
  hastata, *Linn.*
Petrophora
  diversilineata, *Hubn.*
  hersiliata, *Guen.*
Epirrita
  perlineata, *Pack.*
  cambricaria, *Curtis.*
  dilutata, *Borkh.*
Asopia
  farinalis. *Linn.*
  squamealis, *Grote.*
  costalis, *Fabr.*
  olinalis, *Guen.*
  devialis, *Grote.*
Botis
  octomaculata, *Linn.*
  generosa, *G. & R.*
  insequalis, *Guen.*
  marculenta, *G. & R.*
  signatalis, *Walk.*

Botis
  niveicilialis, *Grote.*
  plectilis, *G. & R.*
  gentilis, *Grote*
  magistralis. *Grote.*
  terrealis, *Treits.*
  submedialis, *Grote.*
  marculenta, *G. & R.*
  subdentalis, *Grote.*
  citrina, *G. & R.*
  sumptuosalis, *Walk.*
  Harveyana, *Gr.*
Mesographe
  stramentalis, *Hubn.*
Blepharomastix
  ranalis, *Guen.*
Cataclysta
  fulicalis, *Clem.*
Tetralopha
  asperatella, *Clem.*
Phycis
  indiginella, *Zell.*
Dakruma
  convolutella, *Hubn.*
Argyria
  nivalis, *Drury.*
Crambus
  Leachellus, *Zinck.*
  agitatellus *var.* albocla-
      vellus, *Schl.*
  albellus, *Clem.*
  bipunctellus, *Zell.*
  topiarius, *Zell.*
Schoenobius
  longirostrellus, *Clem.*
Cacœcia
  purpurana, *Clem.*
  cerasivorana, *Fitch.*

Loxotænia
  afflictana, *Walk.*
Ptycholoma
  persicana, *Fitch*
  melaleucana, *Walk.*
Pandemis
  limitata, *Robs.*
Œnectra
  puritana, *Robs.*
Cenopis
  Pettitana, *Robs.*
Dichelia
  sulfureana, *Clem.*
Amphisa
  discopunctana, *Clem.*
Capua
  furcatana, *Walk.*
Eccopsis
  permundana, *Clem.*
Penthina
  nimbatana, *Clem.*
Sericoris
  coruscana, *Clem.*
  campestrana, *Zell.*
Pædisca
  Scudderiana, *Clem.*
Semasia
  formosana, *Clem.*
Timetocera
  ocellana, *Schiff.*
Phoxopteris
  nubeculana, *Clem.*
  discigerana, *Walk*
  spireæfoliana, *Clem.*
Grapholitha
  interstinctana, *Clem.*

The Canadian Entomologist.

VOL. XX.　　　LONDON, MAY, 1888.　　　No. 5

DESCRIPTIONS OF TWO NEW SPECIES OF MELITAEAS BELONGING TO NORTH AMERICA.

BY W. H. EDWARDS, COALBURGH, W. VA.

1. M. Brucei.

Male.—Expands from 1.5 to 1.7 inch. Upper side brown-black, marked with spots of red and yellow in transverse bands ; there are three well marked varieties, in one of which red predominates, sometimes almost to the exclusion of yellow ; in another red and yellow, much as in other allied species ; on the third much yellow, very little red ; in all the spots are small, so that the black surface is more exposed than in many species.

1. The red form. The spots dull ; the common marginal row wholly red, the submarginal row sometimes red on primaries, sometimes red partly replaced by yellow, and secondaries always red and yellow ; the third row is red and yellow on primaries, red on secondaries, the fourth row just the reverse of this ; at end of cell on primaries a short red and yellow band, in the cell four spots, red and yellow alternately, from the arc, the yellow ones very small ; on secondaries, a red stripe along upper side of cell, two small yellow spots in cell ; fringes black at ends of the nervules, yellow in the interspaces.

2. The spots of the second row red and yellow on primaries, yellow on secondaries, of the third yellow on primaries, red on secondaries ; of the fourth red and yellow on primaries, yellow on secondaries ; the two next costa sometimes red on the posterior side ; the yellow spots in cell of primaries large, and a large yellow patch below cell.

3. Nearly all spots yellow ; the marginal red ; no other red on secondaries, or a mere trace of it indicating the spots of the third row, which are otherwise suppressed ; the submarginal row of primaries represented by a few scales only, as are also the spots in cell.

On the under side all these forms agree ; primaries dull red, almost without black ; the marginal spots a deeper red, the next two rows yellow, the submarginal obsolete on lower half, a yellow patch subapical on costa, another outside arc of cell, the two cellular spots yellow, dusted red

Secondaries have all the spots clearly defined, the marginal row red, the second row of yellow lunules, the third wholly red, the fourth yellow, the spots of upper half elongated and cut unequally by a black line from costa to lower discoidal nervule, beyond to base red, with a straight row of four confluent spots from costa to submedian, and a fifth at end of cell

FEMALE.—Expands 1 7 to 1 8 inch.

Varies as the male, but some examples still more widely, the yellow spots being very large On the under side as in the male, except that some examples have the red submarginal spots of secondaries slightly edged with yellow, in the more yellow upper side examples the yellow edging to these spots is broader, and even sometimes extends along the marginal side

This small Melitaea has long been known in collections, but till recently I myself have seen few of them, and knew nothing of its localities or habits. Mr Bruce, who took great numbers of examples, says. " I found it only on 'igh mountain tops (in Colorado), this was strictly the rule These tops are in most cases extensive plains covered with flowers, chiefly yellow Compositæ, and the Melitaeas in question sit on every blossom in numbers, and are very sluggish—or rather I may say, they sit and cling tightly to the flowers to prevent the brisk wind, that is generally blowing at this elevation, from taking them away I have never seen them down the slope lower than a few hundred yards It is an abundant species on the Snowy Range at not lower than 12,000 feet, and must appear early in June, as many of my specimens taken early in July are rather worse for wear "

The species comes also from Montana, Washington Terr., and British America, in the Rocky Mts.

2. M TAYLORI

Male.—Expands from 1 6 to 1 8 inch.

Upper side brown black, the costal margin of primaries next base dusted yellow, marked with red and clay-yellow spots disposed in transverse bands, the hind margins have a common row of red spots, almost confluent on primaries, and a submarginal row of yellow, usually very small on primaries ; on same wings a third row of large yellow spots, and a fourth row red, or sometimes red partly replaced by yellow ; around the end of cell and to lower median nervule a yellow row, sometimes obsolete below cell, the remainder appearing to branch from fourth row ; in the cell four spots, red and yellow alternately from the arc, and a yellow patch below cell. On secondaries the third row is of large red spots, the fourth of large yellow ; a red stripe along upper side of cell and at end ; two yellow spots in cell and another below ; fringes blackish at the ends of the nervules, white in the interspaces.

On under side the spots are repeated, enlarged, nearly concealing the black ground on both wings ; and on primaries are as distinctly defined as on secondaries, the red bright ; the spots of common marginal row confluent, of the submarginal large, crescent ; the red spots of third row on secondaries have each a slight yellow edging except on the posterior side ; next comes a black line, and a row of narrow red spots entirely across wing as in *Rubicunda*, separated by a black line from the dorsal row of yellow spots ; thence to base red, with four yellow confluent spots crossing the area from costa to submedian, and a fifth at outer end of cell.

FEMALE.—Expands 2.7 to 1.8 inch.

Like the male on both surfaces.

The preparatory stages of this species were described by me in CAN. ENT., vol. xvii., p. 156, 1885, as of *M. Rubicunda*, H. Edw., but a better acquaintance with both forms makes it certain that they are distinct species, though closely allied. *Taylori* is considerably the smaller, more constant to one type, the spots of under side not light yellow, as in *Rubicunda*, but either white or white with a mere tint of yellow. *Rubicunda* is a very variable species in all its markings.

I have named this Melitaea for the Rev. Geo. W. Taylor, of Victoria, by whose kind aid very much knowledge has been gained of Vancouver butterflies. I received larvæ from Mr. James Fletcher, Sept., 1884, sent him by Mr. Taylor.

These were in hibernation, lived through the winter, were fed on Chelone glabra, the plant of *M. Phaeton*, and some of them pupated and gave butterflies. I related in the paper spoken of that one larva, soon after waking in spring of 1885, became lethargic, and on 23rd May I returned it to the ice box. On 6th July, I brought it to my room, but after two days, as it had eaten nothing, though it had changed its position, I returned it to the ice box, where it was in good condition on 20th Aug. The larva died some weeks later, instead of passing the second winter as I thought it perhaps might do. Of the extent of territory on the main land occupied by *Taylori*, I am unable to speak.

NOTES ON DANAIS ARCHIPPUS.

BY W. H. EDWARDS, COALBURGH, W. VA.

Now that the observations of my young friend, W. D. Marsh, on this species, have been given in the CAN. ENT. (xx., p. 45), I think no reasonable person can doubt that it is at least three-brooded in New England, and that the late butterflies hibernate there. Very late in the fall of 1887, Mr. Marsh saw individuals flying, long after severe frosts had been felt, and still later, he had butterflies come from pupæ. These late fliers are the hibernators. And early in the spring a hibernator had been seen at Amherst. It seems that Rev. H. W. Parker, when a resident at Amherst, some years ago, saw a hibernated *Archippus*, 12th May, 1871, as appears by his notes published in Am. Nat., vol. vi., 115. This mention had been lost sight of, but has recently been re-discovered by Mr. Scudder, who called my attention to it. Of course this settles the matter, taken together with the observations of Mr. Marsh, as to *Archippus* hibernating in Mass.

Mr. Marsh has stated, and it is an original observation on his part, so far as I know, that a great destruction of *Archippus* larvæ takes place in the fall, owing to the prevalent custom in New England of cutting the grass a second time. Were it not for that, probably hibernated imagos would be as abundant in the spring as they are in West Virginia.

I asked Miss Emily L. Morton, residing at Newburgh, N. Y., to make observations there on *Archippus*, for Newburgh is in sight of the hills of New England, and it is not to be supposed that the behavior of any species of butterfly would be different at Newburgh, in the latitude of Northern Connecticut, from what it would be inside the bounds of New England. Miss Morton wrote me that she had taken hibernated *Archip-*

pus on 3rd, 4th May (1887), at lilac blossoms, and that at the date of writing, June 27th, fresh males of the first brood of the imago were flying Mr. Marsh says that at Randolph, Vt., far to the north, a fresh male was seen a week later, on 4th July

On 16th August, Miss Morton wrote that a new brood of the butterfly was flying in abundance Mr Marsh says that at Randolph, 2 ♀, 1 ♂, perfectly fresh, were taken 11th August

On 20th Sept., Miss Morton wrote: " Fresh examples are emerging every day now, and there are numbers of them in the clover field " Mr Marsh says : " From 30th Sept. to 15th Oct, butterflies from pupæ bred from said larvæ emerge, and besides, many pupæ were found in the fields and the imagos came from them " So running parallel to Miss Morton's account.

On 9th Oct, Miss Morton again wrote " On 6th and 8th of this month, we saw numbers of perfectly fresh examples of *Archippus* We caught several, and in some the wings were still quite fresh, showing their recent advent from chrysalis. On none were there any signs of age " And she adds · " These are doubtless the hibernators " Mr. Marsh had imagos out of bred pupæ so late as 29th Oct and 4th Nov , and saw butterflies on the wing on 5th and 13th Oct. The history is identical in New England and eastern New York.

Years ago I followed up the life history of *Archippus* carefully in West Virginia, and in Psyche, vol 2, p. 169, 1878, and CAN. ENT , xiii., 211, 1882, I showed that the hibernators of this species came out of winter quarters as early as other hibernating butterflies, and with them gathered about the first blossoms of the year, which here are on the wild plum and cherry trees , that eggs were to be found, and old females were to be seen ovipositing on milkweeds but just out of ground , that in a very short time the old hibernated individuals had totally disappeared, undoubtedly dying soon after laying their eggs, as is the invariable rule with butterflies , that within a month a generation fresh from pupae was flying , and that so, certainly three, possibly four, generations of the butterfly followed the hibernators. In fact, that the habits of *Archippus* were in no way abnormal, nor was the species so long lived as others where there is but one brood per year in descent from the hibernators (as for example, in Grapta *Faunus*).

I made observations myself here at Coalburgh last season, to some extent, on this species I found an egg 10th May, on an Asclepias but four inches high   On 27th May, I found a pupa hanging to the outer side of a rail, as I crossed the railway to my garden   I then, in the fall, searched daily for eggs, to see how late they were to be found   On 2nd Sept., I found 2 eggs; on 4th, 1 , on 8th. 1 , on 10th, 1 , on 14th, 1, and saw the female lay this egg; on 16th, found 3 , on 20th, 2 , on 22nd, 1. I found no eggs later than this   Mr Marsh found larvæ up to 30th Sept., though he obtained no eggs apparently later than 5th Aug.   But the eggs to produce his late larvæ must have been laid early in September   On 26th and 27th Sept , I had occasion to drive many miles, and saw great numbers of the fresh butterflies flying about the Actinomeris flowers.   My last imago, from one of the eggs found, was 12 days in pupa and came out 11th Oct.   So that the butterflies were coming out of pupæ later if anything, at Amherst than they were at Coalburgh

It had been said that no one ever found an *Archippus* egg in New England, or on very young Asclepias plants, that could have been laid by an hibernator, though thousands of plants had been searched, at different localities, by many persons   Negative evidence is no evidence at all in such a case   If one thousand plants had failed to produce an egg, the one thousand and first plant nevertheless might have it   The hibernated females are very few, as there is every reason to believe, after hearing of the wholesale destruction over large areas of country of the late larvæ , and Asclepias plants are exceedingly plenty in the spring, thousands of them to one *Archippus* egg, no doubt.   So that a person might very possibly look all day and not find an egg   And on the other hand, the first plant touched might have an egg on it   That the eggs are there is sufficiently proven by the resultant butterflies

ON THE NATURE OF SEASONAL DIMORPHISM IN RHOPALOCERA.

BY T D A COCKERELL WEST CLIFF, COLORADO

In studying the seasonal variation exhibited by various species of butterflies, I have been struck by the fact, that whereas in most instances the form emerging in the spring is darker and smaller than the summer brood, there are also exceptions to this rule, in which the vernal emergence is the lighter. Take, for instance, the genus *Pieris*. The vernal broods of *P. napi* and *P. protodice* are distinctly more dusky than those which have undergone their whole metamorphosis in a single season ; but, on the other hand, the spring emergences of *P. rapæ* and *P. brassicæ* are wont to be pale, and the spring-emerging *P. virginiensis* is pale, and as Mr. W. H. Edwards remarks ("Papilio," 1881, p. 97), more like the summer than the winter form of its progenitor *P. napi*. In Japan, it would appear ("Entomologist," 1888, p. 24,) that the vernal form of *P. napi* is less dusky than the summer emergence.

Hitherto it has been held by the majority of Entomologists that the darkening of vernal forms was due to the cold to which the pupæ were subjected during the winter, and this view seemed to receive ample confirmation when Mr. W. H. Edwards proved experimentally that cold applied to pupæ did produce darkening of the forms.

Supposing, then, that cold is the sole cause of the darkness of vernal broods, why are not *all* vernal broods dark, since they have all been subjected to a greater amount of cold in the pupa-stage than the summer ones?

It seems to me that this question is unanswerable on the supposition that duskiness is the simple effect of cold, and I have therefore been led to seek another explanation of the phenomenon.

On one occasion, I bred a specimen of the European *Geometra papilionaria* Linn., and paid particular attention to the appearance of the pupa before emergence. I noted that although there could be no doubt that the vital organs of the body were gradually formed during a considerable period before emergence, the wing-pigments did not begin to be developed until the last few days. First of all the pigment appeared brown, and only just before emergence did it assume the vivid green characteristic of the insect.

Now suppose that *G. papilionaria* were a species hybernating in the pupa-state, how would cold effect the formation of the wing-pigment? Obviously, not at all, since the pigment is not called into existence until a short time before emergence, that is to say, not until the warm spring sun has wakened the sleeping pupa into new life.

I have not had the opportunity of making careful observations of a similar kind with the pupæ of Rhopalocera since I began to pay special attention to the subject, but I think it will generally be accepted as a fact that the wing-pigments are not formed until a short time before emergence. In all the cases of which I have recollection this has been so.

But I imagine that the ratio between the growth of the wing and the metabolism of its pigment is not always the same, nor is that between the wing-formation and the growth of the vital and reproductive organs constant, and herein I believe lies the key to the solution of the problem.

Rapid metabolism produces darkness of colour, while slow change accompanied by growth gives rise to a larger expanse of wing, on which the pigment is paler, lighter, and often more brilliant.

The vital and reproductive organs of a butterfly will develop *sooner and at a lower temperature* than the pigment of the wings ; and hence in a country where the winters are cold and the summers hot, the hibernating pupæ will have reached a nearly full development by the time the warm weather comes on, except as regards the pigment of the wings. This will undergo very rapid metabolism to be ready by the time of emergence, and the result will be a dusky and small winged form.   On the other hand, if the spring comes gradually, and the winter is warm, the wing-pigment will develop more slowly, the wings will have longer to grow, and consequently the vernal brood will be paler even than that of the summer.

And this is precisely what we find ; *Pieris virginiensis* is a *pale* spring form taking the place of the *dark oleracea-hyemalis* of the more northern portion of the continent, while *P. rapæ* and *P. brassicæ*, which do not exhibit dusky vernal broods, are natives of Europe, where the winters are milder and the advent of spring more gradual than in North America.

It may here be objected, why are not tropical species, whose development is often excessivly rapid, uniformly dusky or black ?   That they are in many cases darker than their representatives in more temperate regions will I think be admitted, but I would point out that they are not by any means in the same position as North American vernal forms.   The vital organs must in any case take a certain time for development, which is always longer than that necessary for the metabolism of the pigment.   So that in the case of any summer brood, however rapidly developing, the temperature being high enough to allow the development of the pigment at the same time as the organs of the body, it has ample time for sufficient metabolism—less indeed than in the case of a warm and gradual spring, but more than in that of a frigid winter and quick coming summer, where emergence must rapidly follow the first wakening to life by the hot rays of the sun.

So I believe that sudden warmth after a period of prolonged cold, and not the cold itself, is the cause of the duskiness of North American vernal forms of Lepidoptera, and I will not hesitate to advance the same reason for the darkness of Arctic species, and of Mr. W. H. Edwards's specimens which he experimentally subjected to cold. I cannot prove anything as yet, but I put forward this theory, which has commended itself to me, in the hope that your readers, who have had much more experience in practical entomology than I, may be able to put it to the test, and either prove its accuracy, or propose some other which may serve better to explain the facts.

I believe there is a phase of melanism caused by moisture, quite distinct in its nature from the duskiness dealt with in the present paper, but I have already dealt with this question elsewhere (" Entomologist," 1887, p. 58,) and need only point out the distinction here. It becomes every day more evident, in dealing with colour-variation. that different colours do not necessarily denote essentially different pigments, and seeming identical colours may be quite unlike in their composition, though we at present do not know precisely what that is.

CAPTURES MADE WHILE TRAVELLING FROM WINNIPEG TO VICTORIA, B. C.

BY REV. W. J. HOLLAND, PH. D., PITTSBURGH, PA.

It was my privilege last summer to accompany the expedition sent out by the National Academy and the U. S. Navy Department to Japan for the purpose of observing the total eclipse of the sun which took place upon the 19th of August, 1887. The route selected by our party was the one just opened to the far East over the Canadian Pacific R. R., and I was the first passenger booked in Chicago for Yokohama, and my colleague, Prof. Todd, was the first passenger booked in Boston for the same port, over the new line. We left Winnipeg on the morning of June 13th, and were borne westward without any detention until the 15th, when, owing to the fact that the railroad bridge at Duthil had been partially carried away by a freshet in the Bow River, we were compelled to lie at Canmore Station for about twenty-four hours. The delay was rather acceptable to me, as it enabled me to do a little collecting in a region wholly new to me. We reached Vancouver upon the evening of June 17th, and on the morning of the 19th were courteously permitted by Captain Marshall, and Captain Webber, the Naval Superintendent of the Can. Pac. R. R., to go to Nanaimo, on Vancouver Island, where the " Abyssinia " took on her coals. Upon the morning of the 20th, while the " black diamonds " were being poured into the hold of the great ship, I took refuge from the dust and discomfort which prevailed on board, and with the assistance of a couple of Indian lads, spent two hours in collecting specimens a few hundreds of yards from where the ship was tied up to the shore. My captures consisted exclusively of Coleoptera. I saw a specimen of Argynnis, and a fine male of *Papilio Eurymedon*, but neither came within reach of my net, and after giving chase for a moment, I reverted to the more profitable task of gathering the beetles, which appeared to be abundant. The result of my collecting at Canmore and at Nanaimo is given in the accompanying lists. I am indebted. to my good friends, Dr. John Hamilton of Allegheny, and Dr. Geo. H. Horn of Philadelphia, for the determination of the Coleoptera.

Species Collected at Canmore, June 15th, 1887.

LEPIDOPTERA.

1. *Papilio zolicaon*, Boisd., 1 ex.	9. *Chionobas Chryxus*,	
2. *Colias* var. *occidentalis* ♂ 1 "	Dbly.-Hew., 1 ex.	
3. *Thecla Irus*, Godt., 4 "	10. *Nisoniades Icelus*, Lint., 3 "	
4. *Lycaena antiacis*, Bdl., 13 "	11. *Heliothis*, sp., 2 "	
5. " *amyntula*, Bdl., 7 "	12. *Rheumaptera*, sp., 1 "	
6. *Phyciodes Montana*, Behr., 1 "	13. *Eupithecia*, sp., 1 "	
7. *Argynnis Freya*, Thnb., 2 "	14. *Nephopteryx*, sp., 1 "	
8. *Erebia Epipsodea*, Butl., 1 ex.		

COLEOPTERA.

1. *Pterostichus Luczotii*, Dej., 1 ex.	4. *Acmaeops pratensis*, Laich., 3 ex.
2. *Trichodes ornatus*, Say, 2 "	5. *Saperda tridentata*, Oliv., 1 "
3. *Dichelonycha Backii*, Kirby, 39 "	6. *Lepyrus gemellus*, Kirby, 1 "

At North Bend Station, B. C , after lunch, I succeeded in taking before the train started four specimens of *Cicindela Oregona*, Lec

My search for Lepidoptera and Coleoptera at Canmore was interfered with by the presence of larger game, and I was so much engrossed by the chase of a lynx that I neglected my entomological opportunities as I have now occasion to regret, inasmuch as the lynx in the end proved missing.

List of Coleoptera taken at Nanaimo, June 20, 1887.

1 *Notiophilus Sibiricus*, Mots , 1 ex.
2 *Pterostichus lustrans*, Lec , 1 "
3 *Amara fallax*, Lec , 1 "
4 *Harpalus rufimanus*, Lec , 1 "
5 *Anisodactylus Californicus*, Dej , 1 "
6 *Silpha Lapponica*, Hbst , 1 "
7 *Coccinella sanguinea*, Linn., 5 "
8 *Anatis Rathvoni*, Lec., 1 "
9. *Psyllobora taedata*, Lec , 3 "
10. *Scymnus Phelpsii*, Crotch, 1 "
11. *Trogosita virescens*, Fab , 24 "
12. *Peltis Pippingskoeldi*, Mann , 3 "
13. *Adelocera profusa*, Cand , 1 "
14 *Alaus melanops*, Lec , 1 "
15. *Cardiophorus tenebrosus* Lec , 1 "
16 *Elater apicatus*, Say, 1 "
17 " var *phoenicopterus*, Germ., 1 "
18. *Agriotes Thevenetii*, Horn, 1 "
19. *Dolopius lateralis*, Esch , 2 "
20 *Melanotus fissilis*, Say, 1 "
21. *Limonius Californicus*, Mann , 1 "
22. *Athous vittiger*, Lec , 1 "
23 " n sp (*fide* Dr Horn) 1 "
24 *Corymbites fallax*, Say, 1 ex.
25 " *inflatus*, Say, 1 "
26. *Chalcophora angulicollis*, Lec , 9 "
27 *Dicerca tenebrosa*, Kirby, 1 "
28 *Buprestis aurulenta (lauta)* Lec., 33 "
29 *Melanophila longipes*, Say, 10 "
30 " *Drummondi*, Kirby, 18 "
31 *Chrysophana placida*, Lec , 1 "
32. *Podabrus piniphilus*, Esch., 2 "
33. *Telephorus Curtisii*, Kirby, 1 "
34 " *divisus*, Lec , 1 "
35 *Clerus sphegeus*, Fab , 7 "
36. *Ptilinus basalis* ♂, Lec , 1 "
37 *Ceruchus striatus*, Lec , 2 "
38 *Asemum atrum*, Esch . 3 "
39. *Tetropium velutinum*, Lec , 2 "
40. *Xylotrechus undulatus*, Say, 1 "
41. *Rhagium lineatum*, Oliv., 1 "
42. *Leptura obliterata*, Hald., 1 "
43. " *chrysocoma*, Kirby, 1 "
44 " *scripta* (var *a*) Lec , 2 "
45 *Syneta albida*, Lec., 1 "

46. *Haltica bimarginata*, Say, 23 ex.	53. *Anaspis atra*, Lec., 8 ex.
47. *Phellopsis porcata*, Lec., 1 "	54. " *rufa*, Say, 1 "
48. *Eleodes cordata*, Esch., 7 "	55. *Eurygenius campanulatus*,
49. *Iphthimus serratus*, Mann., 5 "	Lec., 1 "
50. *Platydema Oregonense*,	56. *Rhynchites bicolor*, Fab., 3 "
Lec., 4 "	57. *Amnesia granicollis*, Lec., 1 "
51. *Helops pernitens*, Lec., 1 "	58. *Sciopithes obscurus*, Horn, 1 "
52. *Cistela variabilis* (var. *c*)	59. *Dorytomus luridus*, Mann, 2 "
Horn, 1 "	60. *Orchestes canus*, Horn, 1 "

While lying in the harbor of Victoria for a few hours, during which I did not have the privilege of going ashore to collect, I climbed to the main-top of the steamer, and while sitting at the cross-trees a specimen of *Pachyta liturata*, Kirby, came flying toward me and settled on my arm. It was promptly captured and tied in a corner of my handkerchief, and is now embodied in my collection. Numerous specimens of *Melanophila longipes* also came on board and sought refuge in the seams between the planking of the deck. I caught a dozen or more, and for two days afterwards, when fully six hundred miles off the coast, a stray specimen would now and then turn up upon the spray-swept deck of the vessel.

The success which attended my efforts to collect at Nanaimo reveals the richness of the locality. I was absent from the steamer about two hours, from 7.30 a. m. until a little before 10 a. m. My collecting was all done in a little clearing made by an Indian for the purpose of planting a few rows of beans and potatoes. The area covered did not exceed 75 yards square. The sun was shining brightly, and about the trunks of the freshly fallen fir trees and under their bark the Buprestidæ and Elateridæ were particularly abundant. It was with pleasure that I recognized *Trogosita virescens* in this high northern latitude, as heretofore it has been represented in my collection mainly by specimens from Florida. Most of the specimens have dark blue elytra, but a few have the typical green. I trust at some future day to be able to explore patiently and thoroughly the length and breadth of Vancouver Island and the coast of British Columbia lying to the East and North.

STRAY NOTES ON MYRMELEONIDÆ, Part 4.

BY DR H. A. HAGEN, CAMBRIDGE, MASS

(Continued from vol xx., page 74)

8 *Brachynemurus Carrizonus* Hag , n. sp

Yellow with black lines , face yellow, above with a transversal narrow black band, separated by a yellow crescent from the antennæ, and by a narrow yellow line between the antennæ from the vertex , a faint median black line goes from the black band nearly to the clypeus ; labrum yellow , palpi short, pale yellowish, maxillary with apical joint, cylindrical, black except on tip, the two preceding joints with a brownish mark in the middle , labials a little longer, apical joint hirsute, black shining except on base, fusiform, thickened, the apical third thin, pointed , on the inflated part an ocellus like spot. Antennæ not fully as long as head and prothorax, strong, clavate, black, faintly annulated, the two basal joints shining brown below, yellow above club luteous , antennæ of female shorter, club broader , vertex elevated, rounded, yellow, before a yellow transversal band , above two black transversal bands, the last one dilated behind on each side of the middle to a larger triangular or square spot , one specimen with the anterior band interrupted in the middle. Prothorax little longer than broad, rounded before. yellow with four black longitudinal bands, the internals approximate , space between the externals with a yellow band, or divided in two elongate spots , the two externals sometimes broader near the head. and a little divergent , one specimen has the externals reaching only the transversal furrow Mesothorax black, with two anterior yellow dots and some near the wings, two yellow angular bands divided from behind on the disk , the hind part yellow with two black approximate anterior spots , metathorax similar but the yellow predominant , sides of thorax black with yellow marks

Abdomen slender, of male longer than wings, very finely clothed with white hairs, black, the two basal segments above yellow with a broad black median band, the following similar, but the black band broader , the last four segments black , appendages pale with long black hairs, as long as the last segment, slender, a little incurved , the last segment below at the end with numerous long black hairs , it can not be ascertained if among the hairs is a triangular plate , abdomen of female a little shorter than the wings, the yellow lateral marks on all segments ; genitals yellow, superiors split with two transversal rows of strong black spines ; below two very small cylindrical appendages.

Legs short, yellowish, strongly sprinkled with black and with black hairs, tip of tibia, of third and apical joint of tarsus black, fourth entirely black ; spurs brown, incurved, as long as the two basal joints.

Wings hyaline, pterostigma small, yellowish white, interiorly a dark dot ; only the last costals before it forked ; venation dark, largely interrupted with white ; along the mediana and submediana the costals marked with dark, also the base of the small forks on the apical and hind margin of the front wings.

Length of body, male 35 m.m. ; female 25 m.m. ; exp. al., 45 to 50 m.m.

Habit., Carrizo Springs, Dimmit Co., Texas, just on the border of ' Mexico ; two males, three females.

It has the appearance of a smaller form of *B. peregrinus*. A larger male, length 38 m.m., exp. al. 60 m.m., is apparently just transformed, with the colors not yet finished, from Tusco, Arizona. I can not separate it from the Texan species.

9. *Brachynemurus Sackeni* Hag., n. sp.

Yellow, variegated with black ; face yellow, with two oblique ovoid black spots near the antennæ ; labrum yellow ; palpi brownish, maxillary with the last joint cylindrical ; labials little longer, last joint fusiform and black on the basal half, with a few hairs ; antennæ longer than head and thorax, black, faintly annulated, clavate, more luteous on tip, below dull, the two basal joints brown shining ; vertex elevated, rounded, black with whitish hairs in front ; yellow with two lacerated black spots on top, which unite anteriorly, surrounding a median heart-shaped yellow spot, two yellow dots behind it, sending to occiput on each side a fine black line ; a black dot near each eye. Prothorax as long as broad, yellow, with two black median lines, separated by a fine yellow line, which is enlarged behind ; on each side a black interrupted line, and a similar one shortly before the side margin, which is clothed with white hairs ; below a black band near the side margin ; mesothorax blackish-fuscous, on each side a yellow maculose band, and some dots ; besides three small black shining dots on each side ; the posterior middle part bright yellow, with three black dots behind, and two in the anterior corner similar to the ocellus-like spots of *M. conspersa;* metathorax yellow, divided by black cross lines ; sides largely black ; thorax between the wings and legs black with many yellow spots and stripes. Abdomen of male slender, longer than wings, densely clothed with long black villosity ; black, each segment with a large yellow spot in middle, a yellow band at the apex, and a yellow band, except on the three last segments, on base ; appendages, long 4 m.m., full as long as the two last segments, thin, cylindrical, a little incurved, clothed with long black hairs ; between and below a short pyramidal tubercle with longer hairs. Abdomen of female similar, as long as the wings ; genitals with a row of black spines, appendages brownish.

Legs very slender, short, pale, hairy, sprinkled with black, femur and tibia with a more or less distinct black ring at base and before tip ; tibia with the three last joints black at tip, fourth nearly entirely black ; spurs brown, as long as first joint.

Wings slightly fumose ; pterostigma whitish after a darker spot ; only few of the costals forked before it ; venation black, largely interrupted with pale ; some transversals near the mediana and submediana, and the small forks near tip and hind margin more or less fumose ; hind wings less marked ; venation and hind margin villous.

Length of body, male 35 m.m.; female 25 m.m. Exp. al. 40 to 50 m.m.

Habit.—Texas, Dallas, Boll, and Waco by Belfrage, May 3 to 7 ; June 10. California, San Francisco, O. Sacken and Austin ; Tucson, Arizona. Seven males and two females.

Two females from Colorado, sub-alpine, July, length 35 m.m.; exp. al. 58, can not be separated from the males, except the larger size ; the description agrees fully, the legs and wings are stronger marked ; the abdomen is as long as the wings, the genitals with a row of strong black spines, the small appendages yellow. The greatest breadth of the wings is 9 m.m. where it is of the males only 6 m.m.

10. *Brachynemurus longipalpis* Hag., n. sp.

Pale yellow, marked with black ; face very pale yellowish, with a small black median spot above ; sometimes between the eyes and the base of the antennæ a faint black stripe and another one on the inner side of the base of the antennæ ; labrum pale yellow ; maxillary palpi pale, of common size and shape ; the apical joint longer than the others, cylindrical, tip a little pointed, light brown ; labial palpi of unusual length, longer than the head, about 3 m.m.; second joint about thrice the length of the last maxillary joint, much stronger, hairy, a little incurved, suddenly thickened above just before tip, where it is brownish ; last joint as long as the second, strongly clavate before the short, fine, cylindrical tip, hairy, yellowish inside, externally brown, blackish on the club. Antennæ nearly as long as head and thorax, strong, thicker to tip, fuscous, annulated with yellowish, the two basal joints and basal half of antenna below yellowish ; vertex elevated, pale yellow, on top a transversal black line interrupted in the middle, where is a black spot, and a second transversal line formed by four black spots, besides some black dots near the occiput. Prothorax a little longer than broad, narrowed before and rounded ; pale with whitish villosity ; two fuscous longitudinal bands, approximate and reaching the front margin ; on each side, more distant, a fuscous band, ending in the transversal furrow with a black spot ; below along the side margin a black stripe ; mesothorax pale yellow with short black bands, forming three forks, open behind, and a similar on the hind middle part ; metathorax with a black cross ; sides of the thorax yellow, with a black maculose longitudinal band. Abdomen of male considerably longer than the wings, slender, with whitish villosity, intermixed with brown hairs on the apical half, fuscous below, above with a broad yellow band, divided by a fuscous line on the segments 1 to 4 ; a yellowish median line on the three last segments, and some lateral marks ; appendages very short, cylindrical, going downwards, a little divergent, yellow with a black stripe above, strongly clothed with black hairs. I can not find below them any middle part or plate. Abdomen of female as long as the wings, blackish-fuscous, with two yellow dorsal bands from the third segment to apex ; genitals light brown with a row of strong black spines ; below two short cylindrical appendages with long black hairs. Legs short, pale yellow, moderately sprinkled with black, with strong black spines and on the interior of the anterior femora with white spines ; tibia with a fine black ring near the base ; tip of tibia and all joints of tarsi black ; spurs brown, strong, as long or a little longer than the two basal joints. Wings hyaline, pterostigma white after a brown spot ; costals simple, a few forked before the pterostigma ; veins fuscous interrupted with pale, near the submediana fumose, forming a more or less visible longitudinal dark line ; near the hind margin and along the gradate veins parallel to tip slightly fumose, venation and hind margin villous, hind wings hyaline

Two females from Nevada have more variegated front wings, nearly all the oblique veins below the submediana, the forks along the hind border are more infumate, which makes the wing look strange, the femurs of hind legs fuscous.

Length of body, male 38 m m, female 26 m.m, exp al. 48 to 52 m.m.

Hab., California, Cap San Lucas, by Xanthus de Vesey, Humboldt Station. Nevada, July 29, by O Sacken. Of the 9 specimens before me, 7 are from California (one female), all alike; the two females from Nevada are stronger colored, but otherwise not different. The great length of labial palpi is a character not to be found in another species

NOTES ON LYCAENA PIASUS, Boisd.

BY W G. WRIGHT, SAN BERNARDINO, CAL.

This is in California the first butterfly to emerge in the spring, appearing in February though it is the accepted representative of the Eastern *Neglecta*, which is not the first to appear there *Piasus* is double brooded, the second brood coming in the latter part of April, and between it and the first brood a few days intervene when no *Piasus* are seen. Both broods are very fond of water, being always found on damp sands of wet places, and at the brookside crossings They are also often seen feeding on willow blossoms A large series gives a uniform expanse of 1.1 inch. I can detect no difference in the markings or size of the two broods

The larval food-plant of *Piasus* is the buds of *Adenostoma fasciculatum*, an anomalous genus which has no representative, even approximate, in the Eastern States. The Spanish name is "chamiso," which is Anglicized into "chemise." It is a heath-like plant, 4 to 6 feet high, resembling a juniper bush more than any other Eastern plant. Every part of it is brittle, dry, and rather resinous, burning freely when quite fresh and green The leaves are very small, round like pine needles, and evergreen, they grow all along the stems in little bunches or "fascicles," whence the specific name The flowers are minute, profuse, in dense terminal racemes on the tips of the twigs, white, scarcely or not at all fragrant, though forming one of the chief sources of honey in the country, and it is notable that while the plant is abundant and flowers so profusely as to whiten the landscape, the seeds have never been found. It grows upon the dry hillsides and covers uncounted square miles of waste land.

This plant, growing at a distance from the usual haunts of *Piasus*, is that butterfly's food plant. While the flower buds are as yet but in their merest infancy, the female *Piasus* of the first brood deposits her eggs, singly, on the bud and between it and the stem. The female of the second brood finds the flowers in blossom. The egg is white, round, flattened, with a depressed point in the center, like other Lycaena eggs.

While *Adenostoma* is entirely foreign to any plant in the Atlantic States or Europe, it is placed by botanists in the Order Rosacæa, and among eastern plants those nearest it are: *Alchemilla*, "lady's mantle ;" *Agrimona*, "agrimona," and *Poterium*, "burnet," though all of these are very unlike in appearance to *Adenostoma*. It is possible that the buds or the immature seeds of other Rosaceous plants might feed *Piasus* larvæ, as cherry, plum, strawberry, etc.

CORRESPONDENCE.

WIND-VISITING MOTHS.

Dear Sir: I have given in the CANADIAN ENTOMOLOGIST a preliminary list of those moths which do not breed continuously in our North American Territory, as defined by Leconte. It has been my theory, stated in numerous papers within the past fifteen or twenty years, that a number of species of moths, found as moths within our limits, are wind visitors. I have been at some pains to point out that the Cotton Worm Moth is, so far as the Central Cotton Belt is concerned and the territory north of this, only a summer breeder, and that it is winter-killed over the larger portion of our continent over which it flies. I ascertained, while in the employ of the Agricultural Department, that, on the coast of Georgia, the earlier or later appearance of the Cotton Worm depended, at least in some seasons, upon the average direction and force of the wind. No continued observations could be taken, but as the general course of the wind is from south to north during the summer, what I heard agreed with my previously published conclusions. My theory as to the Cotton Worm has been ingeniously covered up in his Reports by

Prof. Riley, but I refer to my statements in print and to the fact that the line of continuous breeding is yet unfixed, while it is the primary object to be ascertained by practical entomologists. On page 56 of this volume, Mr. Smith "dissents from the idea" that certain Sphingidæ or Hawk Moths determined from our territory by Mr. Edwards should be taken into our fauna in papers on our fauna. He demands that the right should be made clear by ascertaining that the insect breeds within our territory. I agree with Mr. Edwards that we should take all species found within our territory into our lists and treat them as belonging to our southern fauna, until it is proved that they do not breed with us; and *then* with the remark that they do not breed, but are merely wind-visitors as moths. How can we pass over such a fact, as their being found with us, in silence? Again, seeing the large extent both of our territory and of our ignorance of the conditions under which our moths live, how can we pronounce whether or no these moths may not be summer breeders, or occasional breeders? Who knows that *Philampelus typhon* does not breed seasonally in Arizona? Mexican moths are probably more often found in Texas than we have yet any idea; and Cuban in Florida. Mr. Roland Thaxter has bred the Spanish moth, *Euthisanotia timais* in Florida. This is quite a pronounced tropical form. The moth in numbers is beaten by the wind into the light-houses on the coast at least as far north as New Jersey, probably much higher up. We must keep a busy record of the habits of these moths to understand their geographical distribution and their habits. Any ignoring of them in monographic works will tell against the completeness of such works, while the moths, unhindered by the defects in our literature, will wing their way northward and become at least adopted citizens of our domains every summer. As to the Hawk Moths, the Blue and Green Hawk *(labruscæ)* has been taken in Missouri and in New Jersey. Tropical species of the Owlet Moths allied to *Erebus odora* have been taken so far north as Wisconsin, coming up the valley of the Mississippi. I refer the student to my general paper on the Geographical Distribution of our Moths in these pages, and I earnestly hope that all our wind-visitors will be catalogued, described and put on record, since it seems to me we can get no complete picture of our fauna without them. The limit of their continuous breeding must be ascertained, as also of their summer migrations. Do not our ornithologists take into their works and distinguish between continuous residents, summer breeders, and birds of passage? These moths are our birds. The ornithologists have already a trinomial nomenclature, which we may come to use in time. After awhile the most self-important classificator will come to appreciate the fact, that the laws of Nature are of general application, and that the value of Natural Science is tested by its ability to broaden our views and widen our understanding. It is clear we must compare our results with those reached in other branches of Natural Science.

A. R. Grote, Bremen, Germany.

A RARE MOTH.

Dear Sir: Permit me, in the pages of your valuable journal, to record the capture here of an interesting moth,—the rare and beautiful *Hepialus auratus*, Grote. Towards the close of last July, while strolling through a cool shady ravine at Lancaster, near this city, I came upon my treasure resting upon the leaf of a wild gooseberry bush that grew on a knoll, surrounded by as rich a growth of vegetation as nature can well produce in this latitude. As it hung to the leaf with its wings steeply closed over its back, and the tip of its long body elevated, it was a very difficult object to detect; and in the deep shade in which it occurred, greatly resembled a yellow, partially dead, leaf. The well known larvæ of *Grapta progne*, which feed on this plant, derive perhaps some protection from a similar coloring. May not this circumstance indicate the gooseberry as the food-plant of the golden *Hepialus?* The type specimen of this species was taken by the late Mr. W. W. Hill in the Adirondacks, July, 1877, and was described by Mr. Grote in the Can. Ent., vol. x., page 18. As I find no reference to the capture of another example, I presume the present to be its second recorded occurrence.

E. P. VanDuzee, Buffalo, N. Y.

CELIPTERA BIFASCIATA, BATES.

Dear Sir: Mr. John B. Smith has compared my types of *Celiptera bifasciata*, described as a new species in the Can. Ent., May, 1886, page 94, and informs me that it is evidently identical with *Phurys vinculum*, Guen.

J. Elwyn Bates.

Mailed May 2nd.

The Canadian Entomologist.

VOL. XX.   LONDON, JUNE, 1888.   No. 6

DESCRIPTIONS OF SOME NEW NORTH AMERICAN CHALCIDIDÆ.

BY WILLIAM H. ASHMEAD, JACKSONVILLE, FLA.

Sub-family ENTEDONINÆ.

Astichus Forster.

(1) *Astichus arizonensis* n. sp.

♂. Length .04 inch. Steel blue, finely scaly, with a slight metallic tinge on thorax ; the knees and tarsi white. Antennæ dark blue, the funicle joints excised, pedunculated, with whorls of very long hairs. Wings hyaline ; veins pale, the marginal vein very long.

Hab.—Arizona.

Holcopelte Forster.

(2) *Holcopelte missouriensis* n. sp.

♀. Length .09 inch. Rather robust. Vertex of head, thorax and metathorax cupreous ; face, thorax beneath and at sides, and the abdomen all blue. The scape of the antennæ, excepting at tip, and all the legs, excluding the blue coxæ, waxy white ; flagellum blue-black, pilose. The head is punctate, thorax and scutellum scaly, the latter longer than wide with a median groove ; metathorax with two delicate parallel keels. Abdomen petiolate, truncately rounded at apex, the second segment occupying most of its surface. Wings hyaline ; veins pale brown.

Hab.—Missouri.

(3) *Holcopelte Popenoei* n. sp.

♀. Length .09 inch. All of the head, the thorax, mesopleura and coxæ bright cupreous. Head and thorax punctate ; scutellum delicately scaly with a median groove. The scape of antennæ, excepting at tip, and legs yellowish white ; flagellum cupreous. Abdomen as in *H.*

missouriensis, blue-black, with a slight æneous tinge near the base, in certain lights. Wings hyaline ; veins pale.

Hab.—Kansas.   Prof. E. A. Popenoe.

Both of the above species seem to approach quite closely to *H. albipes* Prov.

(4)   *Holcopelte floridana* n. sp.

♀. Length .08 inch.   All black, shining, excepting a slight æneous tinge on thorax.   The trochanters, apices of femora, all tibiæ and tarsi, white.   The head and thorax very delicately punctate ; scutellum smooth with a median groove.   Abdomen petiolate, pointed ovate, the second segment occupying most of its surface, the following segments short, but all distinctly visible.   Wings hyaline ; veins brown.

Hab.—Florida.

(5)   *Holcopelte microgaster* n. sp.

♂. Length .05 inch.   Blue-black, smooth.   Scape of antennæ, coxæ and metathorax, distinctly blue.   Funicle æneous.   The femora, excepting tips, blue ; tibiæ and tarsi white, the former with a brown blotch. Wings hyaline ; veins yellow.

Hab.—Missouri.

Reared from a Microgaster cocoon.

Pleurotropis Forster.

(6)   *Pleurotropis leucopus* n. sp.

♀. Length .06 inch.   Robust, coarsely scaly.   Dark blue, excepting a slight metallic tinge on the thorax ; the apical tips of tibiæ and all tarsi white.   Metathorax short, with delicate keels.   Abdomen broadly oval, the petiole very short, second and third abdominal segments nearly equal, the following segments shorter.   Wings hyaline ; veins pale yellowish, postmarginal vein wanting.

Hab.—Florida.

Entedon Dalman.

(7)   *Entedon albitarsis* n. sp.

♂. ♀. Length .06 to .08 inch.   Head, antennæ and thorax, blue-black, vertex of head and mesothorax, æneous, distinctly scaly.   Abdomen of female pointed ovate, in male linear ; it, as well as the legs steel

blue , tips of tibiæ and tarsi yellowish-white   Wings hyaline , veins pale
brown

Hab —Virginia.

(8)   *Entedon arizonensis* n. sp.

♀.   Length .10 inch.   Head, antennæ and thorax, fiery cupreous.
Head nearly smooth, vertex narrow , thorax and scutellum very coarsely
scaly.   Abdomen ovate, black very highly polished, the second segment
occupying nearly the whole surface.   Legs blue-black, the anterior and
middle pairs with metallic tingings, the posterior pair all cupreous.
Wings hyaline , veins dark brown

Hab —Arizona

(9)   *Entedon columbiana* n. sp.

♀   Length 07 inch   This species is very close to *E albitarsis*,
and may prove to be nothing but a variety of that species   It differs
however, in being much more robust, more coarsely punctate and in
having the trochanters, extreme tips of femora, all white, as well as the
tarsi, characters that will readily separate the species.

Hab —District of Columbia.

Asecodes Forster

(10)   *Asecodes albitarsis* n. sp

♀.   Length .08 inch   Blue-black smooth, shining.   Head and
thorax with a decided brassy tinge   Scutellum smooth, metallic green
Antennæ (?) seven-jointed, scape blue, flagellum metallic green, pilose
Legs, excepting the three basal joints of tarsi which are white, all blue
or black   Wings hyaline , veins brown, the postmarginal vein is slightly
developed

Hab.—(?)

Omphale Haliday

(11)   *Omphale bicinctus* n sp

♂   Length 09 inch.   Stout, robust, cyaneous, delicately ripple
marked.   Head large, broader than the thorax.   Eyes very large, brown
Antennæ inserted low down on the face , scape slender, yellow excepting
a dusky streak above near the apex , joints of flagellum black, with long
hairs.   Legs, excepting coxæ and femora which are black, all yellow.
Abdomen pointed ovate, slightly longer than the thorax, the second

segment the longest, but extending hardly to half the length of the abdomen; sides with some long hairs. Wings hyaline, with two transverse brown bands across the disk; veins pale brownish, the postmarginal vein longer than the stigmal.

Hab.—Florida.

Closterocerus Westwood.

(12) *Closterocerus cinctipennis* n. sp.

♂. Length .04 inch. Head, pleura, sternum, metathorax and abdomen blue; collar, mesothorax and scutellum golden green, strongly punctate. Head emarginate in front and consequently very thin antero-posteriorly. Antennæ brown-black, hairy. Legs brown, trochanters, tips of tibiæ and tarsi pale or whitish. Wings hyaline, fringed with long hairs, forewings with a brown band extending across the stigmal region and another at the apical margin.

Hab.—U. S.

Sub-family TETRASTICHINÆ.

Anozus Forster.

(13) *Anozus siphonophoræ* n. sp.

♀. Length .04 inch. Black, smooth, shining, impunctured. Head transverse, very thin antero-posteriorly, front deeply emarginated. Antennæ black, (broken). Thorax transverse, collar not visible from above; mesothorax broader than long, parapsidal furrows, deep; scutellum large, smooth, convex, without grooves, broad at base, the scapulæ being very minute; metathorax short; pleura blue-black. Abdomen sessile ovate, yellowish at base. All coxæ black; trochanters, tips of femora and tibiæ, and all tarsi, yellowish. Wings hyaline; veins pale brown, the marginal vein is very thick and about as long as the submarginal, the stigmal and postmarginal veins not developed, wanting.

Described from one specimen reared from an Aphis, *siphonophera* sp.

Euderus Haliday.

(14) *Euderus columbiana* n. sp.

♀. Length .10 inch. Dull brown, or bronzy green, its whole surface including the abdomen strongly confluently punctate. Head transverse, not wider than the posterior part of mesothorax and with only a slight antennal groove in front. Antennæ about as long as the thorax, eight jointed , scape slender, yellowish brown ; flagellum dark brown, about twice as long as the scape, pubescent, the pedicel shorter than the first funicle joint, the latter joint the longest, about twice as long as wide, the following joints being not much longer than wide, sub-moniliform. Thorax : collar transverse, rounded before , mesothorax with parapsidal grooves well defined , scutellum longer than wide. without grooves, rounded behind, sides parallel.   Abdomen conic ovate, cylindric, one third longer than head and thorax together, the segments of nearly equal length   Legs dark brown, trochanters, knees, fore and middle tibiæ, and all the tarsi honey-yellow, hind tibiæ dusky in the middle.   Wings hyaline, fringed with short ciliæ ; the veins brown, the marginal is twice the length of the submarginal, the stigmal short, while the postmarginal is wanting.

Hab —Florida and District of Columbia

Hyperteles Forster.

(15)   *Hyperteles hylotomæ* n sp

♀.   Length .08 inch.   Dark blue, with a faint metallic lustre on thorax.   Antennæ eight-jointed. brown, pubescent   scape brownish-yellow, the joints of the flagellum are about twice as long as thick   Collar transverse, rounded before , mesothorax with a median groove , scutellum with two parallel grooves ͵ metathorax with three keels   Abdomen oval-rotund   Legs pale brownish-yellow excepting the femora, which are blue for two-thirds their length , tarsi pale   Wings hyaline, pubescent, veins pale brown, the marginal vein about twice the length of the submarginal, stigmal vein longer than usual, postmarginal wanting

Hab —Canada.

Described from three specimens sent to me by Mr W. Hague Harrington, who reared them from the eggs of a saw-fly *Hylotoma* sp .

Aprostocetus Westwood.

(16)   *Aprostocetus granulatus* n sp

♀   Length .07 inch   Black, with a coarse, scaly punctation Antennæ, including scape, brown, pubescent   Thorax ovoid, the parap sides distinct, the collar very short, rounded before, the scutellum longer than wide with two grooves on its disk   The abdomen is pointed ovate, longer than head and thorax together, depressed above, rounded below, with an exserted ovipositor, nearly half its length   Legs dark honey-yellow, femora and the tibiæ at base brownish. Wings hyaline, pubescent and ciliated, the pubescence brown, the venation as in *Tetrastichus*.

Hab.—Florida.

Described from one specimen.

(17) *Aprostocetus canadensis* n. sp.

♀. Length to tip of ovipositor .08 inch ; ovipositor .02 inch. Dark blue, with a slight æneous tinge on the thorax. Head emarginated in front, and very thin antero-posteriorly. Eyes brown. Antennæ short, eight-jointed, brown, pilose. Collar short, transverse, rounded before ; mesothorax with distinct, deep parapsidal grooves and a median groove. Abomen linear not quite twice as long as the thorax, concave above, keeled below, the ovipositor being not quite two-thirds as long as the abdomen. Legs honey-yellow, the femora, excepting at tips, blue ; the tibiæ with a brown blotch in the middle, more distinct on the posterior pair ; apical tarsal joints brownish. Wings hyaline, almost devoid of pubescence ; the venation as in the genus *Tetrastichus*.

Hab.—Canada.

Described from two specimens sent me by Mr. W. Hague Harrington, who reared them from the thistle (?) cecidomyia, along with *Solenotus Fletcheri*, on which it may be a secondary parasite and from which it is with difficulty distinguised. *Solenotus*, however, has a larger collar and very broad, thick fore femora and tibiæ.

(18) *Aprostocetus americanus* n. sp.

♀. Length to tip of ovipositor .09 inch ; length of ovipositor alone .03 inch. Smooth, shining black Head emarginated in front and very thin antero-posteriorly. Antennæ eight-jointed, brown, the club wider than the funicle joints. Thorax : collar very short, transverse ; parapsidal grooves deep, distinct and no median groove on the mesonotum. Scutellum convex, slightly longer than wide, with two parallel grooves on the disk. Abdomen sessile, long, linear, without the ovipositor about twice as long as the head and thorax together, very slightly widened just before apex and from thence acuminate and ending in a long ovipositor two-thirds its length, above depressed, below keeled with a few long hairs surrounding apex. Legs honey-yellow, the femora, excepting at tips, brown, the terminal joints of anterior and middle tarsi and the two terminal joints of posterior tarsi, brown. Wings hyaline, with short ciliæ ; venation as in *Tetrastichus.*

Hab.—U. S.

Sub-family TRICHOGRAMMINÆ.

Trichogramma Westwood.

(19) *Trichogramma acuminatum* n. sp.

Female, length .03 ; male, .02 inch. Honey-yellow ; eyes purplish-brown ; legs pale or white. The abdomen in the female is acuminate-ovate, about twice as long as the head and thorax combined, with a lateral and a ventral row of five or six brown spots. In the male the abdomen is obtuse behind, not longer than the head and thorax combined. Antennæ pilose. The wings are strongly ciliate, the fore pair broadly rounded with a dusky blotch beneath the stigma, the hind pair rather narrowed and pointed at apex.

Described from two female and one male specimens, reared from a corn-leaf, and probably parasitic on the eggs of some leaf miner.

(20) *Trichogramma nigrum.*

Female. Length .02 inch. Robust, black, polished. Antennæ short, stout, brown. Legs entirely white. The scutellum is rather high testaceous, the extreme tip white. The abdomen is sessile ovate, not longer than the head and thorax, its dorsum somewhat flat. Wings hyaline, as in *T. acuminatum* without, however, the small blotch beneath the stigma ; veins brownish ; tegulæ white.

Described from two specimens.

(21) *Trichogramma ceresarum* n. sp.

Female. Length nearly .04 inch. Reddish-yellow, rather slender. Eyes brown. Abdomen and posterior femora fuscous, the fore and middle femora pale brown ; tibiæ and tarsi pale The thorax is triangular in front ; the abdomen not longer than the thorax but wider. Wings hyaline. as in *T. nigrum,* but with very strong violet reflections.

Described from two specimens reared from the eggs of the Membracid *Ceresa bubulus* Say.

PREPARATORY STAGES OF CATOCALA PALÆOGAMA, GUEN

BY G. H. FRENCH, CARBONDALE, ILL

Egg —Diameter o4 inch, low conoidal, a prominent bulging ridge round the base of one half of a hundredth of an inch on each side, so that inside of this the egg is o3 inch ; striated with 38 prominent long-itudinal striæ, of which 12 reach the small micropyle, shallow transverse striæ , apex small, not depressed   Color dull, pale, brownish olive. Duration of this period not known, but at least 194 days.

Young Larva —Length .12 inch, of the usual Catocala shape, loopers on account of the first and second pairs of pro-legs being small ; pale brownish yellow, joints 5 and 6 dark, somewhat blackish, joints 7 and 8 whitish, 9 and 10 blackish again ; a faint fine red line on each side of body, very short hairs from the pelifirous spots   Duration of this period three days.

After 1st Moult.—Length .20 inch   Color reniform pale whitish, slightly brown tinted, head darker, a red line on each side with a broken line above it and another below it, of the same color, on the ventre a round red spot on the middle of each joint.   Duration of this period four days

After 2nd Moult —Length .28 inch   On the sides are four rather broad, dark reddish purple stripes, alternating with pale greenish ones, these dark stripes approaching on joint 2 so that there is here only a narrow dorsal light line, the upper line indistinct ; from joint 2 the dorsum widens out in pale greenish so that in the middle of the body this color extends to the region of the subdorsum, its outer part containing the upper part of the lateral stripe which is here broken and of a purplish green color.   The dorsum from joint 5 to 10 has in its centre a series of very narrow elliptical pale purplish green spots extending from the middle of each joint to the middle of the next one back.   Pilifirous spots small and black, head mottled with irregular longitudinal purplish black and pale greenish markings, the purple on joint 2 being of the same color but a little paler on its back part   Ventre with spots of the same dark color in the centres of the joints , feet pale.   Toward the close of this period the larvæ turn darker, many of them being as dark on the whole of the dorsum as on the thoracic segments at the beginning of the period, this color purplish black, with a fine whitish dorsal line , all of them darker than at the beginning of the period.   Duration of this period six days.

After 3rd Moult.—Length .85 inch.   Marked very much as in the preceding stage, stripes and mottlings purplish black, this color enough paler in the middle of the body to be purple, and jet black at the extremities, the two blending into each other and arranged in fine long-itudinal stripes, each of which has a paler centre but which is not so pale as the alternating whitish stripe ; the dorsum paler than the sides. Piliferous spots more prominent, black, the very short hairs black ; head striped with broken white lines as before ; ventral spots prominent only on the middle joints; thoracic feet pale.   The lateral fringe begins to show.   Duration of this period three days.

After 4th Moult.—Length 1.20 inches.   Striped with black very much as before, but each stripe composed of three indistinct lines, making the body pale on joints 5 to 8 and the anterior part of joint 9 and the pos-terior part of joint 10, the rest of the joints darker; the light shade is lilac tinted with a yellow tinge between the joints from the middle of the body back ; joints 2 and 13 so dark as to obliterate the stripes.   Head striped as before, but the dark is orange shading into black towards the mouth; legs orange ; pilifirous spots on the dorsum black with yellow at the base, the lateral ones yellow ; the hairs on the dorsum black, on the sides and head pale yellowish ; a black transverse patch on joint 9 between posterior pair of dorsal piliferous spots ; eyes black ; ventre pale yellow, a yellowish black spot in the middle of each joint ; the substig-matal stripe not separable into lines but irregularly mottled.   Duration of this period five days.

After 5th Moult.—Length 1 60 inches.   Color pale purplish red mottled with black, in some more or less of a yellowish tint, rather dis-tinctly arranged in five light and four dark stripes, the mottlings being thicker in the dark stripes, the pale stripes with darker centres, the outer edge of the pale being almost free from black but mottled in shades of red ; the dorsal stripe with the dark in ellipses that have their broadest part between the joints ; piliferous spots on joint 2 pale yellowish, almost white, tipped with black ; those on joint 3 to 4 white ; those on the dorsum of the other joints dark yellow, pale at base ; those on the sides pale yellowish ; the posterior pair of dorsals on joint 12 very much enlarged ; all large and prominent, each with a short black hair ; joint 9 has a dark patch on the posterior part of the dorsum. Head pale reddish, the same shade as the red ground color, marked with irregular longitudinal rows of white dots; feet pale red; ventre pale yellow with black centres to the joints, those at the anterior and posterior parts of the body small. At this time there is a distinct fringe of fleshy appendages on the sides.

Mature Larva.—Length 2.75 inches; cylindrical, tapering slightly to either extremity, with short lateral fringe. Marked as at the beginning of the period with seven longitudinal stripes from stigmata to stigmata, the lower dark one stigmatal, below this the space to the fringe the same color as the dorsal stripe, making the nine stripes mentioned before. The stripes are very nearly the same color, the only difference being that the dark ones have a little more of the black mottling than the pale ones; the stripes are divided by narrower stripes or broad lines of the ground color, which is dull, pale, smoky red. The thoracic joints are a little darker than the others. Piliferous spots pale nankeen, the dorsal tipped with orange; the space between the posterior dorsals on joint 9 black, only a little elevated; the posterior pair on joint 12 about three times as large as the others; each tipped with a very short black hair. Head, the ground color striped with reddish white that consists of transversely elongated dots; feet the ground color; fringe white; ventre pale yellow, a black patch on each joint. Duration of this period seven days.

Chrysalis.—Length 1.10 inches, depth .35 inch, width .40 inch; cylindrical, tapering from joint 5 back; tongue and wing cases extending back to the posterior part of joint 5, tongue case as far back as wing case; abdominal joints moderately punctured, anterior part of each a little corrugated; head moderately rounded. Color chestnut brown, covered with a white powder as is usual. Duration of this period from 30 to 32 days.

In pupating, the larva fastened leaves together with silk, slightly lining the interior, and into this thin lining the cremaster was fastened.

Food plant hickory.

The eggs from which the larvæ from which these notes were taken were found Oct. 5, 1886, in a crevice in a piece of hickory bark, there being fifty-eight of them in a mass, laid so that they overlapped each other, one edge of each being against the bark. I have since found the shells of other eggs in the crevices of hickory bark deposited in the same way.   The species of hickory upon which they were found was what is known as the Mockernut, or *Carya Tomentosa*.

The eggs hatched, or about one-fifth of them, April 17th, 1887, the rest coming out from day to day after this, and they emerged from the pupæ from June 14th to 16th, giving an egg period as above of at least 194 days, to which it is probable that at least two weeks more should be added ; and from the time of hatching to the emergence of the imagines 58 days, of which one month is in the pupa state.   I have no reason to think that this, or any other species we have here, is more than one brooded.   I am also of the opinion that they pass through changes sooner in the hatching boxes than in their homes in the woods, as I never find this species on the trees before July ; and the same may be said of some other species, though *C. Ilea* should probably be excepted.

After one had moulted, at the last moult, I saw it turn, after its usual period of rest, and eat the cast off skin.

THREE MOTHS NEW TO OUR FAUNA.

BY HY. EDWARDS.

In my article with the above heading, to which my friend Mr. J. B. Smith takes exception, I at once confess that an error occurs, and that the title should have been new to "our lists" and not to "our fauna."   Mr. Smith wrote me a day or two after the publication of the paper, and I *at once* replied that I should have used the word "lists" in the place of "fauna."   I am therefore somewhat surprised that in his printed remarks he did not allude to the correction I had personally made, but that he should take me to task *after* receiving my letter, and charge me with adding the species mentioned to our "fauna," when I had disclaimed the meaning he attributes to me.   But though I am free to allow that the species I spoke of may not with propriety belong to the U. S. fauna, I am by no means willing to admit that they are on that account not deserving of a place in our Check List or Catalogue.   This is, as I take it, not a philosophic account of species belonging to a certain faunal district, but merely the names of those species found to be inhabiting a geographical limit, and is intended chiefly for the purpose of enabling collectors and students to classify their specimens, and in the case of a synonymical catalogue, of referring to the descriptions of species. At any rate, this is the view I take in giving *Pseudosph. Tetrio, Philamp. Typhon* and *Syntom. Epilaris* as being found within our limits, and I hold that they have as much right to a place among N. American, or rather United States species as many that have long been admitted. Of the first named, I have now seen five examples, four taken in Arizona, and one in N. W. Texas. Of these, one was quite fresh and in excellent condition, the others more or less broken and imperfect, though apparently more from careless handling than from either long flight or the age of the specimens. I cannot of course say positively that the species breeds in U. S. territory, but I have as much ground for believing that it *does*, as my friend Smith has for assuming that it *does not*. Then as to *P. Typhon*. The specimen to which I allude was taken by the late Mr. H. K. Morrison in the mountains of N. E. Arizona, as nearly as I can tell, about 20c miles from the boundary line. It is quite perfect, so much so that it may only have emerged from the pupa state within two days, and it seems to me hardly credible that this particular example should have flown such a great distance, and still retain in their purity all its delicate scales. *Syntomeida Epilaris* is from Florida, and I have very little doubt that it will one day be found there in comparative plenty. Indeed, I have good reason to believe that it was taken by Mr. Morrison a short time before his death, and it may possibly be among the Lepidoptera found by Mr. Schwartz during his visit to Key West some little time ago. If we are to discard these insects from our lists because our territory is not their original home, what will become of a large number of the species now included? One third at least of those from Florida, Texas, Arizona and S. California will have to be eliminated, for at least this proportion must be said to belong to a different fauna from the insects of Pennsylvania or Illinois. Mr. Smith calls attention to the fact that he has excluded *Diludia Brontes* from his monograph of the Sphingidæ. I still fail to see on what grounds. *D. Brontes* is found in Florida, and specimens taken by Dr. Wittfeld are in my collection and in that of Mr. Neumoegen. If these insects did not breed near Indian River, where did they come from? Surely Mr. Smith would hardly have us believe that they flew across the ocean from Cuba. I am no believer in the frequent long flight of any species of insects, though it is known that many species travel considerable distances, but I cannot bring myself to think that a specimen say of *D. Brontes* flies from its home in Cuba, and that months or a year after two or three more do the same thing, and that these all find their way to Dr Wittfeld's collecting box. As my friend W. J Florence would say, this is T T. (too thin) It seems more reasonable to believe, as I honestly think is the case with the species in dispute, that a few individuals have established themselves upon our limits, and that they are now gradually taking up new localities and spreading over a larger area. Mr Smith alludes to *Erebus Odora*, and says that " because it has been found in Canada, it would be an absurdity to call it a Canadian insect " Now I think he is unfortunate in this statement. We do not yet know the food plant of the larva of this species, but because we are ignorant of that, it is no reason why it should not breed in Canada, and the evidence is in favor of its doing so I have examined at least forty specimens of *E Odora*, taken severally in New York, Georgia, Arizona, California, Vanc Island, Canada, Michigan, Illinois and Ohio, some of them in absolutely perfect condition, and as fresh as bred specimens, and I am in my own mind quite sure that this species at least has taken up its abode with us, and is as much a resident of the U. S. as *Vanessa Antiopa* or *Pyrameis Cardui* As to Mr. W. H Edwards having " separately called attention to species occasionally found in but not really belonging to our fauna," I respectfully submit that this is a mistake. Mr Edwards has done nothing of the kind He has *discarded* from his Catalogue a number of "species for some time accredited to our fauna, but omitted for want of authentication," which is but saying in other words that had the statement of the capture of the species within our limits been given on undoubted authority, they would have found their place in his Catalogue He has included indeed *Parnassius Eversmanni, Callidryas Philea, Diadema Misippus*, and others, which certainly are not parts of our fauna, but Mr. Edwards holds the same views as I do on the subject, and I claim no more for the three species I alluded to than is claimed for the diurnals I have just mentioned, and that is, that they have been found within our limits, that there is no evidence before us to show that they do not breed therein, and that therefore, when I change, as I am willing to do, the heading of my article to ' our lists " in the place of " our fauna," the three species to which I called attention should be recorded in our catalogues.

THE ORIGIN OF ORNAMENTATION IN THE LEPIDOPTERA.

BY A. R. GROTE, A. M., BREMEN, GERMANY.

Elsewhere I have ventured to call attention to the interesting chapter in Mr. Scudder's book on Butterflies, in which the theory as to the primitive pattern of ornamentation is given. By this we are told that the complex patterns, the seemingly chiselled lines and the eye-like spots, arose from simple transverse shade bands running parallel to the outer margins of the wings themselves. Such bands we yet find on the wings of many Owlet Moths. In the Moths we might expect to find, still existing, a nearer approach to the primitive style of marking than in the higher Butterflies. Mr. Scudder's theory of the primitive pattern is quite independent of the theory as to the origin of the primitive transverse shade lines themselves. Referring to what I have said in my " Essay on the Noctuidæ " and in other places, about the pattern of one wing being reproduced in some species exactly, and in some whole families in the style of a rougher copy, upon the under-lying wing, I have employed the word " photographed " to express the effect produced. The primitive band may then be conceived to have been produced by an *outside* process, the effect of light and shade upon the surface of the wing itself. Its production may have been aided by the movement of the wings (expanding and shutting). The edges of the wings in many ways may be conceived to be first affected. That the primitive Lepidopteron was plain and sombre, we have reason to suppose, judging from what is known of now extinct types from which the whole Order may have been evolved. Under the murky skies of the Carboniferous the colors of the insects remained dull. Upon this plain wing, the first shade or marking may have arisen by a process comparable with photography, the action being produced by the same chemically acting ray of light. The atmospheric conditions then existing are factors in the problem. The shadow originally cast on the wing left a trace in process of time, a deeper tinting which became a permanent shade line or band. The evolution of this primitive shade band is the subject of Mr. Scudder's theory. The manner in which it may have arisen from a shadow has been long the subject of my own thoughts. I am aware that there is a learned opinion that the colors and patterns of insects are developed from the insects' insides, by a process the links in which I am unable to follow, and which it has not pleased the authors of this

inside theory to state.   It seems more reasonable to conclude that the sun
has been the original painter, still improving and beautifying his work.
That the deviations from the original pattern and color have been seized
upon by Natural Selection and that gradual changes have been fostered.
may be conceived under the workings of general evolutionary law

From a study of the subreniform spot in *Catocala*, I, many years ago,
came to the conclusion that the spots in the *Noctuidæ* were modifications
of the transverse lines, and this theory will be found stated in my writings
They may be fragments of original transverse lines, or, as the case seems
to be with the subreniform spots, they may belong to existing transverse
lines from which they have become disconnected   The median transverse
shade is interesting, as it still simulates by its cloudiness, the shade band
of the secondaries and of the under surface of both wings in most *Noctuidæ nonfasciatæ* or *Nocturnæ*.   The primitive transverse shade band
will have been vague and cloudy, and all fine and cleanly cut markings
will prove to be recent in comparison and to have proceeded from nebu-
lous and undefined ornamentation

The instances where the upper surface of the secondaries resemble the
under surface of the primaries occur in the *Ceratocampinæ*, and also in
the *Smerinthinæ*, among other groups   This fact struck me when I was
studying the relationship between the Horned Spinners and the Eyed
Hawk Moths.   As a general rule, the cloudy bands on the under surface
of the wings of the Noctuidæ or Owlet Moths, resemble those on the hind
wings above   The under, or covered wing, bears a certain relationship to
the upper, or covering wing, in coloring and ornamentation   We may
conclude that it has remained longer plain and unicolorous, that its less
exposure in certain groups of the Lepidoptera has allowed it to retain
more of the primitive appearance   The Spanners, or *Geometridæ*, the
Sparklers, or *Pyralidæ*, carry the under wings more exposed and the
markings are continuous and similar on both wings above   This is the
case with the lower or geometridous Noctuidæ. to a considerable extent
The pattern of the wings seems to follow the exposure, as I have elsewhere pointed out   The conditions of the caterpillar stages are widely
different from the environment of the perfect insect, and I have long ago
pointed out that each stage varies independently and unequally, as in the
case of the representative species of *Apatela*, etc , (see my paper in
Annals N. Y Lyceum, N. H)   I have also elsewhere drawn attention to

the law of variation in representative species in the Owlet Moths. This variation is first observed on the upper surface of the fore wings, then of hind wings, while the whole under surface preserves its similarity longest. The uniformity of the under surface in the Noctuidæ seems to be correlated with the habits of the insects themselves, to depend, in fact, upon the conditions of its exposure to the light. I am not here arguing that color in the wings is now dependent upon existing conditions of light. I merely point out that variation both in color and marking proceeds apparently more noticeably upon the more exposed surfaces of the insect in the Noctuidæ, from a comparison of related species inhabiting different parts of the world. In the history of the Lepidoptera former geological conditions have played a part in the evolution of species together with the whole environment. In this paper I merely show the probability that the first transverse markings were the effect of light, and that the more exposed surfaces show most variation in representative species. From my scattered writings I have in part brought these brief notices on this point here together, so that the student may be spared that trouble, and in the hope that the investigation may be carried further.

In the investigation of this subject we must keep the phenomena of color and pattern separate. The test of our theories must lie in the observation of existing variations. In this direction the observations of Mr. Edwards on the influence of cold in the pupa state upon the colors of the imago, are of the utmost value. The class of facts bearing upon the phylogeny of the species must be kept separate from those bearing upon individual variation. But it must be remembered that varieties are in the same sense evanescent species, that species are permanent varieties. The crucial test of our modern idea of species lies in the demonstration of the fact that, in the whole life history, the cycle of reproduction is *now* distinct. To the establishing of this fact repeated observations are often necessary. The whole conditions under which the form is produced must be understood. This is a great field of work, and single instances, however carefully recorded, of breeding from the larva, only partially illustrate the subject. The value of specific determinations from collections of perfect insects depends on the tact and experience of the naturalist and are to this extent tentative. Only where the full round of insect life is known can our determinations be absolutely reliable. The vista of entomological labor is widening as we proceed, so that it is trite to say that the subject is inexhaustible. The most attractive side of the study consists in the curious habits and relationships of the different forms, and here is where the talent of the observer is to be tested. The assorting of collections of specimens is a matter of subordinate tact

CEYLON BUTTERFLIES.

The Lepidoptera of Ceylon, by F. Moore, F Z S., Vol. I , (published under the special patronage of the Government of Ceylon) London, L. Reeve & Co., 1880-81. 4°.

The butterflies of the East India region appear to be now in a fair way of receiving their due share of attention. We have already called attention to Distant's invaluable work on the Malayan butterflies, and to the handbook to the butterflies of India and Burmah, by Marshall and De Nicéville On many accounts neither of these is so important as the earlier work on the Lepidoptera of Ceylon by Frederick Moore, which we desire to introduce to the readers of the CANADIAN ENTOMOLOGIST, principally on account of the very considerable accession to our knowledge of the earlier stages of eastern butterflies which is here given in the plates, and also to draw attention to the notes on the natural history of the insects given by Dr. Thwaites, which are embodied in the text. The work as a whole consists of three volumes , but we speak here of the butterflies only, which are comprised in the first volume, published in 1880-81. It is a large quarto, with 71 excellent colored plates, in which the early stages are in very many instances figured side by side with the butterflies. Notwithstanding that it is published under the special patronage of the Government of Ceylon, the work is a costly one, and to one residing in the United States an embargo is laid upon its purchase by the fact that the duties upon such a work are so high. This single volume cost me $15 for duties and transportation alone. Thus is science encouraged with us !

We are here introduced to a new set of illustrations of the early stages of butterflies, many of which are of extreme interest, and these in every family of butterflies. It is the most important and considerable contribution to our knowledge since Horsfield's memorable volume It is a pity, however, that in many instances no reference is made in the text, either in Dr. Thwaites' notes, or Mr. Moore's descriptive portion, as to the meaning of certain figures which differ strikingly from those of their allies.

Thus the pupa of a species of Cirrochroa is represented as hanging by its hinder end, as in all Nymphalidæ, but bent so at the end of the abdomen, as to lie parallel to the horizontal branch from which it is suspended, much in the way that we find it in our own species of Chlorippe ; but there is no appearence in the figure and no mention in the text of any greatly elongated cremaster with its row of hooklets down the side, which in Chlorippe stiffens the pupa into what would seem to be an unnatural position. We have some interesting additions to our scanty knowledge of the early stages of the Lemoniinæ and an unusual wealth of larvæ and pupæ of Lycaeninæ. Here again is a figure of a species of Spalgis hanging by its tail without the median girt, which is wholly anomalous in this subfamily, but, as there is no explanation of the matter in the text, it is to be presumed that it is not meant to represent the insect in its natural position, the more so as the same is the case in a species of Appias, one of the Pierinæ, represented in two figures as hanging by its tail only, while the whole structure of the chrysalis indicates that it must have had a median girt. Very interesting are the figures of the early stages of the Papilioninæ, which add very considerably to our knowledge, including as they do some figures of the younger stages of the larva—presumably younger from their appendages, though here again no mention whatever is made of the fact in the text. We call attention also to the interesting figure of Gangara, a hesperian living open and unconcealed, as I am informed by Mr. De Nicéville, and which bears long waxy filaments apparently not proper appendages, but as long as the width of the body itself, rendering it an exceedingly conspicuous object.

In the arrangement of families, Mr. Moore follows the rapidly growing company of the best instructed entomologists in beginning the series with the Nymphalidæ and placing the Papilionidæ just before the Hesperidæ. He separates the Lemoniinæ from the Lycaeninæ as a distinct family, and places the Libytheinæ with the Lemoniinæ as was done by Bates ; but he brings the Pierinæ and the Papilioninæ under one family heading. It has naturally pleased the present writer to see that Mr. Moore has had the courage of his convictions sufficiently to subdivide the old and bulky group so long holding rank as a homogeneous whole, the so-called genus Papilio, into a number of genera, including among the seventeen species which he catalogues no less than ten genera, following thus precisely the line which Hübner long ago undertook to establish, and which I adopted in 1872.   SAMUEL H. SCUDDER.

EARLY STAGES OF ARZAMA OBLIQUATA, G. AND R.

BY H. H. BREHME, NEWARK, N. J

EGG —Fusiform, thick in the middle and tapering to a small rounded summit marked by about sixteen longitudinal ribs, which are low, narrow, flat and crossed by a few fine ridges Color yellow-brown Duration about fifteen days

YOUNG LARVA —About 8 inch in length, cylindrical, slender , shape like the other Arzamas Color pale green, with a few long hairs proceeding backwards. Duration eighteen to twenty days.

MATURE LARVA —When fully grown the larvæ are 1½ inch in length, some as much as two inches long They are very slender ; head thick ; color more gray ; body smooth, with no hairs.

PUPA —Length .75 inch , breadth across mesonotum .16 inch, across abdomen 16 inch , greatest depth .22 inches Shape like the other Arzamas Color dark brown Duration sixteen days

The eggs from which these observations were made were obtained on the 26th of October, 1886, by confining a dilapidated female caught flying about the food-plant—the Cat-tail reed The female generally lays her eggs in the middle of the reed, between the long leaves. They began to hatch on the 10th of November, thus giving a period of about 15 days They began to go into pupæ on the 20th April, 1887, making the whole larval period 161 days; adding to this the pupal period of 16 days, makes a total of 190 days from the egg to the imago.

The food-plant—the Cat-tail reed—grows in the meadows As soon as the larva is hatched, it bores at once into the reed and feeds from the top downwards, continuing to feed throughout the winter, until the whole of the reed is eaten out , it then returns to the top, and forms its pupa there The larva is very hard to rear, as it feeds during the winter, and the reed must be kept as wet as possible. I have succeeded by keeping the reeds in a pail of water

The moth generally begins to fly between four and five o'clock in the afternoon, and ceases between seven and eight o'clock. Its flight is very slow It is described and figured by Grote and Robinson, Trans. Am. Ent Soc , vol 1 , page 339

CORRESPONDENCE.

ON INSECTS FEIGNING DEATH.

Dear Sir : I notice in Dr. Hamilton's paper, page 6, the remark that a statement made by me in your pages, namely, " that insects can have no knowledge of death," as such of course and purposely feigning it, is " unsupported " and " dogmatic." I wish to correct these two adjectives, otherwise, as a matter of opinion, I have no further interest with the subject. I cited in my paper the reason for my belief that insects merely kept still and did not move on the approach of danger. I showed that hard bodied insects, as beetles, suffered themselves to drop, while soft bodied caterpillars, equally assuming attitudes of repose and quiet, assisted by their colors and mimicry, clung tenaciously. There is no doubt in my mind that the " keeping still " is the main point, and that the insects have not sufficient mental powers to feign death. Whether insects can have any knowledge of death, as such, may be a matter of opinion, I should as soon credit them with a knowledge of history. Beetles allow themselves to fall by folding in the legs, knowing, from acquired or hereditary experience, that a fall will not hurt them, while in the grass where they tumble they have a place of concealment where they can stop " feigning " and scamper away. While I do not believe that insects can reach the " feigning " process, I know that Dr. Hamilton can, when he says of my paper, which we have all at least glanced over in the pages of the CANADIAN ENTOMOLOGIST, that he " lately saw it in print somewhere." Such carelessness is probably feigned, and whether it is protective may be doubted. It is, however, the privilege of man to keep still, without the danger of being credited with feigning death, a privilege it seems denied to insects. It is well so, since a silent man might run the risk of being buried on suspicion. A. R. GROTE.

NOTES ON COLEOPTERA.

Dear Sir : In my paper in the April No. of the ENTOMOLOGIST, page 66, last line, *Apion herculanum* is printed in error *herculaneum*. On same page I wrote "*prolongata* [Dicerca] breeds so far as known in conifers." This statement admits of a doubt, when the proof is sifted thoroughly. Mr. F. C. Bowditch writes that he collected it on the Colorado mountains on aspen and willow, but never on conifers. It is probably polyphagous, like some other species of this family.

JOHN HAMILTON.

The Canadian Entomologist.

VOL. XX. LONDON, JULY, 1888. No. 7

THE HESSIAN FLY AN IMPORTED INSECT.

BY DR. C. V. RILEY, WASHINGTON, D. C.

As the readers of the CANADIAN ENTOMOLOGIST are aware Dr. H. A. Hagen has argued at length to the effect that the Hessian Fly was, *first*, not imported by the Hessian troops ; *secondly*, that it was not imported from Europe at all, and that it is an indigenous North American insect. In the Third Report of the U. S. Entomological Commission, Dr. Packard has an extended article upon the Hessian Fly, and while he alone is responsible for the general position there taken on this subject, we discussed the matter together, and the views there presented are substantially those which I held at the time, as it was Dr. Packard's desire to arrive at an impartial judgement. The subsequent communication of Dr. Hagen in the CANADIAN ENTOMOLOGIST for May, 1885, seemed, however, positively to set at rest the question of the introduction of the insect by the Hessian troops, as well as of its occurrence in this country prior to the revolution ; because the correspondence which he there published from Mr. H. Phillips, jr., seemed to admit of no further doubt that the first question was settled in the negative, and the second in the affirmative. While in Europe last autumn, I found a great deal of interest manifested in the subject of the Hessian Fly in England, on account of its recent introduction there, and, being called upon, I made some statements at one of the meetings of the London Entomological Society, which will be found reported in the Transactions of the Society for October 5, 1887. I take the liberty of quoting therefrom the following passages as indicating my position in the matter :

"Prof. Riley said it would extend his observations beyond reasonable limits, to enter into the details on which he based his own conviction, which had been substantially expressed in the full paper by Packard, in the 'Third Report of the United States Entomological Commission (1883).' His opinion was that while we might drop the Hessian theory—since Mr. Henry Phillips, jr., as quoted by Hagen (1885), finds mention of the 'Hessian Fly,' in the unpublished minutes of the American Philosophical Society for 1768 (a rather astonishing fact, as it antedates the landing of the Hessians !),—and concede that the insect was introduced some time prior to the revolution ; yet that its introduction *about* that time must be accepted, because Hagen's arguments to the contrary were not supported by [sufficient] evidence."

" Prof. Riley further remarked that he had referred to these conflicting views of leading writers as to the original source and time of introduction of the insect into America, not so much to foreshadow the future conflict of opinion on similar points in England, as to bring out this important fact as a warning to hasty generalisers, viz., that the arguments of Wagner, Hagen, etc., against its introduction into America, were inherently weak from the biologic side.   They are based on the average or normal period of summer development of about seven weeks from egg to adult, and *ignore the impor-tant bearing of exceptional retardation in development whereby the puparia of one summer remain latent and only give forth the flies in the spring or early summer of the ensuing year.*   This fact, recognized by Harris (1852), Prof. Riley said he had evidence of in America in garnered straw, and it was proved by Wagner himself to have occurred in Germany in field stubble.   It was more apt to occur, however, in straw kept dry and packed than in stubble or exposed straw, and is in keeping with many other similar cases of retarded development in insects, some remarkable instances of which he called attention to before the American Association for the Advancement of Science in 1881. It destroyed Hagen's main argument, rendered the introduction of the species possible at almost any season, and made its introduction to America by the Hessians, who left Portsmouth, April 7th, and landed June 3rd, 1777, on Staten Island, quite probable and plausible from biologic grounds."

For the purpose of the present communication, it is not necessary to go into the other arguments which Hagen has brought forward to relieve the Hessians of whatever onus attaches to their accidental introduction of this insect : the more important are, (1) that there was no Hessian Fly in Germany at the time, and (2) that the Hessian troops did not carry straw from regions in which it did occur.   At this late day it would be folly to attach too much importance to these negative deductions, where there are so many possibilities of their both being erroneous in fact.   The evidence as to the introduction and spread of the insect in this country is of a so much more clear and positive nature that it off-sets such nega tive deductions.   With the exception of Mr. Phillips's positive statements, there is only one other recorded statement that would seem to indicate that the Hessian Fly was known in the United States prior to the land- ing of Hessian troops.   This is a statement quoted by Fitch, of Judge Hicock, of Lansingburg, N. Y., who says (Memoirs of Bd., of Agr., 11, p. 169) that a farmer named Jas. Brookins had informed him (Hicock), that upon his first hearing of the alarm upon Long Island, in the year 1786, he (Brookins) detected the same insect in the wheat growing on his farm in Lansingburg.   Fitch remarks in parenthesis, "doubtless 1776 is intended here," evidently on the assumption that Brookins's first hearing of the alarm on Long Island was coincident with the first alarm—an assumption by no means necessary, and one which only complicates the matter. If we grant Mr Brookins's statement to be reliable, there would be nothing remarkable in it as an observation of 1786. But whether for 1776 or 1786 it were folly to overthrow prevailing record and belief by one such unverified statement as this, where the chances are so great of inaccuracy from mere hearsay, and Fitch was justified in stating the strong probability that it was some other insect which was found by Col. Brookins.

Mr. Phillips's statements, as the readers of the CANADIAN ENTOMOLOGIST are aware, are of a very different character. In response to Hagen's inquiries, made to Prof. J. P. Lesley, Mr. Phillips wrote as follows :

"At the request of Prof. Lesley, I have examined our old minutes in reference to the Hessian Fly, and append on next page the results of my search. I know *positively* that before the revolution our newspapers were full of communications in reference to the Hessian Fly *eo nomine*. I cannot call to mind any one paper, but I remember perfectly frequently seeing these articles when reading for other purposes. I cannot find that the committee ever reported."

The following are the extracts from the minutes as furnished by Mr. Phillips :

1768, May 18. Com. on Husbandry to consider whether any method can be fallen upon for preventing the damage done to wheat by the Hessian Fly. [N. B.—Mr. DuHamel has written on the subject.]

1768, June 21. Papers on the Hessian Fly read by Dr. Bond, ordered to be published. See No. 4, original papers.

1768, Oct. 18. Col. Landon Carter, Sabine Hill, Va., observations on the Fly Weevil destructive to wheat ; ordered to be published. [Is published in Vol. 1. of the Transactions of the Society. Cf. Harris, Injur. Ins., pp. 502. Dr. H. A. H.]

And upon being again questioned by Dr. Hagen as to the possibility of error Mr. Phillips writes :

"1. 1768 is not an error. It occurs in the proper place in the old M.S. Vol., and there can be *no doubt* about the fact. *Similiter* the words *Hessian Fly*.

"The term came in use in Pennsylvania from the early German immigrants long before the revolution. I am *sure* the term occurs in our Pennsylvania gazettes long prior to that period.

"2. Cannot say if that paper (of Bond) was ever published. Possibly in some gazette *pro bono publico*. There is no clerical error as to the date and name."

Since this correspondence was published by Dr. Hagen in the CANADIAN ENTOMOLOGIST, the early minutes of the American Philosophical

Society have been published, and the published volume confirms the above statements of Mr. Phillips, as in the minutes for May 18, and June 21, 1768, the term Hessian Fly was printed.

The evidence against the introduction of the Hessian Fly, and even its introduction by Hessians is so easily set aside, and so weak as compared with the positive evidence of such introduction, that I have long wondered at the records of these meetings, and thought that there must be some error. Only recently, however, did I have the opportunity of personally referring to and examining these early minutes in the original. I felt an interest in doing so, because I thought it barely possible to show that they were transcripts from earlier rough minutes, and made subsequent to the revolution, when the term Hessian Fly, then familiar, was inadvertently added by the transcriber. I was therefore much amazed to find that there is really no mention of the Hessian Fly in these old minutes, until the year 1791. I take the liberty of reproducing *verbatim et literatim* the records as they really occur of the three meetings in 1768, quoted by Mr. Phillips in Dr. Hagen's communication :

May 18th, 1768.—" It was recommended to the Committee of Husbandry, &c., to meet on Tuesday, 31st of this month, at the college to consider whether any method can be fallen on for preventing the damage done to wheat by what is called the fly.   N.B. Monsieur du Hamel has written on this subject."

June 21st, 1768.—" The Committee for Husbandry report that they had considered ye affair of destroying the Fly in wheat, and that Dr. Bond had laid before them a paper containing many useful observations on that subject, which Dr. Bond was requested to read before ye Society.   The Society having heard and approved of ye paper request him to prepare it for ye Press, that it may be communicated to ye public without loss of time."

Nov. 15, 1768.—" Colonel Lee transmitted to the Society the ingenious and accurate observation of Colonel Landon Carter, of Sabine-Hall, in Virginia, concerning the *fly-weavil* that destroys the *wheat*.   The Society acknowledge themselves under great obligations to Col. Carter for communication of the conclusions he has formed (on long experience) concerning that insect's propagation and progress, and the methods to be used to prevent the destruction of the wheat by it, and order it to be printed for the public benefit."

It will be seen that in all three " the fly," " the fly in wheat " and " the fly-weavil " are the terms used, and it is susceptible of positive proof that all these popular terms applied then, as they sometimes do yet, to entirely different insects, viz., the grain-weavils, *Sitophilus granaria* and *S. oryzæ*, and the Angoumois grain-moth, *Gelechia cerealella*. Now the minutes, as published, are avowedly abstracted from the original minutes by Prof Lesley, and not full, while the copies of Mr Phillips neither agree with the originals nor with the published abstracts, while in one case, as may be seen, he has changed Nov 15, to Oct. 18.   I can readily understand how Prof Lesley inadvertently used the term Hessian Fly in abstracting from the minutes, if indeed he did so, but it is more difficult to explain Mr Phillips's positive statement after Dr. Hagen's specific questioning.   Mr. Phillips was unable to explain to me how he came to make the error. and just as unable to give me any definite reference that will justify his very positive recollections of having seen the term " Hessian Fly " *eo nomine* in pre-revolutionary literature   When the statement of ocular evidence turns out to be so incorrect we cannot attach any importance to his memory, even where so confidently asserted

With the final disposition of this strongest blow to the general belief that has prevailed for a century among both husbandmen and entomologists, I feel that we must not only accept the general verdict and tradition as correct that the insect was introduced about the time of the revolution, but that there is no very convincing or valid reason for rejecting the other common belief that it was imported by the Hessian troops.   The recorded history of the period does not necessarily include all possible, or even probable facts in relation to the limits of distribution of the insect in Europe, or of the sources from which infested straw may have been derived by the Hessians

In what I have said above I have spoken of the *general* belief and arguments in favor of the introduction of the Hessian Fly to this country, because I am quite aware that others besides Dr Hagen have argued for its indigenous nature , but none of them have perused the question with such single perseverance, and such bibliographical zeal and erudition. He, in fact, deserves our thanks for having brought together so large a body of bibliographical data, because I think it has been the means of confirming not his own conclusions, but the opinion arrived at by Fitch and others.

While in London last autumn I took the trouble to look up and read over the voluminous letters and reports, of which Dr Hagen has published a list, contained in " the proceedings of His Majesty's most Honorable Council, and information respecting an insect supposed to infest the wheat in the Territories of America "   I was thus enabled to verify the accuracy of the list furnished Dr. Hagen by Prof Nichols,   I was fortunate enough to secure a copy of the "Annals of Agriculture," published by Arthur Young, Vol 11, 1789, pages 406 to 613, of which are devoted to these papers. The title in this volume differs only from that given by Dr. Hagen, in having the word "Privy" before "Council," and the contents of the volume from the table of titles given by Dr. Hagen, only in that his Nos. three and seven "Orders of the Council" are omitted in the Annals. The original paper is a quarto volume, and fills in the octavo Annals nearly 208 pages, which will account for the discrepancy in the space occupied by each article, the articles in the Annals not being numbered, I refer to these old papers because they are most interesting as exemplifying the fact, that the late confounding of such terms as "Fly-weavil" for "Hessian Fly" in the minutes of the American Philosophical Society, which has made such a difference in the historic facts, had its counterpart at that time. The more important papers consist of a letter (1788) by P. Bond, Consul at Philadelphia, to the Right Honorable Marquis of Carmarthen, about the injury of the "Hessian Fly" in the Middle States, and supposing that the eggs are laid in the grain, as "seed wheat steeped in a preparation of elder juice effectually secures a crop." Bond probably referred to the true Hessian Fly, but his letter is followed by one from Sir Jos. Banks, President of the Royal Society, to the Marquis of Carmarthen, in which Banks calls the insect "the Flying Weavil," describes the adult as a minute moth, likens it to the clothes moth, states how the eggs are laid upon the grains of wheat and produce a diminutive caterpillar; in fact refers to the Angoumois grain-moth. There is a large subsequent correspondence, and finally Banks recogizes his first mistake and collects a good deal of information about both *Gelechia ccrealella* and the true Hessian Fly, the latter derived from Dr. Mitchell.

Pages 465 and 471 are occupied by an excellent article by Col. Geo. Morgan, of New Jersey, to Sir John Temple, Consul General for Great Britain at New York, which gives a good account of the spread of the Hessian Fly and its origin, states that the name was given by him and a friend early after its first appearance on Long Island, and then treats of the "Virginia Wheat-fly," and also of the "Chintz Bug-fly." It is worthy of note that these papers are preceded in Young's Annals by an anonymous article entitled, "On the Hessian Fly, whose depredations have been very mischevious in America," in which the author recognizes and describes the work of *C. destructor*, describes its annual spread from the points of introduction, and remarks that it must not be confounded with the " Virginia Wheat-fly" *(cerealella)*. The reading of all these papers simply confirms the conclusions which I have expressed in this communication.

Washington, D. C., May 22nd, 1888.

P. S.—In the above communication I have stated merely the facts of the case without any attempt at explaining away Mr. Phillips's misleading statements. The receipt, since the article was written, of the latest part (No. 127) of the Proceedings of the American Philosophical Society, bringing them down to the meeting of May 4th last, induces me to add this postscriptum.

I spent the evening of May 3rd very delightfully with Dr. G. H. Horn, who, as one of the secretaries of the American Philosophical Society, was interested in my intended investigation of the old minutes ; in fact Dr. Horn informed me that Mr. Phillips, knowing that he (Horn) was about to visit Dr. Hagen on his way to Europe, had but a short time before charged him to tell Dr. Hagen, that the latter might feel quite certain of the accuracy of his (Phillips's) statements. I have already indicated my surprise at finding them unverified, and shown how Mr. Phillips was unable to give me any explanation of his mistake.

There was to be an exceptionally interesting meeting of the Society that evening, and I purposely remained in Philadelphia to attend it, and took occasion to call attention to the error in the old minutes above set forth. Mr. Phillips, following my remarks, threw all the blame for the published error on Prof. Lesley who was absent in Europe at the time ; and, having in mind his (Phillips's) communications to Hagen, this conduct struck me as not very magnanimous. I deemed the correction of this error of sufficient importance to go on record, and handed to the Secretary for incorporation in the minutes a brief abstract of my remarks. Judge of my surprise therefore to find the whole matter passed by in the published minutes of that meeting of May 4th last, by the statement of the Secretary that " Prof. C. V. Riley referred to a possible error of transcription in the Volume of Early Proceedings (No. 119), on pages 14 and 15, as to the word Hessian Fly." (! !) Mr. Phillips's conduct in this particular is as remarkable as his correspondence with Dr. Hagen, and I call attention to it that it may no longer obscure the facts of history.

ON DIADEMA MISIPPUS, Linn, IN FLORIDA.

BY W. H. EDWARDS, COALBURGH, W. VA.

About the middle of last November Miss Annie M. Wittfeld, whose untimely death I have spoken of elsewhere, wrote me that she had taken a butterfly of a species which she had never seen before, while it was laying eggs on purslane. She confined the butterfly with the plant and obtained 74 eggs. It was like a Danais, she said, but the caterpillars were like a Vanessan. I wrote her it probably was *Misippus*, a single male of which Dr. Wittfeld had taken several years before. The female of this species is entirely unlike the male in colour and markings, and really imitates a pale Danais. Meanwhile eggs and larvæ at every moult were put in alcohol for me, and after my letter was received Miss Wittfeld inflated two mature larvæ, and with all these stages sent me living papæ, so that I shall be able to illustrate the history of this curious butterfly. This was the last thing Miss Wittfeld did for me, and is an example of the intelligent and painstaking work she was accustomed to.

Misippus is a common species in south-eastern Asia, in Australia, Africa, in parts of South America, and is found in some of the West India Islands. Drury figured the male, and gave New York as one of the localities, but, except these few Florida examples, I know nothing of the occurrence of the species within the United States. As the food plant is everywhere one of the commonest of weeds, it is not improbable that from Florida *Misippus* may spread northward.

In Papilio 1, p. 30, I mentioned the capture of the male spoken of under the name *D. Bolina*, Linn. *Bolina* is an allied but distinct species. The one taken in Florida is Misippus.

SOME NEW NOCTUIDÆ.

BY A. R. GROTE, A. M., BREMEN, GERMANY.

Agrotis agilis, n. s.

Two males in good condition received from Mr. James Fletcher, from Vancouver, belong to a decidedly different species from my *semiclarata*, Essay, Plate 1, Fig 9, though allied, as also to Californian *gravis*, and our Eastern *venerabilis*. Antennæ brush-like. Gray, with a brown tinge. Lines obliterate. Fore wings yellowish gray fuscous, brownish, with a red tinge along costa, this color obtaining before the s. t. line before apices. A distinct velvety black basal streak, absorbing the claviform spot and extending below median vein from base to the faint yellowish brown median shade line. Cell filled in with velvety black on which the complete, rounded, orbicular rests, a little pointed outwardly. Reniform moderate, subequal, transverse, of the normal shape, surrounded almost completely by the cellular black filling. Some black scales along costa marking the inception of the transverse lines, which are here filled in with white, under the glass. The red brown shade obtaining before apices, shows three pale ante-apical costal dots. The s. t. line is marked by cuneiform, dark, subequal shades and followed by a white shade more determinate at costa. Terminal space narrow, darker than the wing. Hind wings rather uniformly pale fuscous ; beneath with an outer shade line and costal border, paler than fore wings beneath, with a thick cellular spot and somewhat whitish at base and inferiorly. Fore wings smoky fuscous, with faint outer transverse shades. On fore wings above, the pale shade is more or less noticeable outside s. t. line at the apex of the wing. Head and collar ochre brown. The collar shows a double black superior line enclosing a reddish shade ; the upper black line edged outwardly with white scales. Tegulae whitish, pale ; abdomen fuscous ; anal hairs ochery. *Expanse* 30–32 mil.

Agrotis hospitalis Gr., Can. Ent. xiv., 184.

This species is allied to *Baja* by the black mark, inaugurating s. t. line, but otherwise it is quite close to *Perconflua.* I think that I am hasty in considering it a variety of the latter species, but the pattern is much the same, although the lines are marked in black in *Hospitalis*, and the color of primaries is a more uniform and darker brown, approaching *Baja.* At any rate this species must be catalogued with *Conflua, Perconflua* and *Hilliana.* In Papilio iii., 29, my late lamented correspondent, Mr. W. W. Hill, records the capture of two specimens of *Hospitalis* in the Adirondack region in July. On a very close comparison with *Perconflua,* taken by the same Entomologist at Centre, N. Y., in August, the shape of the t. p. line is seen to differ from that species. In *Hospitalis* it slopes away downwardly and outwardly from costa much more obliquely ; it is less upright, more outwardly exserted or bent. The species are alike in size, in color of hind wings and in the paler front and palpal tips, contrasting with the darker sides of the face and palpi. There will be nothing gained in throwing these forms together, and they must be bred to decide. The character of the t. p. line escaped me until recently, and speaks for the ultimate distinctness of *Hospitalis*.

Xylomiges Fletcheri, n. s.

The species sent me from Vancouver, by my kind correspondent Mr. James Fletcher, is apparently allied to the forms described by myself from California, under *Xylomiges*, such as *hiemalis* and *curialis:* a specimen of *X. crucialis* Harv. is also before me from Vancouver. *Fletcheri* differs by the more compact shape, the pale fuscous hind wings with darker stained veins. The eyes are hairy, the body untufted, and the color is a stone gray overlaid with whitish, so that the moth approaches *Anytus sculptus* in color. The costa is straight, the wings rather short and full outwardly, with pronounced apices, reminding one a little of *Cloantha*. To the eye the wings appear of a rather light stone gray, but under the glass the whole base of the wing is seen to be overlaid by white scales, as also the coalesced large stigmata, which are outlined in black, completely fused inferiorly, forming an irregular V ; the inner limb of this, the obicular is outwardly oblique ; the outer, the reniform, is upright, sinuate on its outer edge. The white scales appear again over the terminal portion of the wing. The lines are black, fragmentary, marked by different shades on costa. A fine black basal ray. The median lines are waved and inferiorly approach each other, narrowing greatly the median space below the cell ; the concolorous claviform spot, also outlined by black scales, joins the median lines on submedian fold, although moderate in size. The subterminal line is fragmentary, black, appearing between the veins. Head and thorax fuscous gray, a little darker than fore wings, unlined ; tegulæ shaded with whitish ; at the sides with a black edging. Abdomen dusky gray. Beneath the primaries are clouded fuscous ; the secondaries paler than above with a neat dot and an extra-mesial line accentuated on the veins. Antennæ of the male simple ; smaller and shorter-winged than the other species described by me. *Expanse* 30 mil.

Orthosia hamifera n. sp.

This species has been sent me from California, by my kind friend Mr. James Behrens. It is allied to *purpurea*, but larger. The male antennæ are brush-like, female simple. The fore wings are pointed at apices ;

the exterior margin somewhat sickle-shaped ; the eyes are naked ; the tibiæ unarmed. Head, thorax and fore wings brownish wine-red ; the thoracic hairs show a tipping of white scales under the glass. All the markings obliterate, so that the insect in color and appearance reminds one of *Perigrapha transparens.* The markings are indicated by blackish scales. Reniform marked by an upper and lower blackish clouding, moderate, upright, finely ringed with pale. Orbicular more faintly marked, a little oblique, approximate, also finely ringed with pale. The median shade crosses the wing. Lines not discernible ; under the glass the s. t. line is seen to be marked by double black points on the veins. Fringes more clearly red on both wings ; secondaries without marks, somewhat evenly fuscous ; beneath paler, with traces of the reniform on primaries ; secondaries with a dot. This is larger than *crispa;* varying in depth of red, the female the darker. Three specimens. The insect looks like *Gortyna nebris* a little, except in its red color. *Expanse* 35 mil.

DESCRIPTION OF THE PREPARATORY STAGES OF CHIONOBAS JUTTA.

BY REV. THOMAS W. FYLES, SOUTH QUEBEC.

Eggs laid June 17th., scattered, hatched July 1st.

EGG.—Creamy white: one-twenty-fourth of an inch in diameter ; shaped like a nutmeg-melon ; marked longitudinally with zig-zag ridges ; attached by short foot-stalk.

NEWLY HATCHED LARVA.—One-eighth of an inch long. Head large in proportion to body, honey-yellow, granulated. Body attenuated and ending in two pointed prolongations ; pale amber, set with brown tubercles bearing light spines. Dorsal and side lines darker amber. Spiracles dark brown. Head and fore legs bearing a few bristles. The insect feeds with its head downwards on the edge of the leaf. Its food plant is the sedge, *Carex oligosperma.*

The first moult occurred July 6th. The skin was ruptured under the head.

Larva After First Moult.—Length one-fourth of an inch. Colour a delicate shade of pea-green; dorsal, sub-dorsal and side lines a pale warm brown ; spiracles black.   A few small black warts on the body.   Head honey-yellow.

Moulted July 30th.

Larva After Second Moult.—Length three-quarters of an inch.   Colour grey; dorsal and sub-dorsal lines amber, the dorsal having twelve blotches of a darker shade; side lines dark brown.   Under the side line comes a spiracular·line of grey, and then a brown line touching the legs.   Head large, amber coloured ; thickly indented like a thimble, and marked with four longitudinal rows of brown dots.   Under the microscope the body is seen to be thickly set with elongated amber-coloured warts—the brown warts having disappeared.

In feeding the insect has changed its posture, carrying its head up-wards and cutting through the blade till the top falls off ; then eating across, always working from the near edge, systematically shortening the blade and lowering itself when necessary.

Moulted Aug. 14th.   Inert and sickly-looking before the change.

Larva After Third Moult.—Length nine-tenths of an inch.   General colour grey ; thickly covered with light brown hairs.   Spiracular line whitish.   Spiracles kidney-shaped, chocolate-coloured with a yellowish white perpendicular line through the centre.   Dorsal line represented by twelve brown spots ; sub-dorsal lines very faint.   Head large, has five warty dark brown spots on each side.   Mandibles brown.

Moulted Sept. 1st.

Larva After Fourth Moult.—Length one inch and five-sixteenths of an inch.   Head pale brown, indented, set with reddish hairs, and having six longitudinal rows of dark brown dots, also on either side five dark warts. Mandibles brown ; general colour of the body pale green, thickly set with reddish hairs.   Dorsal line dark green, bearing the twelve oblong brown spots.   Pale sub-dorsal lines, and dark green side lines bordered below with a pale streak.   Spiracles dark brown.   Caudal fork has a slight rosy tinge.   Fore legs colour of head.

I left home for England on the 4th of October, having provided a sufficiency of growing sedge, embedded in sphagnum, for the use of *Jutta*.   I returned in February, and found the larvæ fresh and plump, but quite torpid.   They had undergone the 5th moult (probably in October). On the 6th of April they revived.

MAIURE LARVA AFTER HIBERNATION —Length one inch and a quarter. Body pale pea-green, set with light brown hairs. Legs of the same hue of green. Head green with six rows of brown dots, indented. Twelve greenish-brown spots along the back, side-lines dark brown; spiracles black.

After their revival the larvæ ate little, if anything. They pupated April 21st.

CHRYSALIS —Length five-eighths of an inch, greatest breadth one-fourth of an inch. Head-case amber-coloured, with a brown dash on either side. Wing-cases pea-green, outlined and streaked with brown. Thorax prominent, abdomen conical, in colour pale yellowish green, with dorsal line of darker green and numerous longitudinal rows of brown dots. Extremity of abdomen rosy.

The perfect insect appears in this locality from May 31st to June 15th.

PARASITES ON DANAIS ARCHIPPUS AND ANTHOMYIA RAPHANI

BY C. P. GILLETTE, AGRICULTURAL COLLEGE, MICH.

I am not aware that any parasites have ever been reported as attacking the larvæ of *Danais archippus* or the maggots of *Anthomyia raphani.* However that may be, it will be of interest to the readers of the ENTO-MOLOGIST to know that last fall I obtained from a single chrysalis of *D. archippus* over fifty specimens of a new species of *Pteromalus.* The parasites came forth September 13, the chrysalis having been brought into the laboratory a few days before, and inclosed with a bell-jar. Specimens were sent to Mr. L. O. Howard, who has since described the species and given it the name of *Pteromalus archippi.*

The parasites from *A. raphani* belong to the genus *Eucoila,* and are probably a new species also. A large number of pupæ and full-grown maggots of *A. raphani* were put in a jar containing earth, from which the flies began to come forth June 9. The jar remained covered with gauze until September 2, when the parasites began to appear, and in a few days eight specimens were obtained.

In connection with the latter parasite it may be well to note the fact that a red garden mite, a species of *Trombidium,* did excellent service last summer in the College garden by feeding greedily upon the eggs of *Anthomyia brassicæ.* It was not uncommon to find nearly a half tea-spoonful of empty egg shells about the stems of the plants, and in such cases a number of the mites were always to be found just below the surface near the plant.

For experiment's sake three of these mites were kept in a jar of moist earth for a time, and fed each day upon fresh eggs, when it was found by actual count that they would suck, on an average, twenty-eight eggs each and every day.

Many of the plants did well and produced fine heads, that I am certain would have withered and died had not these mites devoured enormous numbers of the *Anthomyia* eggs.

DESCRIPTIONS OF SOME LEPIDOPTEROUS LARVÆ.

BY WM. BEUTENMULLER, NEW YORK.

Datana integerrima, Gr. & Rob.

BEFORE LAST MOULT.--Head and cervical shield shining jet black. Body deep reddish brown, with three very fine, narrow, sordid white stripes along each side, and a broader one below the spiracles, which are black, and another stripe along the middle of the venter. Thoracic feet, extremities of abdominal legs and anal legs jet black, shining. The body is also covered with sordid white hairs. Length 32 mm.

MATURE LARVA.—Body wholly jet black, and covered with very long floss-like, sordid white hairs, becoming yellowish as the larva undergoes its changes to the pupa. Thoracic feet black, shining. Abdominal legs black outside and reddish-brown on the inner side. Length 55 mm.

Lives together in large companies on walnut (*Juglans*), hickory (*Carya*), beech (*Fagus*), and also on oak (*Quercus*), but very rarely.

In several individuals of the brood of this species, in the last stage, there are visible a sub-dorsal, ill-defined, white, longitudinal stripe, and a rather broad wavy lateral stripe below the spiracles, and sometimes there is also a white stripe along the middle of the underside. In all else resembling the typical form.

Datana contracta, Walk.

BEFORE LAST MOULT.—Head and cervical shield jet black, shining. Body black, with four equidistant sordid white stripes along each side, being as wide as the intervening spaces, except the dorsal space which is the widest   Body beneath concolorous to the above with three longitudinal stripes, and the intervening spaces much broader   On each of the 4, 5, 10 and 11 segments two reddish brown patches.   Thoracic feet and claspers of the abdominal legs jet black, with their bases reddish brown. The body is also sparsely covered with sordid white hairs   Length about 30 mm.

MATURE LARVA —The cervical shield now becomes orange yellow, and the stripes creamy white.   Otherwise as in the previous stage Length 55 mm.

FOOD PLANTS.- Oak *(Quercus)*, chestnut *(Castania)*, hickory *(Carya)*.

Datana Angusii, Gr. & Rob.

Head and cervical shield jet black, shiny   Body black, with four very narrow, pale yellow stripes along each side, all being much narrower than the intervening   On the underside three pale yellow stripes   One along the middle, which is the broadest, and one on each side being broken by the legs, the intervening spaces are much wider than those above. Thoracic feet black   Abdominal legs reddish, with the extremities jet black.   On the 4, 5, 10 and 11 segments two reddish patches.   Body with sparsely distributed sordid white hairs.   Length 55 mm

FOOD PLANTS.—Hickory *(Carya)* and walnut *(Juglans)*.

' The following synoptical table may serve in determining the larvæ of the genus *Datana*   The larvæ of *D robusta*, Strk , and *D major*, G. ,& R , are unknown to science.—

STRIPES NARROWER THAN THE INTERVENING SPACES.

Body black, stripes sulphur yellow	*Ministra*
Body black, stripes citron yellow, confluent posteriorly	*Drexelii*
Body black, stripes very fine, pale yellow.	*Angusii.*
Body black, stripes absent.	*Integerrima*

STRIPES AS WIDE OR WIDER THAN THE INTERVENING SPACES.

Body black or red, stripes bright lemon yellow . .	*Perspicua*
·Body black, stripes creamy white	*. Contracta.*
Body black, stripes yellowish, head and anal plates red	*Floridana.*

Hadena turbulenta, Hüb.

Head jet black, shining; mouth parts sordid white. Body above jet black, with a number of fine longitudinal stripes, beginning at the anterior portion of the second segment and running to the end of the tenth segment; last segments black, with a number of white spots. Cervical shield velvety black, with a few semilunate spots on the anterior portion, and posteriorly margined with white. Body at the sides and beneath dull amber yellow. Along the sides are three white stripes; the two below the stigmata run from the anterior portion of the first segment to the last segment, while the remaining stripe runs the same as those above. Thoracic feet black, shining. Abdominal and anal legs dull amber yellow, with a brownish patch, followed by a white one, on the outerside. All the stripes on the black portion of the body are connected in pairs by a fine transverse stripe at the posterior extremity. Lives socially on catbriar (*Smilax*). September.

THE ENTOMOLOGICAL CLUB OF THE A. A. A. S.

We are requested to announce that the next meeting of the Club will be held at Cleveland, Ohio, in the High School Building, beginning at 9 a. m., on Wednesday, the 15th of August. This date is a week earlier than that at first decided upon for the meeting of the A. A. A. S. As this location is central and convenient alike for both United States and Ontario Entomologists, it is expected that there will be a large attendance, and an interesting and enthusiastic meeting. All entomologists are requested to come prepared to aid in the matter; those who desire to present papers should send to the Secretary, Prof. A. J. Cook, Agricultural College, Mich., the subject they propose to discuss in order that it may be announced in the programme.

CORRESPONDENCE.

DANAIS ARCHIPPUS.

Dear Sir: I wish to enquire through your columns whether any progress has been made lately in explanation of the migratory habit of *Danais archippus.* The last information I have got on the subject being from the vividly descriptive pen of Dr. John Hamilton (CAN. ENT., Vol. xvii., No. 11), who showed clearly, that, up to that time, the facts and the theories had failed to agree   Several causes have combined recently to turn my attention to the subject, notably a question from Mr W. H. Edwards, as to its time of ovipositing here, which I could answer only in the most general terms   I have always regarded it as a misfortune that Mr Roland Thaxter, in his account of what he saw in Florida (Can. Ent , Vol. xii, No 2), did not give the month or months in which his observations were made, it might have assisted us much in forming an opinion as to whether they were flocks from the north come for the purpose of going into hibernation or not although the fact of some of them pairing is decidedly against the idea that these, at all events, intended to hibernate.   They make their appearance here about the latter part of May, according as the season favors, the first ones are restless and energetic, like males looking for mates, not in the least broken or damaged, not so rich and bright in color as fall specimens, but fairly good withal.   In a week or so they become more plentiful, and begin to mate and for a time are scarcely seen but in pairs   Shortly after eggs may be found on the flower clusters of the milk-weed, which is not yet in bloom.   They never seem to entirely disappear till fall, fresh hatched specimens mingling with the old battered ones of the early season   Their conduct in spring is quite in harmony with that of species which hatch from the chrysalis here.   If they hibernated in this locality I should expect them to put in an appearance a good deal earlier than they do   I regard it as a particularly interesting creature in every respect , although so common, it is never " vulgar," never in a hurry , it has the easy grace of the leisurely class   I have thought that one who has seen it only in an open country can form but an inadequate conception of the diversity of its movements on the wing.   To see one on a bright summer day, when a stiff breeze is blowing, disport itself about the wide-spreading top of a high tree, is a choice pleasure.   It seems to fairly revel with delight in a gale , now it rolls and tosses and heaves, always heading against the wind , now it spreads its sails to the breeze, and is hurried violently backward and upward ; again it furls them, and, slowly descending and advancing, it describes a variety of the most charmingly graceful curves and waves and undulations imaginable , a thing of beauty to look at, and a joy to think of forever after.   Attempts have been made to attach to it common names.   I have thought, when watching one at such a time, that ' the storm king" would be very appropriate, and quite befitting its regal character.   In my former scrap on this insect, an error in punctuation occurs, which makes it rather confusing.   The " at least every other day " there refers to my visiting the woods, not to the movements of the butterflies.   I have but little of personal observations to add to it, having seen but one small gathering since.   A stream of *Archippus* from the side of a wood attracted my attention.   I entered to watch it go.   There was nothing of the listless attitude of my former observations in this group.   There was a general uneasiness pervading the whole flock, rather difficult to describe.   It did not come from a working of the wings, but of the feet, as if the foothold was not good, and they were trying to secure a better, which produced a rocking motion, whilst continuously throughout the swarm one and another was dropping off to make for the edge of the woods and join in the grand procession.

J. Alsion Moffatt, Hamilton, Ont.

THE CLOVER-ROOT BORER, HYLASTES TRIFOLII, MULLER

Dear Sir :—As far as I know, this insect has not been mentioned in the Entomologist as occuring in Ontario.   The beetle has appeared in this locality, and is doing incalculable damage to the clover fields.   At the time of writing this, the beetles, which have hibernated in the root during the winter, have not all left their retreats, and may be counted by the dozen in roots badly infested.   No doubt the insect has been working in our midst for some time, and at present fully three-fourths of the red clover, *Trifolium pratense,* is dead or dying from the injury caused to the root. The damage has not been all occasioned by the larvæ during the past season, for I found the perfect beetle driving channels in various directions through the roots during May and the early part of June.   My observations correspond so well with the description given by Mr. W. Saunders in the annual report of the Entomological Society of Ontario, 1881, page 43, that I need only refer the reader to his paper.

June 9, 1888.   J. White, Edmonton, Ont.

Dear Sir   Mr Brehme, in his article on "The Early Stages of Arzama Obliquata," after stating its manner of feeding in the reed, says, "It then returns to the top and forms its pupa there"   I would remark that that is not its invariable habit in nature, for I have found the chrysalis in early spring beneath the bark of a decaying stump, corresponding in that respect with Diffusa, and in some instances quite a distance away from the marsh where the reeds grow   From Mr Brehme's dates it would appear to be double brooded with him

J. ALSTON MOFFAT, Hamilton, Ont

ON BOLINA FASCIOLARIS, HUBN

Dear Sir   In the pages of the CAN. ENT I showed that Mr. Morrison's statement that we had re-described *Bolina fasciolaris* Hubn , was an error, based upon a mistaken identification of Hubner's species That my determination was correct, is proved by a letter of Mr. Butler's, published in *Entomologica Americana*, vol iv , p 13, where a specimen of the true *B fasciolaris*, as determined by myself, is alluded to from my collection   This specimen came to me as from "Mexico"   To my knowledge *B fasciolaris* does not occur in our limits, but not improbably it may be found in the south-west.   Mr. Butler thinks that it is highly probable that *B ochreipennis* Harvey is the male of *B. nigrescens* G. & R , and thus repeats the suggestion already made by myself   The species will be known as *nigrescens*, this name being much the older.   The genus *Bolina* of Duponchel is, in my opinion, incorrectly used, and our species should be referred to *Melipotis* of Hubner, as I have done in my Check List, where *ochreipennis* is doubtfully referred to as the male of the preceding species, *nigrescens* G. &. R. (p 39, No 1145)   The sexual distinction in ornamentation in *Melipotis* is peculiar and interesting.

A R. GROTE.

CHANGE OF ADDRESS —Mr C. H T Townsend requests us to state that he has left the Adjutant-General's Office, War Department, and is now an assistant in the Division of Entomology, Department of Agriculture, Washington, D. C.

OBITUARY.

Miss Annie M. Wittfeld, only daughter of Dr. Wm. Wittfeld, of Fairyland, Indian River, Florida, died suddenly of rheumatism of the heart on the 10th April, aged 23.   Fifteen months before—to a day—Dr. Wittfeld had lost his only son by brain fever while down the coast on a boating expedition, and so the stricken parents are desolate.   It is about ten years since Miss Annie began to aid me in obtaining eggs and larvæ of butterflies, and it is mostly owing to her zealous, friendly and intelligent assistance that I have been able to learn the history of so many Florida species.   Her death is a loss to science.   The readers of this magazine will sympathize with Dr. and Mrs. Wittfeld in their bereavement.   W. H. Edwards.

DEATH OF THE "YOKOHAMA NATURALIST."

Particulars have been received of the death in Japan, on the 17th of February, of Mr. Harry Pryer, C. M. Z. S., the Yokohama naturalist, at the early age of thirty-seven.   When Mr. Pryer went to Japan in 1870 he was already known as an active Fellow of the Entomological Society of London.   In the intervals of a busy mercantile career he interested himself in Japanese natural history, and soon became a recognized authority on the subject.   In conjunction with Captain F. Blakiston, he wrote the standard monograph on the birds of Japan, and at the time of his death he was engaged in publishing in English and Japanese an important work on the butterflies of Japan, entitled " Rhopalocera Nihonica."   Mr. Pryer was not only an assiduous collector, but a keen observer and a practical investigator, and his researches on the parasites of the silk worm have been of material advantage to the silk culture of Japan.   His house and garden were filled with valuable specimens and collections of animals and insects, living and dead, and the loss sustained by the European community through his death is shared by the Japanese, who recognize the valuable services he rendered in connection with the establishment and maintenance of the museum at Tokio.—*Pall Mall Gazette.*

The Canadian Entomologist.

VOL. XX.   LONDON, AUGUST, 1888.   No. 8

LIST OF THE SPIDERS, MYRIOPODS AND INSECTS OF LABRADOR.

BY A. S. PACKARD, PROVIDENCE, R. I.

A list of all the known species of terrestrial Arthropods of the Labrador coast may prove convenient as a starting point for future investigations. Hence I have, besides enumerating the species of other groups, revised the lists of Lepidoptera—Mr. Scudder kindly contributing the list of butterflies. For changes in the names of the Tortricidæ I am indebted to Prof. C. II. Fernald's excellent catalogue of the Tortricidæ of the United States.

ARACHNIDA.

The spiders which I collected at various points on the coast were sent to Prof. T. Thorell, of Upsala, for identification and description. Out of ten species collected, seven were new to science. Prof. Thorell's paper was published in the Proceedings of the Boston Society of Natural History, xvii., April 21, 1875.

Epeira patagiata (Clerck).   Square Island, Strawberry Harbor.
  "   *Packardii* Thor.   "   "
Tetragnatha extensa (Linn.)   "   "
Linyphia Emertonii Thor.   "   "   and near Dumplin Harbor.
Clubiona frigidula Thor.   "   "
Gnaphosa brumalis Thor.   Strawberry Harbor.
Lycosa Greenlandica Thor.   "   "
  "   *furcifera* Thor.   Square Island, and near Dumplin Harbor.
  "   *fuscula* Thor.   Strawberry Harbor.
  "   *Labradorensis* Thor.   Strawberry Harbor and Square Island.
Xysticus Labradorensis Keys.   K. K. Zool. Bot. Ges. Wien., 479, 1887.
    Ungava Bay (Turner).

MYRIOPODA.

Julus sp.   Square Island.

INSECTS.

Orthoptera.

Caloptenus. A Pezzotettix-like species, with short wings.   Square Island

Odonata.

Diplax sp., near *rubicundula.* Caribou Island. Dragon flies were very
rare on the coast, and I saw none north of the Straits of Belle Isle.
Æschna sp. Caribou Island. Perhaps another species (identified by Dr.
P. R. Uhler,) also occurred, and an Æschna-like form was observed
at Tub Island.

Hemiptera.

Teratocoris sp.
Deltocephalus debilis Uhler. Hopedale.   A few other species of
Cercopidæ were seen at Caribou Island.
Trigonotylus ruficornis Fallen. Hopedale.
Corixa sp.

Platyptera.

Pteronarcys regalis. Okkak. Hopedale.

Plectoptera.

Potamanthus marginatus Zett. This boreal European May-fly, occurring
in Lapland, we have found in abundance in southern Labrador.
Perla sp. Belles Amoures.
Chloroperla sp. A small greenish species was observed at Strawberry
Harbor.

Trichoptera.

Desmataulius planifrons Kol. Okkak.
Limnophilus subpunctulatus Zett. This Lapland Caddis-fly is the most
abundant species in Labrador, and what are probably its cases are
common in the pools of fresh water. Three or four other species
also occurred, but have not been identified. No genuine *Neuroptera*
or *Mecaptera* (Panorpidæ) occurred.

COLEOPTERA.

Lepyrus colon (Linn.) Cape Chidley (R. Bell).
Pissodes ? sp. Hopedale.
Coccinella lacustris Lec. Okkak.
Leptura sp. Caribou Island.
Criocephalus obsoletus Randall. Okkak.

Argaleus nitens Lec.   Near Cape Harrison

Telephorus fraxini Say.   Hopedale

P lævicollis Kirby.   Hopedale.

Podabrus mandibularis Kirby   Caribou Island.

Sericosomus incongruus Lec   Square Island.

Eanus vagus Lec.   Square Island

E. pictus (Cand.) Horn.   (*E. maculipennis* Lec.)   Caribou Island to
    Square Island.

Cryptohypnus bicolor Germ   Belles Amoures, Strawberry Harbor and
    Indian Harbor.

Byrrhus Americanus Lec.   Caribou Island

B   Kirbyi Lec *(B. picipes)*   Caribou Island.

Atomaria   Not determined.   Caribou Island

Ips sanguinolentus Oliv.   Caribou Island.

Bledius   Not determined

Quedius sublimbatus Mokl.   Blanc Sablon (R. Bell)

Tachyporus n sp.   Hopedale.

Creophilus villosus Gray.   Caribou Island

Agathidium obsoletum Lec.   Square Island.

Silpha Lapponica Linn.   Caribou Island to Hopedale

Philhydrus bifidus Lec.   Caribou Island

Gyrinus picipes Aubé?   Square Island.

G. minutus Linn   Square Island.

G affinis Aubé?   Square Island

Colymbetes picipes Kirby.   Caribou Island and Strawberry Harbor.

C. binotatus Harris (probably).

C sculptilis Harris.   Caribou Island, Square Island, Hopedale.

C. nov. sp.   Square Island

Agabus parallelus Lec   Square Island

A. longulus Lec?   Stupart's Bay (R. Bell)

A. ambiguus Lec. *(A infuscatus* Aubé).   Caribou Island

A subfasciatus Lec   Caribou Island.

A semipunctatus (Kirby).   Caribou Island

A. lævidorsus Lec.   Caribou Island.

A punctulatus Aubé.   Caribou Island

A discolor Lec.   Indian Harbor.

Hydroporus catascopium Say   Square Island and Dumplin Harbor.

H tenebrosus Lec   Caribou Island

H. puberulus Lec.   Sloop Harbor and Dumplin Harbor

H longicornis   Stupart's Bay (R Bell).

H. perplexus Shp   Stupart's Bay (R. Bell)

Trechus micans Lec.   Belles Amoures.

Patrobus tennis Lec   Square Island

P hyperboreus Dejean   Belles Amoures, Straits of Belle Isle, Cape Chidley (R Bell)

Harpalus herbivagus Say , var *proximus* Lec.   Square Island.

Amara obtusa Lec

Amara, near *A. melanogastrica* Esch., perhaps *A. brunni.*

A pennis Dej   Caribou Island.

Amara, "no name."   Strawberry Harbor, Square Island and Hopedale.

A similis Lec *(Stercocerus similis* Kirby).   Caribou Island

A hæmatopus Kirby   Sloop Harbor, Hopedale, Okkak (S Weiz)

Pterostichus adstrictus Esch , var *orinomum* Kirby   Mecatina , Gulf St Lawrence

Pterostichus hudsonicus Lec   Stupart's Bay (R Bell)

Pt , species not determined   Hopedale, Sinker Island, off Cape Harrison (Cape Webuc).

Pt. luczottii Dej.   Blanc Sablon (R. Bell).

Platynus sinuatus Dej.   Belles Amoures, Straits of Belle Isle.

Calathus ingratus Dej   Whole coast

Carabus chamissonis Fischer.   Domino Harbor and Okkak.

Nebria Sahlbergii Fischer   Sloop Harbor, Cape Chidley (R Bell)

Notiophilus Sibiricus Motsch   Domino Harbor, Square Island

DIPTERA.

Scatina estotilandica Rondani, Archiv, etc.   Canestrini iii , fasc. 1, 35, Labrador   Osten Sacken adds . Mr. Rondani, in the same place, mentions *Scatophaga diadema* Wiedemann (Montevideo), as having been received from Labrador.

Helophilus glacialis Loew.   Stett. Ent Zeit. vii , 121.

    "   *groenlandicus* (O. Fabr)

Dolichopus stenhammari Zett   Sloop Harbor, July 19

Therioplectes flavipes Wied.

    '   *septentrionalis* Loew.   Verh. Zool Bot Ges Wien , 1858, 593.

Tipula tessellata Loew.   Cent. iv , 4

Tipula septentrionalis Loew   Cent. iv , 3.

Amalopsis hyperborea O. Sacken.   Monogr. iv., 269.
Dicranomyia halterata O. Sacken.   Monog. iv., 71.

LEPIDOPTERA.

Tineidae.

Glyphipteryx sp.   Caribou Island.

Tinea fuscipunctella Harv.   (= *Œcophora frigidella* Pack.)   Caribou and Square Islands.

Œcophora sp.   Hopedale.

Incurvaria Labradorella Clem.   Caribou Island.

Ornix boreasella Clem.   Caribou Island.

Tinea spilotella Tengström.   Caribou Island, Square Island, " Okkak, June."   Christoph.

Gelechia continuella Zell. Moeschl.   (= trimaculella Pack.) Strawberry Harbor.

Gelechia labradorica Moeschl.   Moravian Stations.

    "   *brumella* Clem.   Caribou Island.

Tortricidæ:

Grapholitha nebulosana Pack.   Strawberry Harbor.

Phoxopteris plagosana (Clem.)   Caribou Island and Square Island.

    "   *tineana* Hübn. (Pandemis leucophalerata Pack.)   Hopedale.

Sericoris bipartitana (Clem.)   Caribou Island.

Pædisca solicitana (Walk.) (Halonota packardiana Clem.)   Caribou Is.

Sericoris turfosana H. S.

    "   *glaciana* Moeschl.   Whole coast ; common.

Penthina capreana (Hübn.)

    "   *murina* Pack.   Caribou Island.

    "   *septentrionana* Curtis.   Sloop and Strawberry Harbors.   (Polar regions, Curtis.)

    "   *intermistana* (Clem.) (P. tessellana Pack.)   Caribou Island to Hopedale.

    frigidana Pack.

Conchylis deutschiana Zetterstedt (Lozopera? fuscostrigana Clem.; C. chalcana Pack.)

Sciaphila osseana Scopoli (Ablabia pratana Hübn.)

    "   *moeschleriana* (Wrcke).

    "   *niveosana* Pack.   Moravian Stations, August.

Pyralidae.

Crambus unistriatellus Pack.   Caribou Island.
   "   *argillacellus* Pack.   Square Island.
   "   *trichostomus* Christoph.   Moravian Stations.
   "   *labradorensis* Christoph.   " Okkak, July."
   "   *albellus* Clem.   Mouth of Esquimaux river, Aug. 3.
   "   *inornatellus* Clem.   Caribou Island, July 15.
Eudorea centuriella Christoph.   *(Pempelia fusca* Harv., *Eudorea* ?
   frigidella Pack.)
Eudorea ? *albisinuatella* Pack.   Okkak.
Pyrausta borealis Pack.   Square Island.
Botys ephippialis Zettst.
   " *torvalis* Moeschl.
   " *inquinatalis* Zell.   (Scopula glacialis Pack.)   Hopedale.

Phalaenidae.

Eupithecia luteata Pack.   Caribou Island, July.
   "   *gelidata* Moeschl.   Moravian Stations.
Glaucopteryx caesiata (S. V.)   Whole coast.
   "   *polata* (Dupon.)   Whole coast.
   "   *phocataria* Pack.
Epirrita dilutata (Borkh.)   Moravian Stations.
Petrophora truncata (Hufn.)   Whole coast.
   " . *prunata* (Linn.)   "   "
   "   *populata* (Linn.)   "   "
   "   *suspectata* Moeschl.   Moravian Stations.
Ochyria munitaria Hübn.   Caribou Island and var. *labradorensis* Pack.
   " *abrasaria* H. Sch.   Caribou Island.
Rheumaptera lugubrata Staud.   Whole coast.
   "   *postata* (Linn.)   Whole coast.
      disceptaria (F. R.)   Moravian Stations.
Triphosa dubitaria (Linn.)   Caribou Island.
Semiothisa dispuncta Walk.   (Sex-maculata Pack.)   Square Island.
Anaitis sororaria Hübn.   Moravian Stations.
Aspilates gilvaria S. V.   "   "
Acidalia sentinaria Hübn.   "   "
   " *frigidaria* Moeschl.   "   "

Noctuidae.

Brephos parthenias (Linn.) Moravian Stations.
Plusia u aureum Boisd.   "   '
   "   *parilis* Hubn.   "   "
   "   *divergens* Fabr.   "   "
Anarta funesta (Thunberg).   "   '
   "   *melanopa* (Thun.)   "   .
   "   *melaleuca* (Thun)   "   "   Whole coast
   "   *vidua* Christoph   "   '
   '   *cordigera* (Thun)   "   .
   "   *algida* Lef   "   '
   "   *lapponica* (Thun)   "   "
   "   *schonheri i* Zett   "   "
   "   *zetterstedtii* Staud.   "   "
Hadena exulis Lef.   "   "
   "   *exornata* Moeschl.   "   .
Pachnobia carnea Thun.   "   '   Whole coast
Mamestra arctica Boisd.   Whole coast
Dianthoecia subdita Moeschl   Moravian Stations
       "   *phoca* Moeschl   "   "
Agrotis septentrionalis Moeschl   "   "
   "   *fusca* Boisd   "   "
   "   *Wockei* Moeschl   "   "
   "   *speciosa* Hubn   '   "
   "   *comparata* Moeschl   "   '
   "   *dissona* Moeschl   "   '
   "   *umbratus* Pack.   "   "
       conflua Fehr .   "   "
Leucania rufostrigata Pack   Caribou Island

Bombycidæ

Hepialus labradoriensis Pack   Caribou Island
   "   *hyperboreus* Moeschler   Moravian Stations.
Laria Rossii (Curtis)   Whole coast
Arctia Quenselii Paykull   Whole coast.
Platarctia borealis (Moeschler)   Moravian Stations
Euprepia caja (Linn.)   Whole coast.

*RHOPALOCERA.

Brenthis chariclea (Schneid). This is the Argynnis boisduvalii of the previous list. A detailed description of the species, drawn up exclusively from American material, will be found in the Proc. Bost. Nat. Hist., Vol. xvii., p. 297.

Brenthis triclaris (Hübn.) = Argynnis triclaris of the previous list. A full description will be found as above on p. 294.

Brenthis polaris (Boisd.) = Argynnis polaris of the former list. A full description, based entirely on Dr. Packard's material, will be found as above, p. 303.

Brenthis frigga (Thunb.) = Argynnis frigga of the former list. The single male obtained in Labrador, with specimens from Colorado, taken by Mr. Mead, form the basis of a detailed description in the same place as the preceding, p. 306.

Eugonia j-album (Boisd.-Lec.) = Grapta interrogationis of the previous list. This is the worst error in that list, and a case of pure carelessness in writing.

Œneis jutta Hübn. = Chionobas jutta of previous list.
  "   *bore* (Esp.) = Chionobas bore of former list.
  "   *œno* (Boisd) = Chionobas œno of former list.

Agriades aquilo (Boisd.) = Lycæna aquilo of former list. An extended description from Dr. Packard's material will be found in the Proceedings of the Bost. Soc. Nat. Hist. vol. xvii, p. 310.

Pieris frigida Scudd. I have not re-examined this.

Eurymus Labradorensis (Scudd.) This is the *Colias palæno*, as well as the *C. Labradorensis* of the previous list. The specimen referred to the former being of the same species as the latter. I will not here venture on a discussion as to the validity of the specific name retained here, but as the species was described and figured sufficiently for determination, and is the common form in south-eastern Labrador, it is easily identifiable.

---

*A revised list of the butterflies obtained in Labrador by Dr. A. S. Packard, by Samuel H. Scudder. (The list was prepared for use in the present work. The species have been arranged in the descending order by the author.) In 1886 I published a list of Dr. Packard's collections in the Proceedings of the Boston Society of Natural History, Vol. xi. The present list is merely a redetermination of the same material, in the light of larger collections since seen. The same order as before is followed. The specimens are mostly in my collection and in that of the Museum of Comparative Zoology.—S H. S.

Eurymus nastes (Boisd) = Colias nastes of former list   I have not re-examined specimens, as they are apparently no longer extant

Pamphila comma (Linn) = Hesperia comma of my former list   The single specimen obtained was not examined by me in my study of the species of Pamphila (Memoirs Bost Soc Nat Hist. ii , 341), and is the only specimen I have seen of P. comma from America. It belongs to the var catena Staud, found in northern Scandinavia and Lapland, and exactly resembles the specimen of that variety figured by me in the memoir referred to above   Moschler has already noted that it is this variety which occurs in Labrador.

Hesperia centaureae Ramb   Nothing to be added.

HYMENOPTERA.

Urocerus flavicornis Fabr   Common on Caribou Island
    "   *cyaneus* Fabr.   Hopedale
Euura orbitalis Norton.   Var. a b   Caribou Island
Nematus Labradoris Norton.   Caribou Island.
    "   *malacus*   "   "   "
    "   *fallax*   "   "
    "   *monela*   "   "
    "   *fulvipes*   "   "
    "   *placentus*   "   "
Allantus originalis   "   "
Macrophya (Pachyprotasis) omega Norton.   Caribou Island
Tenthredo mellinus Norton.   Caribou Island.
    '   *cinctitibus*   "   "   "
Formica herculanea Linn   Whole coast.
    "   *sanguinea* Latr.   Straits of Belle Isle
Vespa maculata Linn   Southern coast, Mecatina Island
    norvegica Fabr   Caribou Island
Bombus lacustris Cresson.   Whole northern coast, common
    "   *kirbyellus* Curtis.   Sloop Harbor and Hopedale.
    '   *frigidus* Smith   Square Island and Hopedale.
    '   *nivalis* Dahlb.   Caribou Island and whole coast northward.

JOHN ABBOT, THE AURELIAN.

BY SAMUEL H. SCUDDER.

It has been a fortunate thing for the study of butterflies in this country that the earlier students were those who devoted themselves very largely to the natural history of these insects rather than to their systematic or descriptive study. It was indeed a natural and healthy result of the poverty of external resources in earlier times ; and I have thought that it would not be devoid of interest to present a few facts concerning the life and industry of one of these earlier naturalists, who worked to such good purpose and accomplished so much, under circumstances that would now seem very forbidding.

A unique figure, perhaps the most striking in the early development of natural history in America, is that of a man of whom we know almost absolutely nothing excepting what he accomplished. With one exception, all our knowledge of his personality comes through tradition. No life of him has ever been written, excepting a brief notice by Swainson in the Bibliography of Zoology, to which Mr. G. Brown Goode has kindly called my attention. It is not known when or where he was born, or when he died ; scarcely where he lived, or to what nationality he belonged. Even the town where he worked no longer exists. His name alone remains, and though we have access to not a little of his writing in his own round hand, his signature cannot be discovered.*

John Abbot was presumably an Englishman, as the name is English, and he is said by Sir. J. E. Smith, to have begun his career by the study of the transformations of British insects. When not far from thirty years old, and probably about 1790, he was engaged by three or four of the leading entomologists of England, to go out to North America for the purpose of collecting insects for their cabinets. After visiting several places in different parts of the Union, he determined to settle in the " Province of Georgia," as Swainson calls it. Here he lived for nearly twenty years in Scriven County, as I am informed by several persons through the kindness of Dr. Oemler, of Wilmington Island, in that State, returning to England probably not far from 1810, where he was living about 1840, at the age "probably above eighty." It is rumored in

---

*Mr. W. F. Kirby has kindly made many researches for me at the British Museum, the Linnæan Society, etc.

Georgia that he owned land there, and all that can be learned of him
comes from persons beyond middle life in that State, who remember hearing their parents speak of him   Col Charles C Jones, the Georgia
historian, informs me through Dr Oemler that 'while he remained in
Georgia, in the prosecution of his scientific labors, his head-quarters were
at Jacksonborough, then the county seat of Scriven County.   Here his
work on the Lepidoptera of Georgia was largely prepared   All traces of
this old town have now passed away "   It is supposed that he also employed himself as a school-master in this place, but this is purely traditional,
and his occasional bungling, not to say ungrammatical sentences, rather
indicate a lack of schooling on his own part   What we certainly know
regarding him is that he entered into relations with John Francillon, a
silversmith in the Strand, London, who had a famous collection of insects
and an extensive entomological correspondence   Francillon undertook to
supply subscribers with drawings of insects and plants by Abbot, as well
as with specimens, the latter of which, says Swainson, "were certainly
the finest that have ever been transmitted as articles of commerce to this
country , they were always sent home expanded, even the most minute ;
and he was so watchful and indefatigable in his researches, that he contrived
to breed nearly the whole of the Lepidoptera   His general price for a
box-full was sixpence each specimen , which was certainly not too much,
considering the beauty and high perfection of all the individuals.   Abbot,
however, was not a mere collector   Every moment of time he could
possibly devote from his field researches was employed in making finished
drawings of the larva, pupa, and perfect insect of every lepidopterous
species, as well as of the plant upon which it fed.   These drawings are so
beautifully chaste and wonderfully correct, that they were coveted by every
one."   It would appear from a note in Kirby and Spence's Introduction
to Entomology (5th ed , iii., 148) that "the ingenious Mr Abbot" also
knew the art of inflating caterpillar skins, and dealt in them through
Francillon   (See many other references in the same volume)   There still
exist in various places, principally in the British Museum, but also at
Oxford, Paris and Zurich, and in this country at Boston, large series of
his drawings of insects and plants   Those in the British Museum are
arranged in sixteen stout quarto volumes, bound in red morocco , each
volume has a printed title page and is dated 1792 to 1809, the dates no
doubt between which they were purchased for the Museum through
Francillon from Abbot, and which probably indicated the period of his

activity in America   In Boston two similar volumes exist, one of which was presented by Dr Gray of the British Museum, to Dr. Gray the botanist of Cambridge, and by him to the Natural History Society, where it may now be seen   The other volume is a collection, perhaps the only considerable one which has never passed out of this country, which was purchased by the Society from Dr Oemler, of Georgia, who inherited it from his father *

In the title page of the last volume of the British Museum series there is a miniature portrait let into the title page, which, tradition says, was painted by Abbot himself, and indeed it bears every mark of this, though there is no memorandum to this effect within the volume   With its peculiar physiognomy it adds considerably to our interest in the original , there seems to be not a little humour in the quaint features and figure, and the spare form hardly gives the figure of robust health which the face would indicate.   Abbot probably returned to England about 1810, at an age of about fifty, and our portrait was doubtless painted at about this time, certainly before he left America, since it represents him in the thinnest of southern costume.   There were old persons living in Georgia up to 1885, but since deceased, who knew him, but apparently none now remain.

Abbot's work was by no means on Lepidoptera alone, as any of the series of his drawings will show   Dr. Hagen, in speaking of the volume in the British Museum containing the Neuroptera, says that all the details are given with the greatest care, and that in almost all cases the species can be identified   The same is the case with most of the drawings of Lepidoptera, though there is a mark of carelessness in some of the figures of early stages which is not found in others ; this is no doubt due to the fact that so many applied for these drawings, " both in Europe and America, that he found it expedient to employ one or two assistants, whose copies he retouched, and thus finished they generally pass as his own To an experienced eye, however, the originals of the master are readily distinguished."

It would hardly appear that he paid more attention to Lepidoptera than to other insects   Yet in the Oemler collection alone there are one hundred and thirty-three plates of Lepidoptera, nearly every one of which

---

*Mr Oemler and Mr " Le Compte ", are both mentioned in Abbot's notes as sending him specimens.

figures a species distinct from the others, and ninety-four of which are accompanied by the early stages   Twenty-two of these are insects figured in Abbot and Smith's work, but the figures of the early stages are in no case identical , they represent the same insect but in different attitudes   Of these one hundred and thirty-three plates, thirty-four are concerned with the butterflies   The drawings of butterflies in the British Museum are contained in the sixth and sixteenth volumes, the former comprising the perfect insects only, the latter the early stages as well, and in this latter series thirty-six species are figured ; while the two Boston collections contain figures of the early stages of all but two of the species represented in the British Museum volume   Swainson states that a series of one hundred and three subjects of Lepidoptera, including none published before, was executed for him " with the intention of forming two additional volumes to those edited by Dr Smith, but the design is now abandoned "

Each set of drawings furnished by Abbot seems to have been accompanied by more or less manuscript, in which the life history of the insect is given in brief form, with the food plant of the caterpillar and the times of the change of the caterpillars to chrysalids, and of chrysalids to butterflies, which shows that Abbot must have been an exceptionally industrious rearer of insects   Indeed the transformations of not a few of our butterflies are even now known only through the observations and illustrations of Abbot   Dr. Boisduval was good enough to present me with three series of manuscript notes entitled " Notes to the Drawings of Insects," all written in Abbot's own hand, and comprising twenty-seven foolscap pages, rather closely written, and describing the changes of two hundred and one species , of these thirty-eight are butterflies.   These, unfortunately, are referred to only by number and by an English name, which Abbot himself applied, apparently to every insect of which he furnished drawings, such as the " reed butterfly," the " ringed butterfly," the " lesser dingy skipper," etc , though he occasionally makes use of such names as the " autumnal ajax," " Papilio antiopa," etc., showing his familiarity to a certain extent with Linnean names.   As the names and drawings are in some instances kept together, the manuscript of those in which they are not connected is still of use   It appears that nearly all the Georgian butterflies were observed and painted by Abbot, and that of about sixty species which he raised he distributed illustrations and notes of the early stages to some of his correspondents.

As is well known by all aurelians, one considerable collection of Abbot's drawings was published by Sir James Edward Smith in two sumptuous folio volumes, but these comprise, as far as the butterflies are concerned, only twenty-four species. This work made an epoch in the history of entomology in this country. Besides this Abbot published nothing. The article credited to him in Hagen's Bibliography was by a Rev. Mr. Abbot, who wrote from England in November, 1798, when Abbot was in this country.

CHARACTERS OF PROTECTION AND DEFENCE IN INSECTS.

BY A. R. GROTE, A. M., BREMEN, GERMANY.

A few years since I described a colony of Spanner caterpillars (*Geometridæ*) belonging to an undetermined species, and the description appeared afterwards in this journal. These larvæ were remarkable for their mimicry, in color and shape and attitude, of dead leaves. There could be no question that they belonged to the category of protective appearance, to which so many green and brown tinted larvæ belong, which share these "cosmical colors." In studying these larvæ we must consider their color, shape and attitude separately. The larvæ of most of the Hawk Moths belong to this category. The caterpillar in repose, or at the approach of danger, assumes a rigid attitude in which it resembles a leaf on a branch of the food plant. The markings along the back often assist this resemblance. The only motion is that imparted by the swaying of the plant on which it rests. When disturbed, the caterpillar of *Thyreus Abbotii* throws itself by jerks from side to side and gives out a crepitating noise. It looks then somewhat snake-like.

The second category is that of defensive appearance. Highly colored, red and yellow larvæ, belong many of them to this category, as also those armed with spines and prickles. These would seem to court observation, which they further aid by their restlessness. It is probable that, by their gaudy appearance, they inspire distaste or fear in their natural enemies. The caterpillars of *Orgyia* are not eaten by birds, nor are those of *Abraxas*. By simulating obnoxious species it has been shown that several kinds of butterflies escape destruction. From these two points of view the appearance of insects must be studied, but it by no means follows that the means to the end have been always perfectly attained.

It is owing to the imperfection of their protection that insects are, as a whole, kept under and an undue multiplication prevented But there is, probably, an effort in these directions to be noted and brought out in the life history of all insects Darwin's law of Natural Selection tends to bring out these characters more strongly by its effect of preserving the best protected kinds. I have noted how the species of *Catocala*, so numerous with us, are preserved , the larvæ by their resemblance to twigs, the moths, from their upper wings, during the day and in repose, corresponding in appearance with the trunk and bark of the trees against which they rest The larvæ of burrowing Lepidoptera resemble in their pale and livid colors those of the Coleoptera or burrowing larvæ of other Orders of Insects. The larvæ of Hymenoptera, which are external feeders, resemble the external feeding Lepidoptera in their greenish tints. There is then a correlation between habit and color. The larvæ of cut-worms *(Agrotis)* resemble the soil in color, where they burrow at the roots of plants.

In South Carolina I collected a number of specimens of an Orthopterous insect, which strikingly resembled the predaceous Cicindelidæ They were active on the leaves of Okra I regret that the specimens were lost, and I could not determine the species. I have observed that certain smooth Chrysomelidæ, living on a species of lily, on the approach of danger folded in the feet and allowed themselves to slide off the leaves, dropping in the herbage beneath where they speedily recovered the use of their legs The snapping beetles, *Elateridæ*, assume a rigid attitude, the short feet tucked in against the under part of the hard body, and look like bits of dead wood or twigs. By their quiet and protective color they seem to expect that they will escape notice This and similar actions in other kinds of beetles and insects is called "feigning death" by some writers. In order to "feign death," as the words intend, some knowledge of death as such and its advantages must be supposed But I cannot think that insects have arrived at any such generalization of ideas Their actions often incompletely answer to their apparent ends It is probable to me that their attitudes of repose are assumed from the experience which they have gradually acquired that in a state of quiet they will best avoid the immediate dangers which beset them and which they cannot escape by flight. A *Catocala* will rest in quiet for hours, but on the near approach of a disturber will take to very quick and instant flight. Trying to capture a specimen once it thus escaped me, but in its endeavor to avoid Charybdis it fell into Scylla, for a passing swallow devoured it in the air.

The characters of protection and defense form an interesting subject in the natural history of external feeding larvæ, such as those of the Lepidoptera, for here the insect must rely on them and can do little or nothing by movement. Therefore they can here be the more readily detected. In tracing descent and relationship between the species, the modifications of the external characters of the larvæ must lead to the best results, to the safest conjectures as to the line taken. Almost all our knowledge as to any species and its habits is fragmentary and incomplete. What piece and parcel we observe we are apt to be very certain about, and we do not hesitate to draw therefrom very absolute conclusions, with an air of authority incommensurate with our knowledge. But in the multitude of counsellors there is in this case so far safety, that each may bring his observations and conclusions to paper, and, if the editor will print them, from the sifting of the whole a picture will in time be drawn which will stand in some proportion to the real truth.

THE ORANGE SPOT IN NATHALIS IOLE, Bdw.

BY T. D. A. COCKERELL, WEST CLIFF, COLORADO.

On November 1st, 1887, I took in this locality (Swift Creek, near West Cliff,) an example of *Nathalis iole*, and was thereby led to examine its characters. The general colour of the upper side of this insect is pale yellow. The primaries are marked with pale black (if one may use such a term,) after the manner described in the text books, and the upper margins of the secondaries also present a black patch, covering the area which is normally overlapped by the primaries. On this black patch, not far from the base of the wing, is an *elongated spot of the most vivid orange*. I first noticed this spot when setting out my specimen, and was led to wonder why the most vivid piece of colouring in the whole insect should be situated where it was invisible under ordinary conditions. Could it be due to some peculiarity in the development of the pigment induced by its peculiar position on the wing? was it a relic of the original colour of the insect, which not being under the same influences as the exposed parts, had not become modified in the course of ages? or was it a secondary sexual character to be exhibited by the raising of the primaries?

Being unable to answer these questions, I put the insect away until January 12th, when I sent it off with other butterflies to Mr. W. H.

Edwards, calling his attention to the presence of the orange spots.   He wrote in reply that he could not tell why some examples of *N iole* had the orange spot and others not, but it was a very variable species   On March 5th I received the box I had sent, and in it my specimen of *N iole*, which, to my great astonishment. had *completely lost the orange spots,*—they having become pale yellow. the colour of the rest of tne wing (except the black portion), only somewhat glossy.   The orange shade on the under side of the primaries, near the costal margin, had not faded in the least   Supposing that the butterfly might have been sub-mitted to some unusual influence while in Mr. Edwards' hands, I wrote to him asking the exact circumstances under which he had kept it, and he replied as follows: "The particular specimen which you sent and I returned never was outside your box and the latter rested on top of one of my insect cases, so that no chemical influence was brought to bear on it   Last year I raised several *iole* imagos from larvæ, and the males I think all had the orange spot; I am sure some had.   On looking at them now (March 16), I find *no orange at all*"   So it is perfectly clear that the orange spot in *Nathalis* is of a peculiar nature, and is further liable to fade, which process is not one of continuous and gradual bleach-ing due to the action of light—because my specimen was all the time in a closed box in perfect darkness. and the orange remained as vivid as ever up to the time that I sent the insect to Mr Edwards—but is more or less sudden, and apparently due to change in the *constitution* of a complex pigment, rather than its destruction   However this may be, I think that however insignificant this question may seem from the point of view of the systematist, it is one which the evolutionist will recognize as demand-ing his careful attention, and this must be my excuse for dealing with it at so great a length

NOTE ON A GERMAN EDITION OF ROSS'S SECOND VOYAGE (1829-1833)

BY A. R GROTE. A M

A copy of a German translation of Ross's Second Voyage lately fell into my hands, and I make the following bibliographical note upon the descriptions of Lepidoptera there given   The translation is by Julius, Graf von der Groben, Lieutenant in K Pr Reg. Garde du corps, and the third part or volume is published in Berlin, 1836   This volume (8 vo.)

contains the natural history, the descriptions of the Lepidoptera occupying pages 238 to 255 inclusive. The following are the references :

Colias Boothii (Curtis), p. 238.
　　" 　*Chione* (Curtis), p. 239.
Hipparchia Rossii (Curtis), p. 241.
　　" 　*subhyalina* (Curtis), p. 242.
Melitæa Tarquinius (Curtis), p. 243.
Polyommatus Franklinii (Curtis), p. 245.
Laria Rossii (Curtis), p. 247.
Eyprepia Hyperboreus (Curtis), p. 249.
Hadena Richardsoni (Curtis), p. 250.
Psychophora Sabini (Kirby), p. 251.
Oporabia Punctipes (Curtis), p. 252.
Orthotænia Bentleyana (Don), p. 253.
　　" 　　*Septentrionana* (Curtis), p. 254.
Argyrotosa (?) Parryana (Curtis), p. 254.

I have identified the moth *Laria Rossii* from specimens taken by Mr. Mann on Mount Washington, N. H.

DESCRIPTION OF A NEW SPECIES OF ANTHOCHARIS.

BY W. H. EDWARDS, COALBURGH, WEST VA.

Anthocharis Pima.

Male—Expands 1.75 inch.

Upper side yellow ; the bases of wings dusted black ; primaries have the basal half of costa white, crossed by dark brown streaks ; the apex also edged white on both margins, and next this is a series of five large, elongated, dark brown spots, almost confluent, filling the interspaces to second medium nervule, each sending a narrow projection to the margin ; on the arc a black rectangular bar, the area between this and the apical spots and costal edge orange ; fringes whitish ; a few blackish hairs at the end of each nervule on secondaries.

Under side of primaries yellow ; the apical area greenish, dusted with black scales ; the orange repeated paler and diffused over cell and second median interspace ; the bar on arc repeated.

Secondaries pale yellow, largely covered by patches of light yellow-green, confluent, forming irregular and connected transverse bands from hind margin to base.

Female—Expands 1 7 inch.

Same yellow ; the apical spots longer and completely confluent, forming a solid patch, the orange paler, the bar on arc less rectangular, broadest on sub-costal, under side as in the male

From two examples taken early in April, 1883, in Pima County, Arizona, by Mr O T. Baron In all 2 ♂ and 2 ♀ were taken This is the only known North American species in which both sexes are yellow The brown apical patch is much larger than in the allied species

BOOK NOTICE

THE BUTTERFLIES OF SOUTH AFRICA.

South African butterflies : A monograph of the extra-tropical species. By
  Roland Trimen, F R S., etc, assisted by James Henry Bowker, F
  Z S, etc Vol I Nymphalidæ, Vol. II Erycinidæ and Ly-
  caenidæ London Trubner & Co, 1887, 8 vo.

All who have studied foreign butterflies at all are acquainted with Trimen's work on the butterflies of Southern Africa, published more than twenty years ago, under the title Rhopalocera Africae Australis It will please them to know that there has recently appeared the first two of three volumes on the same subject, which are based, indeed, upon the old, but wholly rewritten, and with a great wealth of additions, especially on the natural history side These two volumes comprise the Nymphalidæ, Erycinidæ and Lycaenidæ, in all 238 species. The Papilionidæ and Hesperidæ are to occupy the third volume with about 142 species. It will thus be seen that Mr Trimen falls into line with all the principal lepidopterists of England in the serial order in which he here places the different families of butterflies, adopting indeed, exactly the subdivisions and the order Mr Moore employed in his Lepidoptera of Ceylon, which we noticed lately But he does more than that, for, in a long introductory chapter of 44 pp he treats of the structure, classification and distinctive characters of the groups, together with their geographical distribution, their habits and instances of mimicry in an excellent manner, such as is very unusual in a work of this nature It would interest every reader of the Canadian Entomologist. So, too, all the families, sub-families and generic groups are characterized with a fulness entirely proportional to the specific descriptions, rendering the work one of the best introductions to a fauna known to me These descriptions are evidently the work of one who is quite familiar with structure, are not copied from the writings of others, but are introduced in language of the author's own, having a special value quite apart from the rest of the work.   Nor is this all ; for the characters are drawn not simply from the complete stage of the insects, but from the larva and pupa as well, and these same stages are introduced in the generic descriptions.   It is unfortunate that he has not included also the egg.   The work is illustrated so far by ten octavo plates, one of which is devoted to the structure of the wings, the head and legs of the imago ; two to the early stages of a few species, and the remainder to excellent chromo-lithographs of the perfect insects.   The figures of the early stages are an interesting, though somewhat scanty, addition to our knowledge, the most important of which is found in the larva and pupa of D'Urbania, a curious genus of Lycaeninæ, in which the pupa, as well as the larva, is covered with long fascicles of hairs, as long as the width of the body.   Mr. Trimen has been aided by collectors and naturalists throughout Southern Africa to a very great extent, so much so, indeed, that he has added to his title page the name of one of them, Col. Bowker, as joint author with himself ; and the help he has received in this respect may be indicated in part by the considerable number of species which have been added to the list of South African butterflies since the publication of his first work, a total of 380 against 197.   An excellent coloured map of Southern Africa, south of the tropic of Capricorn, is prefixed to the first volume.   We hope the third volume, completing the work, will soon be issued.

SAMUEL H. SCUDDER.

CORRESPONDENCE.

REMEDY FOR ROSE-APHIS.

Dear Sir : Experiments with a weak solution of Creolin upon Rose Aphides and leaf-tying larvæ *(Tortrix)* proved quite successful without any apparent injury to the plants.   Rose bushes syringed with Creolin solution remained for some time after free from insects of any kind so far as I could observe.   More continued use of Creolin must be made to speak with certainty, but it seems to me likely that in this disinfectant we may have a valuable help for garden or greenhouse.

A. R. GROTE.

Mailed August 1st.

The Canadian Entomologist.

VOL. XX. LONDON, SEPTEMBER, 1888. No. 9

CATALOGUE OF THE MYRMOPHILOUS COLEOPTERA WITH BIBLIOGRAPHY AND NOTES.

BY JOHN HAMILTON, M. D., ALLEGHENY, PA.

Quite a number of our Coleoptera are known to associate in their imago or perfect state with the Formicariæ—comprehensively, ants. Very little, perhaps nothing, is known of the larval and pupal life of any of these beetles. Some, like *Batrisus bistriatus*, probably never leave the ants ; but others, like the species of *Cremastochilus*, desert them in the spring, whether afterwards to return and propagate among them is an open question. The association here referred to is common inhabitancy and more or less mutual interdependency, and not mere accidental occurrences under stones, bark and common shelters as seen frequently ; and it is not always easy for the collector to avoid confusion of this kind. By bringing together the most of what is recorded in American literature about these interesting Coleoptera, with this as a basis it is hoped a stimulus may be given to research, and collectors may be induced to search for them more diligently, and make public their observations. It is no easy matter to investigate properly an ant's nest, but patience and labour intelligently directed may meet with ample reward. Larvæ and pupæ should be diligently sought for in the formicariums. Only once or twice is there mention of any larva of a Coleopter having occurred with ants, and that of some Staphylinide that may have only been there as an explorer.

ABBREVIATIONS.

Tr.—Transactions of the American Entomological Society.

Pr.—Proceedings of the Academy of Natural Science, Phil. (2nd series).

An.—Annals of the Lyceum of Natural History, New York.

B. J.—Boston Journal of Natural History.

No Carabidæ are known to me to truly inhabit with ants, but several species hibernate in their burrows whether inhabited or not, as *Panagæus fasciatus*, which I find in autumn and in spring

Ptomophagus parasitus Lec   I take this beetle occasionally in April on the under side of flat stones covering the formicaria of a large black ant *(Formica herculanea ?)*   With this species of ant I once found five specimens of *Hister planipes*, and *Cremastochilus canaliculatus* and *Harrisii* are its guests

Colon   The Classification, p 77, states that some species of *Colon* are found only in ants' nests, but I fail to find further bibliography.

Scydmænus   The Classification, p 84, mentions ants' nests as the residence of some of the species   It might be well for the collector to consider whether the association is other than accidental

S capillosus Lec   Is found in March on the under side of stones, and is said (Pr , 6, 152) to sometimes occur in the nest of a small rufous ant with red legs   I take it sometimes with various small ants but just as frequently by itself, and see no connection besides that of occupying a common shelter.   Georgia, Pennsylvania and New York

S brevicornis Say.   Occurs in the nest of a small black ant   New York and Pennsylvania   (Pr , 6, 153)

S. rasus Lec.   Found with a small fuscous ant   Pennsylvania   (Pr , 6, 153)

Adranes cæcus Lec   Found with a small black ant   June   Georgia and Illinois   (B. J , 6, 84 , N. S., p. 28)

Adranes Lecontei Brend.   Several specimens of this curious insect, which is without eyes and has only two joints in the antennæ, were taken by Mr Charles Dury near Cincinnati, Ohio, with a medium-sized pale brown species of ant, inhabiting a decaying beech log   "On each side of the body and just back of the elytra is a tuft of brown hair, and from it springs a tube from which the beetle exudes a fluid that the ants are supposed to eat "—Dury, Journal of the Cincinnati Society of Natural History, July, 1884

Ceophyllus monilis Lec   Inhabits here with a medium-sized, honey-yellow ant *(Lasius interrimus ?)* that nests under stones.   When the beetle is found, which is not often, from six to a dozen occur in the same nest   I find *Hetærius brunnipennis* with this ant   April and May   Dr Leconte took *C monilis* under bark in August in Michigan   (B J , 6, 73 , Can Ent , 18, 26)

Cedius Ziegleri Lec   Dr Leconte took a specimen at Bedford, Pa , in the nest of *Formica rufa*, though previously he had found it under bark   (Tr, 6, 288 , B. J , 6, 74)

Tmesiphorus costalis Lec   Found with *Formica rufa*   (Tr 6, 287.)

Ctenistes pulvereus Lec.   Taken at San Jose, California, 'with a small piceous ant with testaceous legs."   (An., 5, 214)

Tychus puberulus Lec   With ants. San Jose, California.   (An., 5, 214)

Decarthron formiceti Lec   Found with *Formica Pennsylvanica*. April. Pennsylvania. (B J., 6, 90)

Batrisus Ionæ   Found by Dr Leconte " with a small, opaque, black ant, with rufo-piceous feet and antennæ " May   Mt Iona, Georgia (B J , 6, 94.)

B. armiger Lec   Lives with a medium-sized rufous ant. Pennsylvania (B J , 6, 94)

B. ferox Lec   Found with various ants   Pennsylvania, *loc. cit*

B. cristatus Lec   Found with a large rufous ant with a brownish head   Pennsylvania, *loc cit.*

B riparius Say. Occurs occasionally in Pennsylvania under stones with *Formica Pennsylvanica (?)*, but more frequently under pine bark in Georgia   (B. J., 6, 95)

B globosus Lec   Inhabits with several species of ant in Pennsylvania and Georgia   (B J , 6, 100)

B bistriatus Lec   Taken by Dr Leconte with a large rufous ant, *loc cit.*   I have taken it twice in April with a medium-sized honey-yellow ant.   The ants seem to be very fond of them, and carry them off like their eggs and pupæ, while the beetles appear to be entirely impassive. (Can. Ent., 18, 26)

B lineaticollis Aube   Taken with a large rufous ant. Georgia and Pennsylvania. (B J., 6, 100.)

It is quite probable other species of this genus occur with ants   Five species in California, described as new by Mr Casey since the catalogue was issued, are found in wet moss and under stones near water courses, thus showing great diversity of habit in insects placed in the same genus.

Anchylarthron cornutum ♂ (inornatum ♀) Brend. Gregarious with ants. Mississippi Valley and South Carolina. (Tr , 14, 208)

Trimium puncticolle Lec. Many specimens of this species were taken in an ants' nest by Dr. Horn in Arizonia (Proc. Am Phil Soc , 17, 384)

Homalota An undescribed species was taken with *Formica rufa* at Bedford, Pa , by Dr Leconte. (Tr., 6, 288)

Lomechusa cava Lec About fifty specimens were taken with a colony of black ants [*Formica Pennsylvanica*] inhabiting a white oak log Massachusetts. (Bul Brook Ent. Soc , 2, 4.) Dr. Leconte took it from the mounds of *Formica rufa* in the Alleghany Mountains ; it occurred with yellow ants in Columbia County, Pa , Michigan and Maryland , and in Illinois in large numbers in the nests of *Formica rufa (?)* (Tr , 6, 287)

Oxypoda. A species occurred with *Formica rufa* at Bedford, Pa. Leconte. (Tr., 6, 288.)

Leptacinus longicollis Lec Occurs in the middle States, and usually in ants' nests (N S , p 41.)

Eleusis pallidus Lec. Ants' nests, Lancaster County, Pa (Leconte in New Species, p. 58. This insect is gregarious. I have twice taken a colony early in July under the bark of Balm of Gilead stumps *(Populus candicans)*—once with very small brown ants, and once alone. The association of this species with ants appears to me to be merely accidental (CAN ENT., 18, 27.)

Hister planipes Lec Occurs, according to Dr. Horn, from Massachusetts to Georgia. Here, I took once five specimens in April in a nest of *Formica herculanea*

H. perpunctatus Lec Mr. F Blanchard takes this species at Tyngsborough, Mass., with a brown ant, 4 5 mm long. (Tr., 8, 190)

H repletus Lec. This, according to Mr. Blanchard, is also found in Massachusetts in the nest of a small black ant (Ent Am , 3, 86) It is quite probable *H subopacus* is also a Myrmophile. It occurs in Nebraska, Colorado, and also in Vancouver Island.

Hetærius brunnipennis Rand   Occurs here occasionally with a medium-sized honey-yellow ant in April and May

H Blanchardi Lec.   Mr. Blanchard, the discoverer of this species, took it and *Hister perpunctatus* with the same species of ant   (Tr, 8, 190)

Echinodes setiger Lec   This singular form has occurred variously, in South Carolina and Georgia with a pale ant. (Horn Proc Am. Phil Soc., 1 3, 305.)   Zimmerman found it at Columbia, South Carolina, in April, with a small brown ant.   (Tr.. 2, 253)   And it has been taken in Habersham County, Georgia, in the nest of a small ant under bark.   (Pr , 1859, 316)

Cremastochilus Schaumii Lec.   Dr. Horn frequently found this species in ants' nests in California.   (Tr , 3, 339)

C Westwoodi Horn.   Found in or near ants' nests in Owen's Valley, California, where it is not rare   (Pr. Am Phil Soc , 18, 139.)

C angularis Lec   This species was taken frequently in ant's nests in California by Dr. Horn, who several times saw large black ants dragging the beetles towards their nests   He strongly suspects the fossæ at the anterior angles of the thorax and the finely punctured and perforated patches under the hind angles yield a secretion grateful to the ants.   This species extends to Vancouver

C. variolosus Kirby.   One specimen occurred here with ants.

C canaliculatus Kirby   Is the most abundant species found here ; it is found from April till June with large black ants, perhaps of two species, inhabiting usually under stones or other covering, but not infrequently throwing up small mounds in old pastures and open ground   The nests under stones rarely yield more than two beetles, but the mounds often contain five or six at once and with care will yield a crop every two or three weeks   The beetles are found near the surface, none having been taken below the plane of the base.

As soon as it becomes warm, from the middle of April onward, this species takes leave of the ants and flies away ; like the *Cicindela* it only flies during the hottest sunshine and for short distances, alighting suddenly on a stone or the middle of a dusty road   Its flight is low and heavy, and after it lights cannot take wing again without some delay, and I have seen it flying as late as August.   Whether after having left, the same beetles return and breed among the ants, or whether it is a new brood that claims their hospitality for the winter, is absolutely unknown. I never could satisfy myself as to whether those found in the nests in June had returned or were just preparing to leave. (For some interesting observations on this species and *Schaumii* see Ent. Am., 1, 187.)

C. Harrisii Kirby. I neglected to observe the ant with which I took a specimen.

Dr. Horn incidently mentions that *C. leucosticticus, pilosicollis* and *castaneœ* have likewise been observed in ants' nests. (Pr. Am. Phil. Soc., 18, 384.)

Without much doubt many species of our *Staphylinidœ* will be found to be Myrmophilous as in Europe, where, according to Rev. J. G. Wood, in the Aleocharidæ alone no less than "eight genera contain species that are parasitic and spend their whole lives in the nests of ants," among them *Atemeles emarginatus* and *A. paradoxus* living with *Formica fusca* and *Myrmice ruginodis*, which take as good care of them as of their own young; also *Myrmedona Haworthii* and *Dinarda dentata, Quedius brevis* is said to live with *Formica rufa*, and that wonderful beetle *Claviger foveolatus*, destitute of eyes and mouth, inhabits with *Formica flava*.

Besides the species catalogued here several others in our Fauna are traditionally reputed to dwell with ants, but the observers have either not published the facts or I have failed to find the bibliography.

THE CLASSIFICATION OF THE BOMBYCIDÆ.

(Second Paper.)

BY A. R. GROTE, A. M., BREMEN, GERMANY.

We have seen, CAN. ENT., xix., p. 156, *et seq.*, that the Bombycidæ, or Spinner Moths, are characterized, as a whole, by their short, pectinate antennæ, ample, velvety wings, thick bodies, small heads and sluggish habit, while the pupa is usually contained in a cocoon made by the caterpillar in its last stage. To almost all these characters the sub-family groups offer exceptions, and we have seen that while Dr. Packard follows the tradition of Harris, Latreille and Linnaeus, modern German writers break up the family into independent groups limited by structural features taken from the imago What Agassiz calls "form" still unites these various groups—a certain correspondence in outline and habit. Dr. Packard seeks this in the shape of the clypeus, the piece between the eyes, its relative proportion. In my first paper I have adopted this view, that we have to do with descendants of a former complex and that we may still unite the Spinner Moths under a common family title. Those who differ may merely alter my sub-families into families

Sub-family *Sarothripinæ.*

The single genus *Sarothripus* Curt was first referred to the Tortricidæ, then to the Noctuidæ, and finally as part of the *Nolinæ*, the second sub-family or group of the Bombycidæ In my new Check List the genus is omitted, as I had no knowledge of our N. Am. species The form of the cocoon allies it to *Nola.* The moth is tortriciform and differs from *Nola* decidedly in the form of the wings The fore wings are elongate, sub-quadrate, hardly widening outwardly with acute apices. The palpi are much longer than the head, more erect and prominent than in *Nola* The caterpillar is 16-footed and makes a boat-shaped cocoon The neuration shows a relation to *Nola* and the Lithosians As the hind wings have only two internal veins, we see that the moth is not really a Micro, to which group it was once referred The fore wings have no accessory cell. We shall come back to this accessory cell later and show its importance and constancy in some other groups The antennæ are simple in both sexes The resemblance to *Nola* lies also in the want of ocelli, and this character unites the three first groups, viz., *Sarothripinæ, Nolinæ* and *Lithosiinæ,* again, the elongate palpi, which are, however, equally squamous throughout Of the European genera, *Chlœphora, Halias* and *Earias,* we have no N. Am species, and these probably form a distinct group, *Chlœphorinæ.* Of *Sarothripus* we have one described from the East and one from the West. Now the European species is very variable, and whether we have more than one species, or whether our species is really distinct from the European *revayana,* is not clearly made out. Probably the earliest descriptions of forms of our Eastern *Sarothripus* are those cited by Fernald, Am. Ent , I , 36, the *Tortrix scriptana* and *frigidana* of Walker

Sub-family *Nolinæ*

The fore wings are broad, sub-trigonate, without accessory cell , the hind wings rounded, not as in the *Sarothripinæ,* with the outer margin

indented. No ocelli. The fore wings have tufted scale patches above.
The caterpillars are 14-footed and make a boat-shaped cocoon. The
neuration of our N. Am. genus *Argyrophyes* is given by me, CAN. ENT.,
ix., 236 ; and we have two species, *cilicoides* and *nigrofasciata* (= *Eustrotia obaurata* Morr.). This latter synonym recalls the fact that the ornamentation in this group of small insects resembles that of the Noctuidæ.
In *Argyrophyes* the raised blotches of scales on primaries are metallic.
Of the typical genus *Nola*, I have cited five N. Am. species in the new
Check List.

Sub-family Lithosiinæ.

The long palpi of the preceding groups are replaced by shorter, more
bombyciform appendages. In this group the body is weak and the fore
wings usually narrow, while the hind wings are wide and frail. The ocelli
are wanting. Hence I refer *Crocota* to the following group of *Arctiinæ*.
The costal vein of secondaries springs from the subcostal. No accessory
cell on primaries. The caterpillars are 16-footed and live on lichens. In
the new Check List I cite the genera *Clemensia, Crambidia, Hypoprepia,
Cisthene, Byssophaga* (distinct?), *Lithosia, Euphanessa* and *Ameria*. It
is possible that the two last do not belong to this group.

Sub-family Arctiinæ.

In this group the male antennæ are usually provided with short pectinations ; the ocelli are present ; the palpi are quite short and the whole
appearance is bombyciform. Veins 4 and 5 are near together on both
wings. The moths are usually of larger size than in the preceding
groups ; the wings are ample, held roof-like in repose. The caterpillars
are hairy and make loose cocoons. Our North American genera are
allied to the European, but Dr. Packard has drawn attention to the fact
that onr species are more white and yellow, less red-colored than the
European. In the presence of the genus *Nemeophila* the west coast
fauna more nearly resembles the European. The genera *Crocota,
Kodiosoma, Seirarctia, Leucarctia, Ecpantheria, Euerythra, Halisidota,*
are more especially American forms, outgrowths, so to speak, of *Spilosoma*
and *Arctia*. I wish to correct here Mr. J. B. Smith's reference of *Cerathosia tricolor* Sm., to the *Arctiidæ*. A comparison of its corrected
characters will show that it should be rather referred to the *Noctuidæ*.
The clypeus has an inferior circular rim and presents a sub-central, button-

like projection   This is a Noctuid and Pyralid feature, though a projection
is found in *Copidryas* without the rim   The fore wings have an accessory
cell   The hind wings have vein 5 present, but weak, not absent as stated
by Mr. J B Smith, and this vein is equidistant between 4 and 6, contra-
dicting the characters of the *Arctiinæ*   Mr J B Smith also describes
incorrectly the relative positions of veins 3, 4 and 5 on primaries, as also
the point of emergence of vein 10, which springs from about the middle
of the upper margin of the accessory cell, not from the upper and outer
angle of the cell, whence springs vein 7, giving off 8 and 9   In *Cerathosia* there is a claw on fore tibiæ , the legs are thinly scaled, the palpi
not so short as in the *Arctiidæ*   The moth is lithosiform rather than
arctiiform in appearance, but the ocelli will not allow of its being referred
to the Lithosians , its neuration and total characters exclude it from the
Bombycidæ altogether   The squamation is rather like *Tarache* than like
Arctia   It is not enough that a description of a genus be given , the
reason *why* it belongs to the family must be stated   Added to this, Mr
Smith's description is in itself faulty and inaccurate, and affords no reason
why this author should use such language in correcting Mr Hy Edwards's
reference of certain genera, or take such a tone in correcting my own
writings   In the present day when the Lepidoptera are well known, the
details of structure of the different groups are all given in the writings of
the past fifteen or twenty years in Europe and America

Sub family *Dasychirinæ*

This group is allied to the *Arctiidæ* by the tufted or shaggy caterpillars, the frail cocoons   The antennæ are more plumose, in the female
with short teeth   The palpi are short   The ocelli are again wanting
The legs are short and are usually hairy as in many of the *Arctiidæ*.
The pupa itself is often hairy—an unusual character   The wings are
ample, but in the females of some genera wanting or incompletely expanded   Veins 4 and 5 spring near together, another point of resemblance to the *Arctiidæ*   In fact we cannot but approve of Harris's and Dr.
Packard's arrangements of these groups   *Hepialus* and *Cossus* should
not be interpolated here, but are the lowest groups of the family   In the
Dasychirinæ the body is rather heavy, and there is a disproportion
between the sexes, many males being much smaller and lighter   In the
New Check List I have cited the N Am genera *Parorgyia*, *Carama*

and *Lagoa*. The two latter are curious, and show some resemblances to the following group, *Cochlidiinæ*. *Carama* may be described by Curtis also. The genera *Orgyia* and *Dasychira* are shared with Europe; in the old world the representation of the *Dasychirinæ* seems to be far greater than in the new.

PARTIAL PREPARATORY STAGES OF CATOCALA INNUBENS, Guen.

BY G. H. FRENCH, CARBONDALE, ILL.

April 28, 1887, a single larva of a then unknown Catocala was found on a Honey Locust which proved to be this species. By its appearance it had seemingly passed the first moult. Hence the egg and first stage of the larva is lacking in this account of its life history. If my conjecture be true, my description will begin with the conventional " after the first moult." Length, .26 inch. Color pale greenish, the anterior two and posterior three joints whitish; four purplish red stripes on each side, the lower somewhat broken; head mottled, but not heavily so; piliferous spots black, with short black hairs. Shape as usual with Catocala larvæ. Duration of this period unknown.

After 2nd Moult.—Length, .40 inch. Color, pale dull purplish rose in nine longitudinal stripes alternating with pale greenish white lines, the rose darker on the head and joint 2, shading into the pale rose on joint 3; the dorsal stripe a narrow line on joints 2 to 4, broken between the joints and narrow on the last three joints; stripe 2 (counting the dorsal one) contains the dorsal piliferous spots; stripe 3 without any piliferous spots; stripe 4 with the lateral piliferous spots; below this a broken and irregular stripe that contains the lowest piliferous spots. These stripes are of the double line kind, each edge darker than the middle, though there is little difference in any of them except the lowest or number 5, which has more or less of the greenish white in its centre. Piliferous spots black, conspicuous, the short hairs black; head reddish purple with mottlings of broken white lines. Duration of this period four days.

After 3rd Moult.—Length, .80 inch. Color, pale green, with seven dark reddish purple stripes on each side, composed of contiguous dots; head striped with purplish black and white; the dark on joint 2 black, gradually shading into the purple, yellow tinted between the joints, piliferous spots black, joints in the middle of the body with black patches on the venter. The posterior pair of piliferous spots on the dorsum of joint 9 are, like other species, more approximate than the others and the intervening space elevated, the elevation containing four spots in a transverse row with a patch of pale yellowish back of these   Duration of this period five days.

After 4th Moult —Length, 1 20 inches   Color, pale green, almost white, with a slight yellow tinge. more distinct underneath the top of joint 2, the legs and a substigmatal stripe distinct yellow, the transverse folds between the joints with more of the yellow tinge   Head striped with dark reddish purple (this was black before) and white, the markings arranged as before but the stripes are almost obliterated on the body except on joints 2 to 4, and the transverse folds between the joints where they are distinct as to the rows of black dots that mark the boundary of the stripes, faint traces of these on the middle of the joints, the black on the venter small except on the middle joints   Piliferous spots black, not very large, a prominent black patch on each side of the posterior part of joint 9, composed of three spots, a short dorsal orange line between them, the posterior pair of spots on the back of joint 12 more prominent than the others, no lateral fringe, but a slight fold above the pro-legs, the anterior two pairs of pro-legs pretty well developed

Mature Larva —Length, 2 25 inches   Color, sordid white, a little green tinted, very obscurely striped as at the beginning of the stage, the bordering blackish dots marking the boundary of the stripes most distinctly on the intersegmental folds, the black on joint 9 the same as before with a very short orange stripe between, the substigmatal pale stripe orange on joints 5 and 6, joints 2 to 4 with the rows of spots distinct Piliferous spots small, black ; venter white, tinted a little with yellow, black only on the joints bearing feet, no fringe   Duration of this period nine days

Chrysalis —Length, 1 05 inches, diameter, .40 inch, of joint 5, 30 inch, tapering from joint 5 to the end, rather strongly indented on joint 1, tongue and wing cases equal, extending back to posterior part of joint 5 ; cremaster two long hooks at the tip, two shorter at the base, outside of these and a little removed from them several other short hooks, abdominal joints slightly punctured, the tongue and wing cases shallowly cornu-gated, terminal joint deeply on dorsal and lateral parts, head rounded. Color, chestnut brown, as usual coated with a white powder.   Puparium a slight lining to the leaves that were fastened together with silk.

The larva pupated May 17th, and the imago appeared June 20th, giving a pupal period of about a month, which is about the same as the other species that have been bred   One feature of the species is that the larva has no lateral fringe   As given before, the food plant is Honey Locust

May 12th, another larva was found that differs from the above description only in being darker, and as a natural result the stripes more distinct, the light stripes having an orange tint   After this two more were found, one of which had all the light stripes quite distinctly orange tinted.   The head was reddish purple striped with numerous white lines, or rather broken lines   Like the other, the venter had the black only on the joints bearing legs   This one had passed the last moult when found, and produced the imago June 17th, showing that keeping the first in confinement had not materially interfered with its time of pupating or its other changes

ON THE CHALCIDEOUS TRIBE CHIROPACHIDES

BY WILLIAM H ASHMEAD, JACKSONVILLE, FLA

Below I give an analytical table for recognizing the genera in the tribe *Chiropachides* Thomson   It will be seen that I have placed in this group the genus *Schizonotus* Ratzburg, which Dr. Arnold Foerster, in his Hymenopterologische Studien (1856), says is identical with *Seladerma* Walker, an opinion in which I cannot concur, my type of *Schizonotus Siebaldi* Ratz not agreeing at all with Walker's definition, also the genera *Mesopolobus* and *Platymesopus* Westwood, which were subpressed by Walker and other authorities, and placed in the genus *Pteromalus*, they agree in all essential characters with this group, the anterior femora being very similar to *Chiropachys*, the type of the tribe.

Two new genera will be found characterized in this group the characters of which, as given in the table, being sufficient, it is hoped, to enable them to be easily recognized.

The arrangement proposed is as follows :—

Tribe *Chiropachides* Thomson

TABLE OF GENERA.

Posterior tibiæ with one spur   3
Posterior tibiæ with two spurs
Eyes not hairy   .   .   2
Eyes hairy.
Abdomen sessile, long pointed ovate, marginal and postmarginal veins
    somewhat thick, the latter being longer than the marginal ; stigmal
    vein short, one-third the length of the marginal ; sculpture coarsely
    pitted .   .   .   .   .   *G. 1, Dasyglenes* n g.

2   Collar transverse quadrate, separated from the mesothorax by a deep
    incision at the posterior angle , pedicel of antennæ lengthened,
    funiclar joints much broader than long, the club obliquely truncate
    from below.   .   *. G. 2, Schizonotus* Ratzburg
Collar not so formed
Collar transverse, rounded before, narrowed in the middle.
Anterior femora exciso-dentate , wings with two transverse bands .   . .
    .   .   .   *G 3, Chiropachys* Westwood.
Anterior femora simple , wings with one transverse band   .   . .
    ..   .   .   .   .   *G. 4, Acrocormus* Forster.

3   Abdomen petiolated   6
Abdomen sessile, long or pointed ovate.
Marginal vein of anterior wings not thickened   . 5
Marginal vein of anterior wings thickened
Antennæ with transverse ring-joints.   .   4
Antennæ with ring-joints large not transverse
Marginal vein but slightly longer than the stigmal...   .
    ....   *. G. 5, Pandelus* Forster.

4   Stigmal vein and postmarginal vein short. .. *G. 6, Metacolus* Forster.
Stigmal vein longer than the marginal , ♀ with the antennal joint stylate
    at the apex . ..   .   *G 7, Raphitelus* Walker.

5   Parapsides only indicated anteriorly , anterior margin of collar sharp.
Stigmal club very large   .   .   *G. 8, Dinotus* Forster.
Stigmal club small or moderate,

* ♀ With marginal vein at least thrice as long as stigmal ; funiclar joints broader than long; middle tibiæ in ♂ with a small hirsute lobe, outwardly near tip.... ....*G. 9, Mesopolobus* Westwood.

** ♀ With marginal vein not twice as long as stigmal ; anterior tibiæ flat ; middle tibiæ in ♂ broadly dilated, foliaceous.............. ....*G. 10, Platymesopus* Westwood.

6. Collar rounded before ; mesothorax lengthened with three keels. Marginal vein more than twice longer than the stigmal ; parapsides indicated anteriorly..·.....................*G. 11, Rhopalicus* Förster. Marginal vein but slightly longer than the stigmal ; parapsides complete . ...*G. 12, Brachycrepis* n. g.

Dasyglenes n. g.

♀ Whole surface, including the abdomen, very coarsely reticulato-punctate, and sparsely covered with a pale pubescence. Head large, slightly broader than the thorax with deep antennal grooves, the grooves converging and meeting at apex. Antennæ inserted slightly above the clypeus, the latter with a sinus in the middle. Eyes hairy. Collar transverse, contracted and produced anteriorly into a short neck, the neck with a delicate medium carina. Mesothoracic parapsides delicate but complete. Scutellum convex, as broad as long, slightly prolonged over the metathorax and ending in a slight projecting ridge at the apex. Metathorax short, with a delicate medium keel. Abdomen sessile, much longer than the head and thorax together, acuminated, the tip projecting slightly beyond the wings when folded. All femora swollen, the fore pair much more so than the middle pair ; the tibiæ are very long, the three basal joints of which are as long as their tibiæ ; the middle and posterior tibiæ longer than their femora, and the tarsi not nearly as long as their respective tibia ; the posterior tibiæ are armed with two strong, divergent apical spurs. The submarginal vein, of anterior wings, is one and a-half times as long as the marginal, the marginal and postmarginal veins thick, the latter much lengthened, gradually acuminated, ending at the rounded edge of the apical margin of wing ; stigmal vein short, about one-third the length of marginal, slightly bent, the stigma small and slightly emarginated at the apex. ♂ Unknown.

Dasyglenes osmiæ n. sp.

♀ Length .25 inch. Cyaneous, coarsely pitted, pubescent. Flagellum of antennæ brown. Legs dark red, pubescent ; femora infuscated. Wings hyaline, veins brown, the whole surface is covered with a fine brownish pubescence   Described from one ♀ specimen reared from a bee, *Osmia* species, living in Catalpa twigs

This genus shows strong affinities with *Cleonymus* Latreille and *Aeroxys* Westwood but is readily distinguished from both by the thickened fore femora, had it not been for this character I should have placed it in the genus *Cleonymus*

Chiropachys Westwood

Chiropachys colon Linn., Faun So Ed, ii, p 413, *C quadrum* Walk., Ent. Mag, iv, p 14, *Pteromalus bimaculatus* Swederus.

This common European chalcid must now be added to our fauna, specimens having been taken in the United States that cannot be separated from types received from Europe

The species described by Mr Edward Norton as *Chiropachys nigrocyaneus*, Trans Am Ent. Soc, ii, p 327, is not a *Chiropachys* but belongs to the genus *Pachyneuron* in the tribe *Sphegigastrides*

Dinotus Forster

Dinotus elongatus n sp

♀ Length 13 inch.   Dull metallic brown. confluently punctate. sparsely covered with white hairs   Head much wider than the thorax, the width of the vertex nearly twice the length of the eye   Ocelli red, Eyes ovate, brown   Antennæ 13-jointed, filiform, pubescent, the long slender scape, pedicel and the two ring-joints, honey-yellow, flagellum brown, the first funiclar joint the longest following joints slightly subequal, the club short. three-jointed, slightly thicker than the funicle, and not longer than the first funiclar joint.   Collar very short, transverse, parapsides only indicated anteriorly.   Metathorax not very long, not keeled, metathoracic spiracles long oval, metapleura slightly pubescent.   Coxæ smooth, bluish-green. with tufts of white hair anteriorly   Legs honey-yellow, excepting the femora which are brownish in the middle   Abdomen sessile, pointed ovate, one-third longer than head and thorax com_ bined, concave above, and of a dull greenish metallic lustre, each segment laterally with some short hairs   Wings hyaline, sparsely pubescent, veins yellowish, the marginal hardly twice the length of the stigmal, the latter terminating in a slight knob, while the postmarginal is slightly shorter than the marginal   Described from one specimen captured at large

Brachycrepis n g

This genus is very similar to *Rhopalicus* Forster, but the prolonged metathorax has three distinct keels, the abdomen has a short rugose petiole, the marginal vein of the front wings is but slightly longer than the stigmal and the parapsides complete   The anterior femora are very much swollen , the antennæ are subclavate 13-jointed with two ring joints, and are inserted slightly below the middle of the face ; the pedicel is about as long as the first funiclar joint.

Brachycrepis tricarinatus n sp.

♀ Length .13 inch.   Dark blue with a slight metallic tinge on the head and thorax, confluently punctured.   Eyes dark brown.   Antennæ 13-jointed, black, except the scape beneath, which is brownish-yellow ; flagellum pubescent , the first funiclar joint the longest, the others slightly subequal, but gradually growing wider toward the club, the fifth and sixth joints being wider than long   Collar transverse, narrowed in the middle   Mesothoracic grooves distinct, but very delicate as they approach the scutellum   Coxæ, femora and tibiæ, excepting their tips and the last tarsal joint, blue-black , tips and the other tarsal joints, honey-yellow   Abdomen long ovate, about the length of the thorax, blue-black with a very slight metallic tinge near the base beneath   The second segment, counting the petiole as the first, is the largest, the others gradually subequal , each segment with a single row of delicate white hairs.   Wings hyaline , veins pale brownish, the submarginal vein as long as the marginal and postmarginal together, delicate, the marginal is but slightly longer than the stigmal, the latter clavate with a slight uncus

Hab —Riley Co , Kansas   Prof E A Popenoe.

CAN INSECTS DISTINGUISH BETWEEN RED AND YELLOW ?

BY T. D. A. COCKERELL, WEST CLIFF, COLORADO.

In this neighborhood (Custer Co , Colorado,) one very frequently finds a yellow spider of the genus *Thomisus* or allied thereto   seated in the middle of the umbels of *Ligusticum montanum* Benth   and Hook., and on other yellow flowers   This spider, so seated, has nothing to cover it from direct observation, and from its size and colour would be conspicuous enough elsewhere , but on the yellow flower, sitting in the depression in the centre of the umbel, it is quite invisible unless specially looked for. Thus concealed, it waits until some insect—frequently a small bee, or a butterfly of the genus *Pamphila*, settles on the flower—but no sooner is the insect intent upon the nectar of the blossom, than the cunning *Thomisid* has it in its grasp, and is sucking its life-juices away. On one occasion, also, I found a white *Thomisid* spider seated on a white umbel, and equally concealed here by its whiteness, it had secured and was feasting on a bee. So far good. It may be argued that spiders of this family have been accustomed to sit on flowers, and being variable in colour (as in fact they are) natural selection has so arranged matters that yellow spiders preside over yellow flowers, white over white, and so on. But perhaps, also, the spider has " an eye for colour," since he (the yellow one) occasionally sits on a small species of sunflowers which has yellow rays and a dark brown disc—and here, although the spider always sits in the *middle* of a yellow umbel, he sits on the *rays* of this sunflower, knowing altogether better than to expose himself to observation on the brown disc. But, to come to the point to be discussed, there is a species of geranium found here (*Geranium fremontii* Torrey,) having *pink* flowers—yet the *yellow* spider sits on these, apparently unconcerned at the difference of colour. Now, it is a curious thing, that throughout living organisms, whether birds (*e. g. Fringillidæ*), mollusca (*e. g. Tellinidæ, Helicidæ*), insects (*e. g. Zygænidæ, Sesiidæ, Cheloniidæ, Ichneumonidæ*), or plants, that the red and yellow pigments seem to stand in this relation to one another, that the red is a more complex form of the yellow, and hence occasionally reverts to it, yellow being in all cases the primitive color. In *Geranium*, it is true, there are not (to my knowledge) yellow-flowered varieties, but then, there are both pink and yellow-flowered species of *Oxalis*, in the same natural order. Therefore, it is conceivable that the yellow *Thomisid* first came to sit on geranium flowers at the time when these were yellow, and has continued the habit—but still, since it appears to understand the difference between brown and yellow on the sunflower, why cannot it tell that pink and yellow are not the same ? Does it not look as if, to this spider, these colours were indistinguishable ?

Also, the geranium-frequenting spiders do not starve, although to human eye they are very easy to be seen—does not this, again, look as if the insects frequenting those flowers could not distinguish between pink and yellow, and so, not seeing the spider, fell unwittingly into its grasp ?

This is the question I wish to ask, and to answer it, it is necessary to have observations of a more extensive nature on the relation of yellow insects to pink flowers, and *vice versa.* I have myself noticed that (in Kent, England,) *Gonepteryx rhamni* appears to be exceptionally fond of settling on pink flowers, but it seemed to me rather that the butterfly was conscious of the contrast between the colours and its own conspicuousness arising therefrom.

May I rely upon your readers to supplement these notes, and so clear up this question?

CORRESPONDENCE.

DICERCA PROLONGATA.

With reference to Dr. John Hamilton's note on p. 120, I may say that I have found the larva of this species boring in *Populus tremuloïdes* in Colorado, concerning which details were published in the " Entomologists' Monthly Magazine" for March, 1888, vol. xxiv, p. 232-233.

T. D. A. COCKERELL.

CAPTURES IN 1887.

Dear Sir: My additions to the list of Canadian Lepidoptera for the past season is of the most meagre description. I took a good many micros, new to me ; but as usual, with them a large proportion were single specimens of a kind. I sent to Prof. Fernald 17 specimens which I had in duplicate ; of these three turned out to be variations of kinds that he had previously named for me ; three proved to be all one ; one, *Depressaria heracliana* Dege. was new to me, but already in the list, and one *Eccopsis nitidana* Clem. is new to the Canadian list ; the rest were unknown to him. Three years ago I captured at Ridgeway, along with Limacodes, to which I thought it belonged, a moth new to me, and which has been from that time until lately awaiting a name. During the past winter, Mr. Johnston, of this city, was making some exchanges with Miss Emily L. Morton, of Newburgh, N. J., and received from her a specimen labelled *Adoneta spinuloides* H. S., in which I recognized my unnamed Bombycid. Miss Morton acknowledges her indebtedness to Mrs. Fernald for the correct identification of most of her Lepidoptera. On the 11th of July last I came on an assemblage of Pyralids in the grass under the shade of a butternut tree, where I had taken refuge from the excessive heat. At first

I thought it was *Botis magistralis*, on closer inspection I doubted its identity—it was like, and yet unlike. I concluded that if it was *Magistralis*, it was an unusually fine specimen, so I took a quantity of it anyway. and all the more willingly as it was quite abundant in the very spot where I wanted to stay for a while. On comparing them, I was still undecided, whilst in communication with the Rev Mr Hulst, about some Geometers, I sent to him a specimen and received for it the name *Botis quinquelinealis* Grote These three names are then the only presentable result of my last season's work in this direction.

J. ALSTON MOFFAT, Hamilton, Ont.

KNOWLEDGE OF DEATH IN INSECTS

Dear Sir · An incidental remark in one of my papers, page 6, of the present vol., has attracted the attention of a correspondent of the ENTOMOLOGIST, as may be seen by turning to page 120 I was then entirely unaware that I was meddling with an '*ipse dixit* of Mr Grote's, or was touching one of his 'chips,'" but, in common with the readers of the ENTOMOLOGIST, I know it now While Mr Grote certainly had the right to show, if he could, that the alleged assertion, whether made by himself or not, was not " unsupported," was not " dogmatic ," yet he had no right to assume that I had seen his paper, and even on that assumption no right disposed person, while differing from me, could take legitimate offence at my words, which are strictly scientific. The cause is said to be weak, when the advocate resorts to the *argumentum ad hominem* to overcome his opponents *argumentum ad rem ;* * ⁺ * Let us see where Mr. Grote stands, his words are · " It is by *the keeping still* that the insects seem to me to appear to feign death,' of the existence of which latter they could have no knowledge " Few or none will dispute the first part of the quotation It states exactly what such insects do, that is, " keep still ," but this does not prove that insects can have " no knowledge of death ," no proof of this is anywhere offered, nor is the assertion in any way limited or qualified , hence " unsupported," " dogmatic " are appropriate adjectives, and though not made by me with any reference to or knowledge of Mr. Grote's paternal claim Now see how he " corrects " the adjectives " unsupported," " dogmatic " (ib , p 120) His words now read " Whether insects can have any knowledge of death, as such may be a matter of opinion," etc , quite a different statement from his former postulate, that insects could have no knowledge of death. The reader will notice how *ingenuously* " dogmatic " is disposed of by this change of base Now, as to what he doubts not is the main point, that is, " the keeping still," that is only what these insects do, a mere act, and one to which even Mr. Grote himself attaches a motive, "the approach of danger." But why " keep still " on the " approach of danger "? His answer cannot be surmized Writers have expressed various opinions about this " keeping still," " death mimicry," " feigning death," as practiced by certain insects and other animals, but I have not seen any statement that they can have no knowledge of death, except that claimed by Mr Grote and a similar one in a Pittsburg newspaper Dr Lindsay, in his work " Mind in Animals," in treating of death-feigning, says " This must require great self-command in those that practice it;" while Professor James, of Harvard College, in an article in Popular Science Monthly, June, 1887, on ''Some Human Instincts," says · ' It is really no feigning of death at all and requires no self-command It is simply a terror paralysis, which has been so useful as to become hereditary '' In commenting on this the newspaper man makes the remark I took exception to, my notice of which, without at the time being able to state where I had derived it, brought out Mr. Grote, whom I would most assuredly have quoted had I been aware of his assertion   JOHN HAMILTON, Allegheny, Pa

---

ARZAMA OBLIQUATA, G AND R.

Dear Sir   In reference to Mr. Moffat's remark in the July number of the CANADIAN ENTOMOLOGIST, that the larva of this moth does not always form its pupa in the reed, I wish to say that I have taken between fifty and seventy-five chrysalids this spring, and all of them were in the reeds where the larva had been feeding. I believe that the larva sometimes goes out of the reed and wanders in other directions before going into pupa, but this is not often the case. My friend, Mr Doll when breaking an old cedar stump apart last spring, found in it the chrysalis of *A obliquata*, but the larva had been feeding in the stump Could that have been the case in Mr. Moffat's instance ?

HERMANN H BREHME, Newark, N. J.

The Canadian Entomologist.

VOL. XX.   LONDON, OCTOBER, 1888.   No. 10

THE CLASSIFICATION OF THE BOMBYCIDÆ.

(Third Paper.)

BY A. R. GROTE, A. M., BREMEN, GERMANY.

Sub-family *Cochliinæ*.

A study of the American genus *Lagoa* in its various stages of growth shows a manifest approach to the present group, so that we are warranted in following the *Dasychirinæ* with the *Cochliinæ*. This sub-family is remarkable for its peculiar larvæ, called " slug caterpillars " or " saddle-backs." The first name is given on account of their snail-like appearance, the form being elliptical or oval, the false feet replaced by swellings on the abdominal segments, so that the larva lies flat and close to the leaf. The head is also retractile. The cocoon is egg-shaped or circular, firm and spun between the leaves. The moths are not unfrequently green and brown as are the larvæ, and the name " saddle-backs " is given in allusion to the bright green quadrate patch which covers the back in some species. Dr. Packard calls one species *monitor*, in allusion to the singular shape and armature of the larvæ. The moths are of various shades of brown, often with green patches, sometimes with darker lines and shades on primaries. The ocelli are wanting and the tongue is short. The North American genera fall into two series : one in which the male antennæ are pectinate, the other brush-like or sub-simple. To the first series belongs the typical genus *Limacodes* of Latreille, and to this series belong the two European species representing two distinct genera. As compared with Europe, our fauna is rich in *Cochliinæ*. We have two species belonging to the Asiatic genus *Parasa*, with grass-green thorax, and the fore wings largely green. The larva of *Parasa chloris* H.-S., is described by Mr. Henry Edwards, Papilio iii., 128 ; that of *Parasa fraterna* Gr., by the same author, Ent. Amer. iii., 169. (I here correct a statement of mine, that the sub-family *Chloephorinæ* does not occur in North America. Mr. Henry Edwards describes *Earias obliquata* from Florida, a form unknown

to me, the genus belonging to this sub-family which I distinguish from the
Sarothripinæ)   I do not know any forms of *Cochliinæ* from California ;
if the sub-family is feebly represented there, it will be a fresh example of
the resemblance between the West Coast fauna and the European.   No
Cuban forms were included in the collection described by me.   The
geographical distribution of the North American Bombycidæ merits attention.   On the islands of the West Indies, there seem to be no typical
Spinner moths, that is to say, no *Attacinæ, Ceratocampinæ, Platypteryginæ,
Lachneinæ*.   In the new Check List, I included the only West Indian form
of this group known to me, *Heuretes picticornis* G. & R., the types of which
are in the Royal Museum in Berlin.   Fifteen other genera are included in
my list, and although one or two of these are probably synonyms, not
being identified by me, enough is shown to prove the richness of our fauna
in this group.   Sepp figures a South American species of *Empretia*.
The group is probably widely distributed and belongs to the older forms
of the family.

Sub-family Psychinæ.

The larvæ of the present group are still more curious than those of the
Cochliinæ from their habit of living in a case.   The thoracic feet alone are
developed, and the undeveloped abdominal feet present a resemblance to
the slug caterpillars, so that we have a reason for bringing the groups
together.   The cocoon-making habit is not alone displayed by the mature
larvæ, for so soon as the little Psyche larva leaves the egg it fashions a tiny
sack and begins its wanderings, dragging its shelter after it.   In most of
the genera, the females are apterous and worm-like, but in the North
American genera with broad, falcate wings, *Perophora* Harris, and
Lacosoma Grote, the females are winged like the males.   Sepp figures a
South American broad-winged form, and Herrick-Schaeffer, from the venation refers this section of the sub-family to the *Attacinæ*, notwithstanding
the sack-bearing larvæ.   The neuration will hardly guide us in this group,
since certain European genera have apparently three internal veins on the
secondaries like the Microlepidoptera.   Perhaps they are wrongly reckoned
here.   Some of the moths resemble the *Dasychirinæ*.   This resemblance
is seen in *Psyche;* but the American genera *Thyridopteryx* and *Oiketicus*
have long-bodied males with partly glassy wings and short antennæ, and
look more like the *Cossinæ*.   As compared with Europe, we have apparently
very few species of *Psyche;* in fact only one species is well known, viz.,

Psyche confederata Gr., now described in almost all its stages   The life-history of almost any species in this group will be found replete with curious facts, and instances of parthenogenesis are recorded among the European genera   The moth *Phryganidia californica* Pack., is apparently incorrectly described as belonging to this sub-family, and Butler refers it to the *Dioptidæ*, a group not studied by me   The *Psychinæ* occur in the West Indies, and South America, the genus *Oiketicus* also in Ceylon   This group seems to be, with the *Cochlinæ*, of very general distribution, and to belong to the older forms of the family, retaining perhaps some characteristics of a primitive form of the moths.   It may even be that the cocoon or sack was, in past geological ages, more common as a part of larval habit, and that it was later on restricted to the pupal condition.   The *Sphingidæ* and groups making no cocoon may have been thrown off from the genealogical tree of the Lepidoptera at later periods. In North America there seem to be but few species of *Psychinæ*, generally distributed, the genus *Oiketicus* being tropical and sub-tropical, *Platœceticus* a Floridian form, the other genera ranging from Canada to the Southern States, while from the west a few species belonging to the more typical section of the sub-family have been indicated   The broad, falcate-winged genera seem to belong east of the Rocky Mountains, and are reported from the region east of the Andes in South America   Hence, their distribution is paralleled by that of the *Ceratocampinæ*.

Sub-family *Notodontinæ*

Although we have found some reasons for our sequence of the preceding groups, there is here somewhat of a break   For instance, the *Sarothripinæ, Nolinæ, Chloephorinæ*, make a similar cocoon, in the two first the labial palpi are elongated   The *Lithosiinæ* resemble these more or less in form and the absence of ocelli, but their colors and shorter palpi are more like the succeeding *Arctiinæ*, again the *Dasychirinæ* resemble the latter in their hairy larvæ and style of pupation   There is an approximation to the *Cochlinæ* in the Dasychirid genus *Lagoa*, and the *Cochlinæ* and *Psychinæ* approach by the rudimental abdominal feet of the larvæ, but the *Notodontinæ*, although they fit in with succeeding groups, differ greatly from the *Psychinæ*   I have described a Psychid genus from Cuba, which has something of the Notodontid form, which is that of the Noctuidæ, and which latter several genera of this group greatly resemble Indeed, there seems to be some doubt as to whether the genus *Edema* is, as I believe, a Notodontid, or a Noctuid.   We may take also into consideration a certain similarity of the abdomen in *Limacodes* and *Ichthyura*, among the superficial resemblances which induce the bringing in of the *Notodontinæ* here ; but the position chiefly recommends itself to me in that we obtain a better sequence for the ensuing groups.

In the *Notodontinæ*, the neuration of the secondaries approaches the *Noctuidæ* in that vein five of the hind wings is (when present) situated midway between four and six from the cross-vein.   The form varies, but most of the genera have long wings, and the abdomen exceeds the secondaries.   The costal vein of hind wings does not spring from the sub-costal or upper margin of the cell, but is free from the base.   The head and thorax are usually thickly haired, the latter being sometimes peculiarly tufted at the sides.   The male antennæ are usually pectinate, the female simple.   The caterpillars are often naked, that of *Notodonta stragula* almost sphingiform.   That of *Apatelodes* is hairy, and Abbot's figures induced the generic name.   They have fourteen or sixteen feet, and sometimes the anal claspers are wanting *(Cerura)*, and the body is terminated by two thin prolongations.   It is this form of the larva which prepares us for the *Platypteryginæ*, in which the anal projection is single.   This sub-family is known to English entomologists under the name of " Pebble Moths," in allusion to the ornamentation, which consists often of shaded spots or blotches.   In repose, the wings are folded close to the body.   In this position *Datana* looks like a broken twig, the shaded thorax, with its raised tufts at the sides, like the top of the twig at the break.   *Datana* is related to the European *Phalera bucephala;* the same mimicry is displayed, but here the colors are paler, and the deception even more apparent.

The American genera are remarkable for their odd forms, and in some cases for the number of species.   Among the most unusual is *Apatelodes,* closely related to the South American *Parathyris.*   The fore wings are broad, curiously outlined, with sharp tips ; and the soft gray color, the tufted abdomen, present a resemblance to the Sphingid genus *Cressonia,* so that I have called the species of *Apatelodes*: False Hawk Moths.   The larvæ of several rarer Notodontids have been described by Prof. French, to whom we are much indebted for life-histories of our North American moths.

Sub-family *Platypteryginæ.*

The moths of this family are frail, geometriform, with falcate or sub-falcate primaries, with short maxillæ and palpi, and pectinate male antennæ,

The caterpillars have the anal claspers replaced by a single projection, have fourteen feet and make a cocoon between the leaves, and are probably double brooded, the pupa of the second brood hibernating   I have described the larva of *Dryopteris*   an allied genus has been described by Walker, from Japan, which I have not been able to compare critically with our two North American species of *Dryopteris*   Mr Henry Edwards records the European *Fronia lacertinaria* from Canada, and it seems that we have a second species in the *Prionia bilineata* of Packard   We have two species of *Platypteryx* Lasp *(= Drepana* Schrank*)* from the east, the one more whitish, Walker's *arcuata*, the other more of a buff yellow, my *genicula*   The European genus *Cilix* of Leach, is apparently absent in our fauna   In the shape of the wings this little group resembles the following *Attacinæ*, if we may compare such frail species with the giants of the family   The neuration shows also some approach to the typical Bombyces   The hind wings have eight veins, but the inner of the two internal veins is incomplete , vein five is nearer to four than to six   The fore wings are twelve veined and a certain look of miniature Attacids is due to the conformation of the wings.   We have a Geometrid genus *Drepanodes*, which, with its pointed primaries, looks like *Platypteryx*, and it is possible that Stephens has so mistaken the species

STRAY NOTES ON MYRMELEONIDÆ, PART 5

BY DR H A HAGEN, CAMBRIDGE, MASS

Dendroleon pantherinum Fabr

Myrmeleon pantherinum Fabr , Mantissa, 249 3—Ent Syst ii 93, 3—Brauer Neur Austr , 64

Myrmeleon ocellatum Bork in Scriba Beitr ii , 165, pl ii, f 5.

Dendroleon pantherinum Brauer, Wien Z. B. G xvii , 963 pl. 14, f 3

The species was described (1787) by Fabricius, from a specimen wanting prominent parts, antennæ and legs   The descriptions by Villers, Olivier, Gmelin, Latreille and Walker, are simply copies

Borkhausen, in 1791, described the sa mespecies as *M ocellatum*, from a specimen found in Darmstadt, Hesse.   The description and figure are good, and Burmeister believed the N. American species to be identical   Prof Brauer has given a new description in Neur. Austriaca.   The species is a very rare one, found, besides in Austria and Hesse, fifty years ago in Silesia and Hungary   The discovery of the larva in the Prater, near Vienna, on trees, and the raising of the imago by Prof Brauer is one of his numerous splendid discoveries   He made for the species the new genus *Dendroleon*   Both species are recorded as *Glenurus* Hag in my Synopsis Hemerob   This genus was proposed exactly at the same time with *Dendroleon*, but the latter one should be retained for those species.

The N American species and the European are very similar, but the rarity of both prevented the exact knowledge of their differences.   I have seen of the European species only three specimens, one from the Rhein Mus Berol., one from Austria, and one from Hungary in Frivaldsky's collection.   The latter one I have compared carefully with Burmeister's types in Winthem's collection in 1852.   As since this time nothing is published about the differences of both species, I give here my manuscript notes

D. pantherinum is of the same size, but a little more robust ; prothorax plain-luteous, without the fine black granulation of *D. obsoletum* ; a large black dorsal band on metathorax and basal segment of abdomen , *D. obsoletum* has mesothorax, metathorax and basal segment above in the middle only with a very dilute blackish color   Abdomen with segment second and third black, the fourth and fifth above light brown , *D obsoletum* has on all segments, or at least on second and third, a transversal yellow band.   Legs yellowish brown , fore legs with a ring around the apex of femur middle of tibiæ, and third and fourth joint of tarsus all black , middle and hind legs with a broad dark ring before the middle of femur, which is externally nearly connected with the apical ring ; the apex of tibia and a median ring, which is wanting on hind legs, black. The coloration of *D. obsoletum* is very different, as stated in the description.   Wings with the venation less close, the areoles larger , veins in both wings more fuscous , front wings in the basal third of the space between fourth and fifth longitudinal vein with four fuscous spots, the most apical one longest, about 3 mm. (wanting on *D obsoletum*) , the ocellate spot on the hind margin is complete *(D obsoletum* wants always the apical half of the iris around the spot), hind wings with a quadrangular (round in *D obsol.)* spot near the costa, and ring of spots on the apex of hind margin

Dendioleon obsoletum Say.

Formicaleo obsoleta Say , Journ Acad. Phnad viii , 44, 1—Say, Ed
    Lec ii , 413, 1.
Myimeleon obsoletus Hag , Syn N. Am Neur 225, 2
Myrmecolcon ocellatus Burm. ii , 995. 1—Walk 401, 172
Myimeleon nigiocinctus Rbr 398, 20—Walk 361, 101—Glover Ent
    Amer Neur., pl v , f. 15 (the figure is a fair one)

Body slender, abdomen little villous. Head narrow, face luteous,
between the eyes a broad shining black band, notched on the inferior
margin , vertex luteous ; antennæ as long as head and thorax, slender,
elongated, clavate on tip, blackish fuscous, pale in middle , palpi short,
pale , maxillary ones with the three apical joints equal , labials not longer,
apical joint fusiform , prothorax elongated, narrower anteriorly, luteous,
faintly granulated with black , thorax dull luteous, above darker , on each
side above the legs a broad black longitudinal band ; below pale ; abdomen shorter than the wings (I believe I have not seen a male), blackish
brown, with a yellow dorsal, transversal band on the middle of each segment, or at least on the second , the parts in the last segment light brown,
with black hairs ; above split longitudinally , below on each side a short,
flat appendage , legs very long and slender, with short hairs, shining
black , anteriors with base of femur and tip of tibia brown , hind legs
with a luteous band before the tip of femur, or luteous, tip black , tibia
pale, black on tip and after base , or black pale at base , tarsi long,
black , the basal joint sometimes luteous , spurs luteous, as long as the
two basal joints , apex incurved , claws luteous , wings hyaline spotted
with fuscous , front wings with the inner half of an ocellate spot on the
middle of the hind margin , a double spot at the pterostigma, an apical
interrupted series, and some dots along the mediana ; hind wings with a
larger orbicular spot before the pterostigma. and some spots near the tip
and the apical part of the hind margin ; venation white, some of the forks
and the longitudinal veins interrupted with fuscous. Length of body, 20
to 26 mm , exp al , 46 to 67 mm.

Mr Sanborn, Mass. Agric Rep., 1862, p 161, states —" Specimens
of this insect are sometimes found which differ either with the wings not
spotted, but hyaline or sprinkled with fuscous, or costal space with a
double series of areoles, or without spurs " Apparently Mr. Sanborn has
here confounded several species

Habit.—Canada, Ontario, Mr Saunders , southern peninsula of Michigan, Mr. Harrington , N. Hampshire, Mr Leonard in T. W Harris's coll There is a very indifferent figure of Harris's specimen by F. J Sanborn (it is reproduced in Dr Packard's Guide, f. 604), in his Rep , 1862, Mass Agric , p 160 Mr Sanborn, who had a most general and reliable knowledge of insects in this country, says —" It is of common occurrence throughout the country, and this is the only well-known ant-lion in N England " But I have to state that Harris's specimen is till now the only one from N England seen by me , N York, in Winthem's coll and by Mr. Akhurst , Missouri, St Louis, Mr Engelmann , Illinois, Galena, Mr Bean , Maryland, Mr. Uhler , N Carolina, Morganton , S. Carolina, Aiken , Virginia , Georgia, June 7 and August 21, in pine woods, rare, in Abbott's figures in the Brit Museum , Alabama, figured by Mr Gosse in his letters from Alabama p. 242 (I have not seen this book), Liskiyon, Cala Mr Behrens Mr Th Say states only "this species is rather common "

The range of this species is very large, and probably a larger one to the south and west The size is not very variable, except one specimen from South Carolina, and one from Cala , to which belong the smallest given dimensions Very probably the larva ascends trees as the related European species , and the larva from Washington, D C , described by me years ago, probably belongs to this species   (Stett Ent Z , 1873. p. 271. n 7)

Myrmeleon immaculatus De Geer.

M immaculatus De Geer in., 564 (365). pl. 27, f 8—Retzius 59, No 202—Walker 401, n 174

M melanocephalum Oliv Encycl viii , 127, No 33

M. immaculatus Hag , Syn N. Am , 231. 14, partim

Face shining, black , epistom and mouth yellow , the black color covers sometimes more or less the epistom, notched anteriorly , a fine yellow ring around the eyes, more or less interrupted near the antennæ, and enlarged below near the mouth.

Labrum short, twice as broad as long, rounded laterally, largely notched anteriorly

Palpi light brown, darker in more adult specimens , maxillary moderately long , thin cylindrical , three apical joints sometimes black, with a small yellow basal ring , last joint cylindrical. truncate on tip , labial about as long, second joint arcuate, thin, enlarged on tip , last joint of the same length, subarcuate. largely fusiform above, shining black. tip thinner, yellow

Antennæ a little shorter than head and thorax, clavate, dull black, more or less annulate with yellow basal joint above yellow, below the basal joints shining black.

Head broad , vertex transversally ovoid, elevated ; anteriorly finely rugose ; a number of very fine elevated lines originating together between the antennæ, and then diverging , the color and pattern of the vertex varies much , the main color is dull black, with a yellow transversal band, which is entire or more or less divided and may be wanting entirely , two pitchy black transversal bands are divided by a middle longitudinal band, consisting of two anterior and two posterior approximate twin spots, all these pitchy black shining flat spots and bands may be differently shaped , besides there is on each side near the eyes on the vertex a posterior linear flat spot, and another behind this on the occiput , the yellow transversal band fills the space between the two pitchy black bands, and is always interrupted in the middle by longitudinal band ; the yellow band is entirely wanting in the N England, Michigan and N York specimens, it is more or less indicated in the specimens of the Southern States, and always present in the Western States and Colorado

Prothorax short, nearly once broader than long , sides about straight , front margin semi-circular, dull brown , the front margin, two large spots on the part before the transverse sulcus, and two smaller ones after the sulcus, and the membrane between the prothorax and mesothorax luteous or yellowish , some black hairs on the sides of prothorax , thorax pitchy fuscous to black above and below the margins sometimes a little luteous

Abdomen of female much shorter than the wings , of the males less shorter and more slender , pitchy black , the basal half principally of the females or newly transformed specimens with a large dull luteous spot, covered with short and fine whitish villosity

Female genitals the same of *M mobilis*, but the black appendages a little shorter and thicker, with very long black hairs , male genitals similar, but the spoon-shaped part a little shorter

Legs of the Southern specimens similar to *M mobilis,* the specimens from the Northern and Eastern States and the Rocky Mts much more black ; the anterior tarsi and larger parts of tibiæ entirely shining black, but all intermediate colors are to be found, spurs and sometimes the claws brown.

Wings similar, variable in size, shape and coloration ; the most striking difference is the hind margin of the hind wings, which is never (in 3c specimens) sinuate in the apical half, but performs a flattened curve, a little more incurved on tip, the mediana and subcosta are darker and the space between them is blackish, where they are not interrupted with yellowish, sometimes the transversals below the mediana and some other veins are fumose, pterostigma white.

Length of body, 25 to 36 mm, exp al., 60 to 76 mm   Breadth of hind wing, 5 to 7 mm   The smallest specimens are from Colorado

Habitat —30 specimens male and female are before me, Ludington, Mich, Mr. Pierce (raised), Keene, N. H., Mr F. H. Foster (raised) ; Peabody, Mass, Mr G H. Emerton (raised) ; Albany, N York (raised by myself), Maryland, Mr Uhler, Virginia, Alleghany Mts, and Washington, D. C, O Sacken, Morganton, N. Carolina, Mr H. Morrison, Waco, Texas, Mr. Belfrage, Denver, Golden City, Manitou, Colorado, by O. Sacken ; Wasatch Mts., Utah, Rocky Mts Dr Anderson, Lake Tahoe, Cala., O Sacken, Sylvania, Cala, Mr Ricksecker (raised) ; Oregon, Mr. H. Edwards ; Washington Terr., Yakima River, Mr. S. Henshaw.

The imago appears everywhere in June and July   The larva hybernates and transforms in the pupa about May

The description and the figure by De Geer, though both not sufficient, proved that his species was the one here described ; there is no N. American species known, which makes this determination doubtful.   There can be no doubt that *M. melanocephalum* Oliv. is the same species   Olivier's specimen was collected by Bosc near New York, De Geer's in Pennsylvania   Burmeister's type, now before me, is *M mobilis*   It would be useless to speak about two species described by Walker, without comparing his types.   The same applies to Prof Taschenberg's species

When I published the Synopsis N. Am Neur, I knew only three specimens, which are still before me   I had them separated in two species, but the insufficient material seemed to make it more prudent to unite them provisionally.   Both species are very similar, and the only palpable difference is the hind margin of the hind wings sinuated in the apical half of *M. mobilis*, and convex in *M. immaculatus*.   I have raised myself both species, and have the full grown larvæ in alcohol.

(To be Continued)

THE CHALCID GENUS RILEYA.

BY L. O HOWARD, WASHINGTON, D. C

An interesting interference in the adoption of the generic name *Rileya* has recently taken place between Mr Ashmead and myself, and, as I am of the opinion that this name should apply to the genus of Encyrtinæ defined by myself, rather than to the genus of Eurytominæ defined by Mr Ashmead, I state in this note the circumstances of the interference, and print in full the paper in which my description occurred.

At the meeting of the Entomological Society of Washington, held June 7, 1887, I read the paper in question and handed the manuscript, after reading, to Mr Smith, the Secretary, with the request that he publish the generic description in full in his abstract of our proceedings in Entomologica Americana.   June 9 this periodical for June was received, and I found upon reading Mr. Ashmead's " revised generic table of the Eurytominæ," published upon pages 41 to 43, that he had decided to use the same name for a genus of that sub-family   The name is there given, *not as a new genus*, but as one already described, and the few words given to it in the table fail to sufficiently characterize it.   Noting these points, I did not recall my description from Mr Smith, and it was published in the July number of the same periodical (received July 5)   I inferred from the fact that Mr Ashmead entered the genus as " *Rileya* Ashm ," and not " *Rileya* n g ," that his description had been sent away for publication, but had not appeared, and this inference was shown to be correct when upon July 14, first copies were received of Bulletin No. 3 of the Kansas Experiment Station, which contained in an appendix Mr. Ashmead's full description of this genus

I am individually inclined to think, therefore, that as Mr. Ashmead did not give his few words in the generic table to *Rileya as a new genus*, his mention of it there amounts simply to the mention of a manuscript name, and as the full description of *Rileya* Ashmead *as a new genus* was not published for some days subsequent to the publication of my genus, the latter should bear the name   Were this a mere matter of credit for a genus, I would not waste words upon it, and were it any other name I would give way without hesitation to my friend Mr Ashmead, but my desire to establish the genus in Professor Riley's name, and to apply it to this extremely interesting and beautiful form, is so great that I am led to assert my claim, which of course will stand or fall upon its merits

The original paper as read before the Entomological Society of Washington, June 7, is as follows :—

"One of the most beautiful insects I have ever seen was sent in considerable numbers to Dr Riley, from California, by Mr Koebele, in 1886 It was captured by Mr Koebele, as stated in his notes, while searching for a species of *Dactylopius*, which lives upon the Passion Flower at Los Angeles   His account of the actions of the little parasites upon this plant is interesting enough to quote ·   'A number of the parasites were collected on a plant, and some of them were noticed depositing their eggs.   Busily they ran up and down the branches, and if they met with a grown insect, this was touched from behind with their antennæ from five to fifteen seconds, then either the parasite would run off or turn around and thrust an egg into the insect, which, when the parasite approaches, keeps perfectly quiet, but if operated on, will turn the posterior part of its body rapidly around in a circle, and its enemy will, after the egg is left, walk quietly off without facing its victim again.'

"This little parasite, although only about a millimeter and a-half in length, is a perfect gem in color.   It is a fleck of brilliant green-gold, and its structure is very strange to one not familiar with the peculiar group of genera to which it belongs   The remarkable antennæ, with their concave leaf like scape, peculiar pedicel, and broadly flattened flagellum carry to an extreme a conformation seen only with the three genera—*Mira, Anusia* and *Cerapterocerus*—of the sub-family *Encyrtinæ* of the *Chalcididæ*   I have always supposed that the preliminary tapping of a Bark-louse, with the antennæ, as described by Mr Koebele above, and as often noticed with other parasites, was for the purpose of ascertaining by a tactile sense or by sound whether the Bark-louse was already inhabited by a parasitic larva, and it is altogether likely that this extraordinary development of the antennæ in these genera is of use in this direction, and was developed in response to some such need, for it will be noticed that this conformation occurs in the female sex only, and that the males of such of these genera as have known males have antennæ of the ordinary pedicillate whorled type.

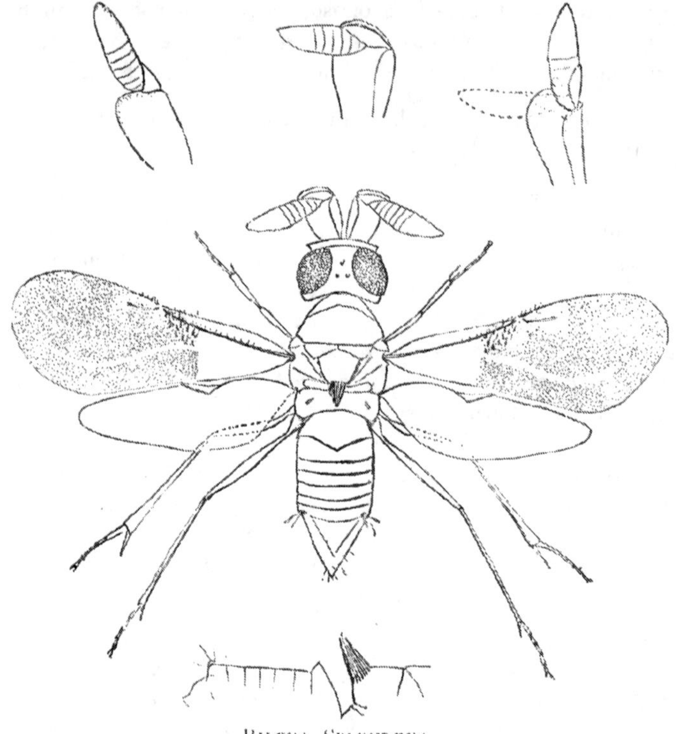

RILEYA SPLENDENS.

"The relationships of this California parasite, although it forms a new and in some respects abnormal genus, are plainly with the European genus *Cerapterocerus* of Westwood *(Telegraphus* Ratz.*)*, of which two species have been described, viz., *C. mirabilis* Westwood, and *C. corniger* Walker, of both of which we have authentic specimens in the collection of the National Museum, through the courtesy of Dr. Mayr, of Vienna. The formei has been reared from a Lecanium on peach by Tschek, from a Lecanium on plum by Kollar and Rogenhofer, and from coccids on grass by Kollar and Knechbaumer, while the latter has been reared by Kriechbaumer fiom coccids on plum and grass

"I have, with Dr Riley's kind permission, dedicated this remarkable and beautiful genus to him, in acknowledgement of the work which he has done in making known the life-histories of American hymenopterous parasites, not less than in acknowledgement of the opportunities he has given me, and the assistance and encouragement he has rendered me in the study of the interesting family to which it belongs.

"*Rileya*, Gen. nov   Female   Moderately stout, resembling somewhat *Cerapterocerus* Westwood (see Mag. Nat. Hist. vi, 1833, page 495, see also Snellen van Vollenhoven, Schetsen, Tab. vii, see also Mayr, Die Europaischen Encyrtiden, Verh d k k. Zool. Bot Ges Wien 1875, page 747, see also Ratzeburg, Ichn d. Forstins. ii, 1848, page 152, under name *Telegraphus*), but differing as follows: The face is not elbowed in the middle so as to give a triangular profile to the head, but is gently rounded, and has a strong glistening transverse clean-cut ridge just above the insertion of the antennæ, which are stouter and with a more concave scape than with *Cerapterocerus*   The mesoscutellum has a strong tuft of erect black hairs as in *Chiloneurus*, but which is lacking in *Cerapterocerus*   The stigmal vein is given off immediately at the junctuie of the submarginal with the costa, and is a trifle longer than the postmarginal. The submarginal is three and one half times as long as the stigmal   The postmarginal, the distal third of the submarginal, and the wing disc below this last heavily clothed with short stout bristles   The body is highly polished and the wings are not hyaline   The metanotal spiracles are large, long-oval and oblique, and the abdominal spiracles are very prominently tufted   The ovipositor does not protrude, except in specimens killed in the act of oviposition

"*Rileya splendens*, Sp. nov   Female.   Length, 1 63 mm, expanse, 3.8 mm ; greatest width of fore wing, 0.53 mm.   Front with a delicate round-oval punctation, cheeks with delicate longitudinal striation, and a perfectly smooth band bordering the eyes, mesoscutum very delicately shaggieened, scutellum and scapulæ smooth, mesopleura and abdomen smooth   General color metallic green, the most brilliant reflections given off from the cheeks and the proepimera, antennæ also with metallic reflections, but darker in general effect , mouth-parts honey-yellow , abdomen bluish-metallic below , all legs metallic , joints 2, 3 and 4 of tarsi honey-yellow. Distal two-thirds of wings (fore) dark brown , the proximal limit of the color very definite, and the color deepest at this point, becoming lighter at tip of wing , a narrow, longitudinal, slightly curved, hyaline line arises at the middle of the proximal border of the infuscation, and extends rather more than half way to the tip of the wing.   Described from many female specimens   Los Angeles, Cal , A Koebele '

ANNUAL MEETING OF THE ENTOMOLOGICAL CLUB OF THE AMERICAN ASSOCIATION FOR THE ADVANCEMENT OF SCIENCE

The annual gathering of the Entomologists of North America, in connection with the meeting of the A. A. A S., took place this year in the city of Cleveland, Ohio.   While much regret was felt at the absence of many eminent Entomologists who have always taken an active part in the work of the Club, and at the consequent smallness of the attendance, the meeting was much enjoyed by those who were present, and the valuable papers read were received with great interest.

The first session was held at 9 a m. in a class-room of the Central High School Building on Wednesday, August 15th ; the President, Mr. John B Smith, of Washington, in the chair.   In the absence of the Secretary (Prof. A. J Cook, of the Agricultural College, Mich) Professor Herbert Osborn, of Ames, Iowa, was requested to act in his place. Owing to the smallness of the attendance the Club adjourned till 1 15 p m., when the President read his annual address on " Entomological Collections in the United States."   In this interesting and valuable paper, which, as well as the other papers read at the meetings of the Club, will, we understand, be published in full in *Entomologica Americana*, the writer gave an account of all the great collections, both public and private, in the United States   Among general collections he especially mentioned those of Mr Bolter, of Chicago, and Mr. Henry Edwards, of New York , in Coleoptera he specified the collections of Dr. Horn, of Philadelphia, Mr. Ulke, of Washington, and Messrs. Hubbard and Schwarz, and Lieut. Casey , in Lepidoptera those of Messrs. Henry Edwards, Neumogen,

Strecker. Graef, Tepper, Holland, W H Edwards, Lintner, Bailey. and
Meske, in special departments of Lepidoptera those of Mr W H.
Edwards, Rev. Dr Holland, and Mr. Bruce in Butterflies, in the
Hesperidæ that of Mr E. M Aaron, of Philadelphia, in the Sphingidæ
that of Mr E. Corning, of Albany, in the Geometridæ that of the Rev.
G D. Hulst, of Brooklyn, and in the Tortricidæ that of Prof Fernald,
of Amherst. Mass. He also noticed many other collections in various
orders for which we must refer the reader to the address itself

After hearing the address the meeting adjourned till the next day
The following persons were in attendance during the sessions —John B
Smith, Washington, D C. , Prof. H Osborn, Ames, Iowa, Prof F M.
Webster, Lafayette, Ind , Dr D S Kellicott, Buffalo, N Y ; Mr. and
Mrs O. S. Westcott, Chicago, L. O Howard, Washington ; J. Mackenzie,
Toronto; A B Mackay, Agricultural College, Miss , D A Robertson,
St Paul, S. H Peabody, Champaign, Ill , Dr C. V. Riley, Washing-
ton ; S B McMillan. Signal, Ohio, Rev. L C. Wurtele and Miss Wurtele,
Acton Vale. P Q., and others.

The Entomological Society of Ontario was represented by its President. Mr. J. Fletcher, of Ottawa, and the Rev C J S Bethune, of Port
Hope.   .

On Thursday, August 16th, the Club met at 1 p m and entered upon
the consideration of the President's address, this naturally led to a
discussion upon the best materials for boxes, &c , in which to preserve
collections Mr Howard stated that the boxes in the Museum of
Comparative Zoology at Cambridge, Mass, had their bottoms made of
Italian poplar. Mr. Fletcher asked for the experience of members with
poplar, tulip-tree and other woods as regards cracking and splitting
Dr Riley said that there was no wood that would not split, warp or
crack, the only remedy was to have the materials kiln-dried and then
soaked in shellac and alcohol. He adopted the form of boxes used in
Washington for the sake of convenience rather than otherwise. The
cabinets in Europe were not subjected to the same dry heat as in
America. and were consequently not a guide to us in this respect

Mr Fletcher stated that there are only two noteworthy collections of
insects in Canada . (1) that of the Entomological Society of Ontario at
London It is not very large, but is very good as representative of the

Canadian fauna, while it contains many specimens from the United States and other countries. The collection of Lepidoptera is especially good and well named, having been revised by Mr. Grote before it was sent to the Philadelphia Exhibition, in 1876 In Coleoptera and other orders great care has been taken to have the specimens well named. The collection is open to any one who desires to examine it (2) The collection of Lepidoptera in the National Museum at Ottawa is very good. The nucleus was formed by the purchase of about 8,000 specimens from Captain Gamble Geddes, of Toronto. It is now being added to by the officers of the Geological Survey, who bring to it from time to time rare specimens from out-of-the-way and little known regions There are several private collections of value, but it is unnecessary to specify them. Mr Fletcher agreed with Mr Smith that "types" of new species should be placed in some national collection where they would be accessible to all students. For his part he should always be glad in future, as in the past, to place "types" whenever possible in the National Museum at Washington.

A discussion then arose as to what is meant by a "type." Mr. Fletcher understands the term to mean all the specimens actually before a describer when he is making out his description of a new species Some writers, however, call all specimens types that may afterwards be identified by the describer as agreeing with the originals. Mr. Howard agreed with Mr. Fletcher that only the material before a describer at the time is to be called "type," other specimens should be marked "determined by the author." Dr. Riley thought that all the materials determined by an author might be called "types of that species," provided that they do not vary from the original specimens Prof. Webster considered that all typical material should be placed in some national depository where it would be perfectly safe, and instanced the loss of the Walsh collection by fire as a calamity to science , collectors should be willing to sacrifice their types for the general good of science Mr Smith was also of opinion that only the specimens before the author at the time of making the description are "types," and that specimens determined afterwards are not really "types" Mr. Fletcher referred to *Chinobas Macounii* as an example Mr. W H. Edwards had eleven specimens before him when he described the species ; these are types, though most of the specimens were imperfect. During the past summer the speaker had obtained from the original locality a good supply of specimens in perfect order, and although these agreed with the original description perfectly, they should only be labelled as " typical," and he was of the opinion that the describer even would not be justified in labelling them "type."   Professor Osborn agreed with the last speaker.

(To be Continued.)

CORRESPONDENCE.

NOTES ON IPS.

In vol. xvii., p. 46, of the CAN. ENT., Dr. John Hamilton gives some notes on *Ips fasciatus* and allied forms.   He says:—" The form *fasciatus* is the most common here (Allegheny, Penn.), and is that into which all the others are resolved ; in it the elytra are black with an irregular broad basal, and a sub-apical fascia, yellow ; individuals are met with totally black without any spot ; others have only a small basal and sub-apical spot yellow (more often reddish) ; others add to these a humeral lunule ; others have various other spots, and by the gradual dilation and coalescing of these through a series of specimens, the full form *fasciatus* is reached."   He further says that he has never met with these black and spotted forms at any other time than in early spring, usually during April. As the season advances these entirely disappear and the fasciate form alone remains, continuing till autumn.   Judging from my observations of these forms at Montreal, I cannot quite agree with Dr. Hamilton's opinion. I find that in the fasciate form the colour is bright clear yellow, while in all the spotted specimens that I have seen the colour is very pale yellow, almost white ; the difference in this respect being very marked.   With respect to seasons, I find that the spotted form, or what I take to be *4-signatus*, occurs during summer as well as in spring, as the following notes will show:—April 24th, 1886, found *Ips fasciatus* and the spotted forms common at a bleeding stump on Montreal Mountain, *4-signatus* being most abundant.   June 12th, 1886, found several specimens of *Ips 4-signatus* in a small hole in the bark of an oak tree, where the sap was oozing out.   August 5th, 1886, found a specimen of *Ips 4-signatus* on a tombstone in Mount Royal Cemetery.   August 15th, 1886, found a specimen of *Ips 4-signatus* on a tomato on the breakfast table.   July 26th,

1888, found a specimen of *Ips 4-signatus* in a jug of milk   The last "find" was a rather curious one, but the specimen was quite fresh, and had evidently been "supplied" with the morning's milk.   No specimens of *fasciatus* were observed during the summer months, so that my experience appears to have been just the reverse of Dr Hamilton's

F B. CAULFIELD, Montreal

INSECTS FEIGNING DEATH

Dear Sir   I have read with much interest Mr. A R. Grote's communications upon the subject of "Insects Feigning Death," glad always of the opportunity of learning from the older members of the entomological fraternity   But in this case I am not sure that I comprehend the gentleman's meaning.   In the June number of the CAN ENT. he expresses a doubt in regard to insects possessing any knowledge of death, and hence considers that they are not mentally capable of feigning death.   In the August number he again takes up the subject and says, " It is probable to me that their attitudes of repose are assumed from the experience they have gradually acquired, that in a state of quiet they will best avoid the immediate dangers which beset them, etc "   Immediate dangers of *what ?* Physical pain, a knowledge of which they have gained by frequent captures and escapes ?   It strikes me that it is not only not this, but death itself which they seek to avoid   With no knowledge of death, as such, why should they seek to avoid it ?   Is it not true that all animal life is doomed to die sooner or later ?   And is not a knowledge of the fact that it is something to be feared and avoided as long as possible, necessary to the perpetuation of species ?   Surely even insects would not seek to avoid that of which they have no knowledge.   Does not the very presence of the sense of fear presuppose a knowledge of death, in the sense of annihilation ?   If the larva of a *Geometer* has learned, no matter whether by experience or instinct, that by assuming a certain rigid position resembling a portion of the twig upon which it is itself located, it is thereby enabled to escape destruction in common with the twig, might not another species, by the same course of reasoning, learn that, to assume the same inanimate position as a dead companion who is not carried away, it also might escape ?   Beetles belonging to the genera *Chlamys* and *Exema*, of the family *Chrysomelidæ*, will often drop from a seemingly safe position on the stem of a plant to the exposed upper surface of a leaf of the same, remaining there perfectly quiet without making any further attempt to escape, their only protection being the form and color of their bodies, which very strongly resemble the excrement of caterpillars. After all have we not reason to believe that life, to an insect, embodies all that is precious; the alpha and omega of all that is worthy of being cherished and protected? Knowing as we do the great variety of methods by which insects seek to protect this life, is it so highly improbable that they should hit upon the plan of feigning its absence? The question is an interesting one, though difficult, and, perhaps, impossible to solve; yet it certainly involves nothing that should lead us to forget that we are fellow-workers.

F. M. WEBSTER, Lafayette, Ind.

DANAIS ARCHIPPUS.

Dear Sir: In view of the discussion now going on respecting this insect, it may not be amiss to give some observations from this locality. *D. archippus* (alias *plexippus*) is an exceedingly common butterfly in Custer Co., Colorado, from the end of April throughout the summer. At the present time it is abundant near my house, at about 8,400 feet alt., especially frequenting the flowers of *Oxytropis lamberti*, and also seeming much attracted by a patch of *Trifolium pratense* that has sprung up in a timothy field. But the peculiar thing is, that so far as I know, *Asclepias*, the food-plant, does not occur nearer than some four or five miles away, and at perhaps nearly a thousand feet lower elevation. The only larva I have seen here was an immature one brought to me July 3rd, which had been found on *Asclepias* at about 7,300 feet alt., some six miles from here. Yet the specimens of *plexippus* found up here at 8,400 feet are perfectly fresh and undamaged (much more so than *Papilio asterias*, which breeds up here), and further, are frequently to be seen paired.

July 22nd.   T. D. A. COCKERELL, West Cliff, Colorado.

NOTICE.—The Annual Meeting of the Entomological Society of Ontario will be held in the City Hall, Ottawa, on Friday, October 5th. It is hoped that there will be a full attendance of members.

Mailed October 3rd.

The Canadian Entomologist.

VOL. XX. LONDON, NOVEMBER, 1888. No. 11.

AN EXTREME CASE OF SEASONAL DIMORPHISM IN COLIAS.

BY T. D. A. COCKERELL, WEST CLIFF, COLORADO.

It was thought strange when it was proved that *Colias keewaydin* and *C. eurytheme* were seasonal forms of a single species. Still stranger did it seem when Mr. W. H. Edwards proved by breeding that *C. eriphyle* (alias *Hagenii)* was also a form of *eurytheme*, but even after this I was not quite prepared for the conclusion, forced upon me by irresistible facts, that in this locality the orange and yellow forms were not only of one species, but actually alternated seasonally, the former being the summer, and the latter the winter form. The locality in question is the eastern slope of the Sangre de Cristo range, in Custer County, Colorado, in the neighborhood of Swift Creek, at altitudes varying from about 7,800 to 8,400 feet. Only two forms of *C. eurytheme* are found (exclusive of the pale females), and neither of these agrees precisely with those already described, so that (" West American Scientist," 1888, p. 42,) I called the orange one *intermedia,* and the sulphur yellow form *autumnalis*, this last being very close to *C. eriphyle.*

The facts of the case are best shown by extracts from my diary, all bearing upon this locality :—

July 13th, 1887.—Arrived here, found *intermedia* flying abundantly, and so until the middle of August, when I left for a trip to the western slope. No *autumnalis* seen.

October 22nd.—Returned to this locality ; a few worn *intermedia* seen, the last of brood.

November 9th.—Caught a ♀ *autumnalis*, the first I had seen.

May 13th, 1888.—Caught a ♀ *autumnalis*—the first of the year. Soon after *autumnalis* became common, but no *intermedia* seen. The first ♂ was caught May 19th. (The ♀'s of both forms of *eurytheme*, and also of *C. alexandra*, seem to emerge here sooner than the ♂'s.)

June 4th.—The first *intermedia* of the year seen.

June 8th.—*Autumnalis* still abundant, but some *intermedia* seen.

June 12th.—*Intermedia* becoming common, and *autumnalis* scarce.

June 26th.—*Intermedia* abundant, a single *autumnalis*, a ♂, taken, and this is the last seen.

C. eurytheme var. *intermedia* is now (July 17th) abundant, and *C. alexandra* is flying very freely. It is a curious circumstance that the so called " albino " females (var. *pallida*) do not appear to occur in *autumnalis*, or if they do are very rare, while they are so frequent in *intermedia* that I have sometimes fancied they even outnumbered the typical females. In both forms, I think, the females outnumber the males.

From the above facts, I think that it is hard to come to any other conclusion than that the orange and yellow forms alternate, and that this should be so, presents perhaps one of the most remarkable cases of seasonal dimorphism at present known.

There is a very large Asiliid fly found here, which occasionally preys upon *C. eurytheme* var. *intermedia* in the perfect state.

DESCRIPTION OF A NEW SPECIES OF ORTHESIA FROM CALIFORNIA.

BY WILLIAM H. ASHMEAD, JACKSONVILLE, FLA.

In a collection of Hemiptera sent me some time since for identification, were two male specimens of a coccid, and a single white waxy sac, from which one had issued, attached to the upper surface of a small, oval leaf, which at the time, from a superficial examination, I took to be a mealy bug, *Dactylopius longifilis* Comstock; but recently on a more careful examination I find to be a species of that interesting genus *Orthesia* Bosc.

But a single species has been described in this genus in our fauna, *i.e.*, *Orthesia Americana* Walker. A good description of what is supposed to be this species was given by Prof. Comstock in the U. S. Agricultural Report, 1880, page 349. As the present species does not agree with that description, it is apparently undescribed, and below I give a description of it, naming it in honour of its discoverer, Mr. Hy. Edwards, who took it at Grass Valley, Nepa County, California.

Orthesia Edwardsii n. sp

Male sac —This is broadly oval, pure white, .15 of an inch long by .12 of an inch in breadth. It was evidently formed by a secretion of fine, waxy flakes. the regularity of which has been lost as the insect reached maturity, the dorsal disk being entire, and the flakes only being partially distinguishable at the margins.

Male.—Length 12 inch; style about 04 inch Entirely black, excepting a reddish cast on the mesothorax, scutellum, metathorax, abdomen at sides and beneath, and the epipleura of the mesothorax , while the head beneath the insertion of the antennæ is pale yellowish white. Head small, nearly quadrate, being but slightly narrowed posteriorly. The eyes consist of 5 or 6 ocelli placed at the side of the head, while the mouth consists of two large, quite prominent ocelli Antennæ very long, the points of which have four or five irregular nodose swellings, with irregular whorls of long, delicate bristles ; the first two joints are very short, not as long as wide, the 3rd and 5th joints the longest, about an equal length, the 4th, 6th, 7th, 8th and 9th shorter and gradually subequal. the 10th or apical joint more thickened, fusiform, about four-fifths the length of the penultimate joint Thorax short, less than one-half the length of abdomen ; the prothorax is hardly distinguish-able from above, being but a delicate ridge or collar; mesothorax quite short, somewhat trapezoidal in outline, and obliquely ascending towards the scutellum, but with a depression in the middle, the lateral lobes distinct , scutellum highly convex, polished, with some short hairs on the disk, abruptly transversely divided by a deep, yellowish fissure posterior-ly. Metathorax very short. Legs very long, rather slender, black, and with a long, fine hair pubescence ; tibiæ longer than their femora, slender, cylindrical ; tarsi less than one-third the length of tibiæ and more slender, gradually acuminate toward apex and terminating in a small, delicate claw ; no digitules Abdomen, on the dorsum wrinkled, at sides towards apex covered with a white, waxy substance, and terminating in two very long caudal setæ, more than double the length of the insect, rather thickly covered with a white, waxy substance, especially at base, so that in reality they are much more slender than they appear. Style long, blackish. Wings two, white, of the ordinary shape, but I can detect a spurious vein, springing from near the base of the longitudinal vein, between it and the costal margin, and running parallel with it to half the length of the wings. I have examined many male coccids, but never before noticed this spurious vein, and consequently think it of great importance. Halteres linear, terminating in a hook with two teeth , one of the halteres is attached to a fold or thickening in the front wing, and as has before been observed, evidently greatly assists the insect in its flights , the other one was loose, and thus enabled me to make out the two small teeth

STRAY NOTES ON MYRMELEONIDÆ, PART 5

BY DR H A HAGEN, CAMBRIDGE, MASS

(Continued from page 191.)

Myrmeleon mobilis Hag.

M. mobilis Hag.   Stett. Z , vol xxi , 368 , vol. xxvi , 444.   (No description)

M immaculatus Burm   Vol. ii , 994, 5 (not De Geer)--Hagen Syn N Am 231. 14, partim

The face above the epistom blackish brown, shining ; mouth and a ring around the eyes yellowish ; palpi yellowish , maxillary thin, apical joint cylindrical, notched on tip , labial of same length, apical joint fusiform. the conical tip notched

Antennæ as long as head and thorax, thicker at tip, which is clavate, fuscous, annulated with yellow, except on club , basal joint yellow above, second black ; antennæ below largely yellow.

Head dull luteous, with some flat pitchy-fuscous spots , vertex transverse-ovoid elevate, anteriorly finely rugulose , on the middle two pairs of twin bands, one behind the other , the anterior pair with hind end of its band bent outward , a round spot on each side of the bands , the posterior pair straight , on each side two triangular spots near the eye , behind the vertex on each side a transversal band, near the eyes

Prothorax broader than long, sides about straight, front margin semi-circular, luteous with some black hairs besides ; anterior part before the transverse sulcus on each side with a black crescent and indistinct median band , hind part on each side with an indistinct black mark , thorax dull luteous, with some indistinct brown shadows besides and below.

Abdomen much shorter than the wings, slender, dull luteous, more yellowish on the apex, articulations pale, covered with very short pale villosity.

Female—Last segment short, yellow, split below near the ventral margin with two, thick, black shining cylindrical appendages, which are as long as the segment and covered with very long black hairs and spines, out of the superior part of this segment is protruded an additional short segment with two short quadrangular yellow plates with black margins, and below two transversal rows of very strong black spines.

Male—Abdomen not longer than of the female, ventral part of last segment not split below, yellow with long black hairs, forming a large spoon-shaped part, there are no cylindrical appendages; the additional segment forming two yellow plates which are shorter but much more prolonged below and a little enlarged, margin black with long black hairs below without the rows of spines, above on dorsum with a bunch of hairs.

Legs slender, pale, with black hairs, the femur, tibia and all joints of tarsus black on tip, a fine black ring on tibia not far from the knee ; spurs as long as the basal joint, straight fuscous   Wings long, narrow, front wings with the costa straight, curved strongly on tip, which is short, about rectangular ; hind margin very slightly incurved, so that the wing is broadest near the apical third, hind wing nearly as long, a little narrower, sharply pointed, hind margin a little sinuate on the apical half, broadest near the middle of its length, hyaline, hairy, veins fine, dark, subcosta, mediana and submediana interrupted with pale yellow, pterostigma small, whitish

Length of body, 30 to 34 mm, exp. al. 80 mm.

Hab —Burmeister's type from Savannah. Georgia, very probably collected by Dr Zimmermann, it is a female, and was described out of Winthem's coll, the label, *immaculatus* De Geer, in Burmeister's handwriting, is still on the pin   I have raised male and female in July, 1883, out of larvæ from Alabama, given by Prof Lyon ; I have the full grown larva, larva skin, nympha skin and cocoon   The larva is called Doodle, and it is a favourite pleasure of children to kneel in the sand near the holes and to sing in a monotonous way, " Doodle, Doodle, etc." It is believed that the animal comes out to receive food   But I have to remark that the larva of *Tetracha Carolina* is treated similarly.

The type is just transformed, as is proved by specimens from Alabama, which made their transformation on the same day, one has all four wings developed, one only the fore wings, and the third has all wings crumpled. Nevertheless they have all the same colours of the type, and it is to be supposed that older specimens will show a darker coloration

I have never seen more specimens When I published the synopsis I had before me the type of Burmeister and two specimens of *M. immaculatus*, and believed all three to belong to the same species.

Myrmeleon formicalynx L

The synonymy need not be repeated here ; compare Stett. Ent Zeit , 1866, p 439

Face shining black, above with two impressions, which are variable in shape and size, and an engraved spot in the middle between the antennæ ; around the eyes a yellow ring, interrupted near the vertex , epistoma yellow, with two black spots connected with the colour of the face ; mouth yellow

Maxillary palpi slender cylindrical, black shining, pale on tip , apical joint notched on tip, third joint incurvate , the two basal joints globular, dull yellowish, the second blackish externally , labial palpi longer and stronger, shining black , second joint incurvate, thickened on tip , last joint thick, ovoid, with an engraved spot externally before the tip, which is pyramidal, pointed

Antennæ shorter than the thorax , tip clavate, dull black, below shining black on base ; basal joint yellow, below black in middle, and with a yellow ring around the base

Head dull black anteriorly, with rare white hairs, finely rugose, the lines diverging , vertex transversally ovoid, elevated, divided by a more or less pronounced median impression, on top with a transversal corrugated band, and some glossy flat spots , two approximate anteriorly and two posteriorly, and on each side a larger round one , behind the vertex near the eye an oval similar spot.

Prothorax short, broader than long, enlarged behind, rounded before, dull pitchy black , margin yellow except in middle anteriorly , yellowish near the thorax , on each side with some longer black hairs , mesothorax and metathorax pitchy black ; the body paler.

Abdomen slender, compressed, shorter than the wings, pitchy black ; apical margin of the last segments pale , villosity white, rather scarce.

Female genitals with two transverse rows of black bristles, two cylindrical black appendages with very long black hairs, and between them an advanced black part of the margin with strong bristles. (Rambur says with two appendages "formant deux petites saillies an peu plus épaisses " —which I cannot find)

Male genitals similar to *M mobilis*, the spoon-shaped part shorter, triangular, yellow

Legs slender, reddish-yellow , apical half of femur black; tibia blackish , the posterior legs externally reddish-yellow, except on tip ; tarsi blackish, sometimes yellowish at base , spurs about as long as the basal joint, straight , claws brown

Wings in shape and venation like *M immaculatus*, with the hind margin convex , hyaline ; veins black, interrupted with yellow ; pterostigma milk-white blackish interiorly

Length of body, 25 to 32 mm.; exp. al., 55 to 84 mm. Breadth of hind wings, 6 to 8 mm

· Hab.—Everywhere in Europe, only England and the islands in the Mediterranean excepted A pair collected in Castilia by Staudinger is quoted by myself Stett Ent Z , xxvii, p 290 A Costa figures it from Naples In Russia it is known from Livland to Astrachan and Nertschinsk, Siberia

I have eight specimens, male and female, before me from Sweden, Prussia, Silesia, Switzerland. The imago flies from July to September. I have raised this species, which is common in Germany.

In the collection of Linnæus a specimen of this species *on the characteristic Linnean pin, bearing in his own handwriting on the label the name "formicalynx,"* is still present I have seen it in 1857 and 1861.

The high authority of my friend McLachlan, and the emphasis with which he declines to acknowledge this specimen as typical (Tr. Lond. Ent. Soc., 1871, p. 443), oblige me to state why I hold decidedly the contrary opinion Mr. McLachlan bases his objection solely on the fact that the specimen is identical with the Swedish species, and that the African habitat, given by Linnæus for his *M. formicalynx*, must belong to a different species (though the few words of the diagnosis given will apply to this insect so far as they go —McL), because no specimen from Africa is known to him , and "that the collection of Linnæus has been mal-treated by additions, destruction and displacement of labels " The dis-covery of a true African specimen would make McLachlan's objection untenable Nobody would be surprised that an insect, with such a large distribution, and found in Castilia and Naples, should be found in Africa For the statement of the displacement of labels in the Linnean collection McLachlan quotes the preface of Staudinger's Catalog der Lepidopteren, 1871, p xvi –xvii This quotation is indeed very unfortunate, as the Ger-man original is essentially different (p xvi) from the French translation (p xvii.) which is alone used by McL —" C'est malheuresement un fait certain que l'acquéreur de la collection de Linné a eu la deplorable idée de remplacer quelquefois des exemplaires endommagés par des exem-plaires frais—*vielleicht* vorhandene schlechte Exemplare durch bessere ersetzte." So long as McLachlan gives not any other evidence for his opinion, it is apparently not admissible.

Concerning the Neuroptera in the Linn. collection, I have published (Stett. Ent Z., vol. vi , 1845, p 155) the list *still before me*, made in 1844 by Mr R Kippist, then Secretary of the Linn Soc

Of the 83 species described in Syst Nat. Ed . xii., were present 50 species, but 17 of them were later additions, with labels written *not by Linnæus*, but probably by Mr. Smith, with the occasional addition " exdescript Linn " These 17 species are marked *only with pencil* in Linnæus's own copy of Syst Nat Ed , xii The other 33 species have labels in Linnæus's own handwriting, and are marked in the copy of Syst Nat. Ed., xii , with ink From these alone it is certain that they were in the collection of Linnæus, and *among these is M. formicalynx*. I have compared myself the collection in 1857 and 1861. I found nothing changed and no indication of displacements

Illiger's paper, 1801, in his Magazin, vol. i., p 7

Westwood's paper of the Linnean Staphylinus (Tr. Ent Soc . Ser. I., vol iv , p 45), Schaum "neber zweifelhafte Kaefer Linné's nach seiner Sammlung," Stett. Ent. Z , 1847, p 276 , Haliday ibid., 1851, p 131 ; Motschulsky, 1855, Etudes. Ent, iv , p 25, will show that the sweeping charges in McL paper can not be considered as warranted

The description of *M formicalynx* in Ed x is the same as in Ed xii , excepting the clerical error " antennæ setaceæ " for clavatæ, as given in the character of the genus. The quoted figure of Rœsel well represents this species. The insects in Linné's collection have been labelled by him in accordance with Ed. x of his Syst. Nat. At this time the imago of the Swedish species (1758) was unknown to him, and was only published later (1761) in the Ed. 11, of his Fn Suecica It is evident that Linnæus has believed Reaumur's species and the Swedish one to be identical, as he says in Ed xii, "Alae nostratis obsque maculis fuscis," and as he has called this species *M formicarium*, instead of *M formicaleo*, as in all his anterior works   Now every student of Neuroptera, since half a century ago, knows very well that Linné has combined two different species, and that a new name would be needed for one of them, but as a second species had been *described also by Linnæus* this name was accepted for the Swedish species as *M formicalynx*. Therefore, indeed, no mistake and no uncertainty was possible. McLachlan has given no proof for his opinion that *M formicalynx* from Africa belongs to a different unknown species. McLachlan's quotation l c, p 441 and 442, "In the first edition of the Fn. Suec, 1746, he (Linné) says of an anthon *alae obsolete nebulosae*," is not to be found at all in this book, and could not be found, as Linné described only the larva   The words *obsolete nebulosae* occur in no work of Linné, nor in any other work known to me describing this insect, but I have now the kind information by McL. that those words were taken out of the interleaved copy of the Fauna Suecica, and that my friend is now sure that they belong not at all to *Myrmeleon.*

McLachlan proposes to use the name *M. formicarium*, which every body has used for more than a century, since Syst Nat, Edit. xii, 1767, for Reaumur's species, *for the Swedish species*   McLachlan proposed for Reaumur's species at first the name *M formicaleo* used by Linné in Ed x and by Poda, later he proposed to call it *M. Europæus*, which was adopted by Mr Redtenbacher and Prof Brauer, though the latter remarked that if a new name was needed *M. nostras* Fourcroy *would have the priority.*

Concerning such changes of names, should be studied the excellent dissertation of Dr Elias Fries, Ofver Vexternes Namn Upsala, 1842 (also in Fries's Botaniska Utflygter, T i, p. 113, and German Transl in Hornschuch Archiv, 1855, T. 1), where also about Linné's collection, the former idolatry and the later belittling in England, excellent advice and notice will be found.

Myrmeleon formicarius, Linn.

The curious habits of this insect are known for nearly two centuries and quoted so often that in my Synops. Hemerobidarum, p 439, about half a page is filled by them   There is much written pro and con about this name   I believe the change of the name is simply a matter of taste, and I remember with merriness the page on which the late R. Crotch, my old friend McLachlan and myself were hacked to pieces for our heresy in nomenclature by A Lewis   I consider the paper of McLachlan, Tr. Lond Ent Soc, 1871, p 441, to be a very fair one   Of my two objections one has been removed by himself as I mentioned by *M. formicalynx.*

Myrmeleon rusticus Hag

M rusticus Hag.   Syn N Amer Neur. 233, 17.

Front a little convex, nigro-piceous, shining, above with two transverse small impressions , epistom black, or on each side with a yellow oval spot, which may encroach a little on the front, and a triangular yellow middle spot, largest anteriorly , rhinarium bright yellow, labrum largely notched, brownish , maxillary palpi yellowish, apical joint a little darker, cylindrical, notched at tip, scarcely longer than the preceeding ; labial palpi longer, yellowish, second joint thin, incurved, thickened at tip ; apical joint about as long, strongly ovate, blackish, with an impressed spot outside, suddenly contracted before end, which is thin, pyramidal, a little incurved , head below and a narrow ring encircling the eyes bright yellow , antennæ strongly clavate, longer than head and prothorax, dark, annulated with yellow

Vertex obscure ferrugineous, shining, elevated, with a median furrow, dull grayish in front above the antennæ , a yellow spot on each side near the eye , two flat interrupted median stripes and on each side a larger flat shining spot.

Prothorax short, broader than long narrowed before, front margin rounded , clothed on margins and behind laterally with short white villosity , dull yellowish. with two approximated median bands more visible before the furrow, and on each side with a broader dark fuscous band more visible after the furrow , thorax dull pitchy, obscurely margined with dull yellow , besides, below the wings pitchy with a few yellow spots.

Abdomen shorter than the wings, luteo-fuscous , posterior margin of segments, and sometimes a faint middle line, yellow.

Genitals of male and the last segment black, below a row of strong black spines , an inferior conical part with long black hairs ; abdomen of female shorter, the superior parts blunt, below a row of black bristles ; two small appendages (probably) inferiors.

Legs yellowish, not very short, the intermediate finely sprinkled , femora and tibia darker inside, except in the middle pair , tibia with an apical dark ring ; tarsus about longer than tibia, tips of joints darker ; spurs scarcely as long as first joint, straight, dark

Wings hyaline, moderately pointed , pterostigma small, milk white, a small dark dot before it , venation pale, median and submedian veins distinctly interrupted with fuscous ; costals simple

Length of body, ♂ 30, ♀ 26 mm., exp. al. 54 to 60 mm

Hab —New Mexico (formerly W Texas), Pecos River, August 4th, Capt Pope's Exped , Mexico, Matamoras, same expedition.

THE ANNUAL MEETING OF THE ENTOMOLOGICAL SOCIETY OF ONTARIO

The Annual Meeting of the Society was held in the City Hall, Ottawa, on Friday and Saturday, October 5th and 6th, 1888   A Council meeting was held on Friday morning at 10 30 o'clock in a Committee room of the City Hall, at which the following members were present ·— The President, Mr James Fletcher, Ottawa , Mr. E Baynes Reed, Mr W. E Saunders and Mr J M. Denton, London , Rev C J S Bethune, Port Hope ; Rev. T W Fyles, Quebec , Mr James Moffat, Hamilton , Mr. H. H Lyman, Montreal.   After the transaction of routine business, the sum of $200 was voted to the Library Fund for the purchase of books and the binding of periodicals and pamphlets   An Executive Committee, to consist of the President, the Editor, the Secretary-Treasurer and the members of the Council resident in London was appointed to deal with the financial affairs of the Society and to provide for the representation of the Society at the annual meeting of the American Association for the Advancement of Science   The work of arranging the Society's collections and putting them in good order was directed to be continued, and Mr Moffatt was requested to do for the Coleoptera what he has already so successfully accomplished with the Lepidoptera

In the afternoon the Society met at 2 o'clock Mr W H Harrington was present in addition to those above mentioned   Mr. Lyman exhibited a series of specimens of the different species of *Callimorpha* which he had described in his paper last year (C. E. xix , p 181) and remarked upon their various peculiarities. He thought it most desirable that names should be attached to the different varieties, even though they may hereafter be found to belong to the same species. Messrs Fletcher, Fyles and Moffat made remarks upon the subject. and agreed that all distinct forms should have separate names.

Mr. Fletcher gave an account of his visit to Nepigon, Lake Superior, early in July, in company with Mr. S H. Scudder, of Cambridge, Mass., for the purpose of collecting the eggs of various rare species of butterflies. He described the various modes they had employed in order to induce the females to deposit their eggs, and recounted the great success achieved in securing the eggs of no less than seventeen species of butterflies and capturing a number of others.

Rev Dr Bethune exhibited a number of specimens of *Colias eurytheme*, chiefly of the form *eriphyle*, which he had taken at Port Arthur on the 1st of September last, and gave an account of his trip to the Nepigon River, exhibiting a large number of specimens of butterflies and other insects captured there on August 21st, 22nd, and 30th.   Among these may be especially mentioned *Colias interior* and *eurytheme*, *Argynnis electa, atlantis, chariclea* and *bellona, Phyciodes tharos, Grapta faunus* and *progne, Pyrameis huntera* and *cardui, Limenitis arthemis*, etc

Rev. T W Fyles read a paper on *Chionobas Jutta*, in which he recounted his success in rearing the insect through all its stages

Mr Fletcher and Dr Bethune spoke of the desirability of issuing a series of papers on popular and economic entomology in the CANADIAN ENTOMOLOGIST, and urged upon the members present the necessity of co-operating in the work The Editor also drew the attention of the meeting to the duty of at once providing the material required for the Annual Report of the Society

The President laid on the table specimen sheets and plates of Mr. Scudder's great work on the Butterflies of the Eastern States and Canada, which were examined by the members with much interest. He also brought up for discussion the subject of the disease known as " Silver-top" in hay, which is believed to be caused by a species of Thrips, and requested the members to investigate the matter in their various localities. The only remedy at present suggested is the plowing up of old hay-fields which are found to be the most seriously attacked The depredations of Grasshoppers during the past season were next consider- ed. Mr. Fletcher suggested that much might be done to reduce their numbers by cutting the hay about the 20th of June, if practicable, and thus preventing the maturity of the insects by depriving them of their food before they were able to fly to a distance for it. Mr. Denton reported that the Chinch Bug had been observed in the Township of Delaware, near London, and that it was likely to become very injurious if measures were not taken to counteract it

The meeting adjourned at 5.30 p m.

EVENING SESSION.

In the evening the Society held a public meeting in the Council Chamber of the City Hall at 8 o'clock, at which there were about sixty persons present, including the Hon. C. W Drury, the recently appointed Minister of Agriculture for Ontario; Mr John Lowe, Deputy Minister of Agriculture for the Dominion of Canada , Prof. Saunders, Director of the Experimental Farms of the Dominion , Sir James Grant, M D., Mr. R B Whyte, President of the Ottawa Field Naturalists' Club , Mrs. Macleod Stewart , Mrs R. B Whyte, Mrs Davidson, and several other ladies as well as a number of farmers and gardeners from the city and neighbourhood.

The proceedings of the evening began with an able and practical address from the President, Mr James Fletcher, of Ottawa, upon " Insects Injurious to Crops " (The address will be published in full in the Annual Report of the Society.) The speaker stated that it was a well-known fact that at least one-tenth of all the crops grown in this country was destroyed by noxious insects. In order to combat these insects it was necessary to know their life-histories, and to acquire and disseminate this knowledge was the main object of our Entomological Society He described in simple terms the two systems of structure in insects, in accordance with which one class live by sucking out the juices of plants and the other by biting and gnawing the substance, and related the various means adopted to counteract the ravages of each In his position as Dominion Entomologist he found it possible to give to nearly all enquirers useful information about the insects that might be affecting their crops or gardens. He then referred to many common injuries and related the best means of dealing with them, and gave an account of what might be termed the "first-class pests" of the season, among these he specially mentioned the cut-worms and grass-hoppers, which had been more than usually numerous and destructive in many parts of the Province. He concluded his address, which was listened to with great interest and attention for upwards of an hour, by expressing the pleasure it gave to the members of the Society to observe the growth of their science in popularity, a fact evidenced by the attendance that evening of so many distinguished persons.

The Hon. C. W. Drury next addressed the meeting. He said that he had not come to deliver a speech, but he had travelled five hundred miles in order that as the head of the Agricultural Department of Ontario he might show the importance which the Government he represented attached to the work of the Entomologists. He considered that the small grant annually made to the funds of the Society was amply repaid by its practical work, and mentioned as an instance the immense saving to the country effected by the discovery of the remedy for the clover-seed midge

Sir James Grant spoke in graceful terms and delivered a very interesting address. He described the importance of Entomology in its various aspects, and referred to the work of some of its greatest masters, from Aristotle and Pliny, in ancient times, to LeConte, who had described so enormous a number of species of beetles and whose lamented death was so great a loss to science. He described its relation to other departments, especially to medicine, and mentioned as an instance the fact that bacteria had been introduced into the blood by the bite of mosquitoes. He paid a high compliment to the President for his practical and interesting address, and for his enthusiastic devotion to the science which had deservedly won for him the recognition of the Dominion Government.

Professor Saunders rose to move a vote of thanks to the President for his valuable address. He gave a short account of the history of the Society and its work, and mentioned the fact that there were only two of the original members present besides himself, viz.: Dr. Bethune and Mr. E. Baynes Reed, who had been concerned in its organization twenty-five years ago. Sir James Grant seconded the vote of thanks, which was put to the meeting by Dr. Bethune and unanimously carried.

Rev Dr Bethune then proceeded to give a brief address, in which he strongly urged the importance of encouraging young people in their instinctive fondness for collecting insects It was not only a most useful pursuit from an educational point of view, but led to great results in developing a love for science and a steady increase in the number of its votaries. As one of the pioneers of the Society he was delighted to see for the first time at one of its meetings the Provincial Minister of Agriculture and also the Dominion Deputy-Minister, he expressed his pleasure also at the presence of so many ladies. and trusted that they would bring to the aid of Entomology all those gifts of deftness and neatness which they so eminently possessed For their encouragement he mentioned that the most distinguished entomologist in England at the present time is a lady, Miss E Ormerod, of St Albans.

In acknowledging the vote of thanks, Mr Fletcher took occasion to refer to one point which he had overlooked, namely, the injuries inflicted by "that miscreant, the English sparrow," whose extermination he strongly advocated The Hon Mr Drury stated that this destructive bird was no longer under the protection of the Act of Parliament respecting insectivorous birds, and that everyone was at liberty to aid in reducing its numbers The meeting then adjourned

SATURDAY'S SESSION

Saturday, October 6th —At 10 o'clock a m. a meeting of the Council, was held for the transaction of business, and after its adjournment the Society continued its proceedings The reports of the Secretary-Treasurer, the Librarian, the delegate to the Royal Society of Canada, the Montreal Branch, and the delegates to the Entomological Club of the American Association for the Advancement of Science were presented and adopted

The following gentlemen were elected officers for the ensuing year —

President—James Fletcher, F R S C , F L S , Ottawa

Vice-President—E Baynes Reed, London.

Secretary-Treasurer—W E Saunders, London.

Librarian—E Baynes Reed, London

Curator—Henry S Saunders, London

Council—J. M. Denton, London , J Alston Moffat, Hamilton , Gamble Geddes, Toronto , W H Harrington, Ottawa , Rev T W Fyles, M A., South Quebec (and the former Presidents, who are ex-officio members viz., Prof. Saunders, F.R.S.C., F.L.S., F C.S., and Rev. C. J. S. Bethune).

Editor of the CANADIAN ENTOMOLOGIST—Rev. C. J. S. Bethune, M.A., D.C.L., Port Hope.

Editing Committee—The President, Prof. Saunders, J. M. Denton, H. H. Lyman (Montreal), Dr. W. Brodie (Toronto).

Auditors—J. M. Denton and E. B. Reed.

Delegate to the Royal Society of Canada—H. H. Lyman, Montreal.

Papers were read by (1) the Rev. T. W. Fyles on " The Hypenidæ of the Province of Quebec;" (2) Mr. J. A. Moffat on "Some Curious Proceed ings of the Larvæ of *Euchœtes egle* Feeding upon the Milk-weed ;" (3) Mr. W. E. Saunders on the English Sparrow, strongly recommending its extermination ; (4) Rev. T. W. Fyles on " The Sphingidæ of the Province of Quebec." Mr. Fletcher, in discussing this paper, remarked upon the colours of *Sphinx 5-maculata*, and said that the dark forms seemed to be hardier than the pale green; he had observed also in *Papilio asterias* that some green pupæ emerged much sooner than the brown ; he had obtained no less than four broods of this insect this year. (5) Rev. T. W. Fyles read "A Memoir of the late Philip H. Gosse," and exhibited a photograph of this eminent naturalist and his late residence. (The above papers will all be published in the annual report of the Society.)

Mr. Moffat stated that he had taken *Papilio cresphontes* this summer at Hamilton, and that he had seen in that neighbourhood a specimen of the now rare *Pieris protodice.* Mr. Fyles mentioned that he had taken *Grapta gracilis* and *faunus* at Quebec in September, *Hepialus gracilis* in the Township of Dunham, and *Hepialus auratus* in the Township of Brome. Dr. Bethune had found *Grapta J. album* numerous at Port Hope in September, and brought some living specimens to the meeting ; these will be taken care of during their hibernation, and efforts will be made to obtain their eggs in the spring.

The following gentlemen were elected members of the Society :—Rev. Prof. Symonds, Trinity College, Toronto ; Rowland Hill, London ; Mr. Brown, *Free Press*, London ; A. L. Poudrier, Donald, B. C. ; Arthur M. Bethune, Port Hope ; E. M. Morris, Toronto.

It was decided to hold the next annual meeting in London immedi- ately after the close of the meeting of the American Association in Toronto in August.

After passing a vote of thanks to the Mayor and Council for the use of the City Hall the meeting adjourned.

BOOK NOTICES

ENTOMOLOGY FOR BEGINNERS, for the use of Young Folks, Fruit Growers,
Farmers and Gardeners   By A. S. PACKARD, M. D.   New York
Henry Holt & Co —1 vol , 8 vo , pp 367

It is with much pleasure that we draw the attention of our readers to
the publication of this work.   For many years past, we have been re-
peatedly asked to recommend some book that would serve as an introduction to the study of Entomology, and enable young collectors to make
a satisfactory beginning in the pursuit.   Hitherto, we have been unable to
mention any single work that would answer the purpose, and we have felt
constrained to tell enquirers that they must procure several books for
instance, Kirby & Spence's Entomology, Harris's Insects Injurious to
Vegetation, etc , and even then not have what they want   Dr Packard's
new book is certainly one that has long been wanted, though we fear that
it is a little too technical in its language, and too abtruse in its treatment
of some of the subjects to exactly meet the requirements of beginnerst
We think, too, that the author has not been judicious in the arrangemen
of the matter , the first two chapters on the structure of insects and their
growth and metamorphosis will, we fear, prove rather repellant to one
who has collected a few specimens and wants to know something about
them and what to do with them   They are carefully written, and give an
admirable summary of what every student of Entomology requires to
know , but they are a little beyond the youthful mind, or the uninstructed
powers of the ordinary farmer   We, therefore, strongly advise all beginners
who procure this book—and we recommend them to get it without fail—
to commence their reading with Chapter vi , which contains very interesting
and useful directions for collecting, preserving and rearing insects ; they
might then turn back and read Chapters iv. and v on insect architecture,
and insects injurious and beneficial to agriculture.   By this time, we have
no doubt, they will have become so deeply interested in the work that
they will not be discouraged by the drier details and the harder words in
the remainder of the book   The third chapter, which fills over a hundred
pages, gives an admirable synopsis of the classification of insects, and
should enable a beginner to arrange with some degree of system any
specimens that he collects   The author has departed from the usually
received divisions of insects, and sets forth no less than sixteen orders ,
this number he obtains by sub-dividing the Neuroptera, Orthoptera and
Diptera   To the new orders thus formed, he applies the novel terms
Plectoptera, Platyptera, Mecaptera, etc.   We feel rather doubtful about
their general acceptance, and think it a pity that they should have been
put forth in an elementary work of this kind before they had been dis-

cussed and approved of by Entomologists in general. We do not, however, wish to disparage the work ; it is certainly a valuable compendium,
and we cordially recommend it to our readers who are beginners in Entomology. The book is well written and excellently illustrated throughout,
and must prove a great help to the science by furnishing young students,
in a convenient form, with information that hitherto they could not readily
procure.   C. J. S. BETHUNE.

THE BUTTERFLIES OF THE EASTERN UNITED STATES AND CANADA,
    with special reference to New England, by S. H. SCUDDER. Imp.
    8 vo. Cambridge, pp. 1–40 and 105–208, Part I, 1st Nov., 1888.

For some months Lepidopterists and Librarians have been anxiously
awaiting the appearance of Mr. Scudder's monumental work on the
Butterflies of New England, which, as is well known, has been constantly
engaging the attention of this keen observer and careful student for the
last 20 years. Through the courtesy of the author we have been favoured
with advance sheets and plates of Part I, which is to appear on 1st Nov.,
1888. From the well known high character of Mr. Scudder's past work,
doubtless much will be expected by the scientific world of this long
promised book. Judging from the number under consideration we
believe few will be disappointed. No work has ever appeared, in any
branch of science, where such thorough and complete information is given
of the objects discussed, nor which has been so copiously and accurately
illustrated. An Introduction treats, with the greatest detail, of the general
structure of butterflies from the egg to the imago, and includes a chapter
upon their classification. This is followed by a systematic treatise in
which " not only every species," (embraced within the scope of the work)
" but also every genus, tribe, sub-family and family is described and dis-
" cussed with a fullness never before attempted, except in individual
" cases, including in each instance not merely the perfect form, but, when
" possible, the egg, the caterpillar at birth and in the succeeding stages,
" and the chrysalis, together with the distribution, life-history, habits and
" environments of the insect, in which a great accumulation of new facts
" and observations is embodied."

In the Part before us we have pages 1 to 40 of the Introduction covering the structure of the egg, the caterpillar and the chrysalis, and the
beginning of the description of the perfect insect. There is then a break
and the pagination continues again at page 105, where the second section

begins with a short chapter on the families of butterflies. This is a reproduction, slightly altered, of the table of classification which Mr Scudder has already published in the CAN ENT, xix, 201, in which he divides the butterflies into *Nymphalidæ, Lycaenidæ, Papilionidæ* and *Hesperidæ*, an arrangement virtually the same as that given by Bates and adopted by Packard, in which the genera *Œneis* and *Cercyonis* are considered the highest of the butterflies

At page 109 the systematic treatise begins with the *Nymphalidæ* or "Brush-footed butterflies" With this family, as with sub-families and genera throughout the work, when possible analytical tables are given for their arrangement, based upon the egg, the caterpillar at birth, the caterpillar at maturity, the chrysalis and the imago The first sub-family is the *Satyrinæ*, including six genera, of which *Œneis* is described first Under each species we find first complete and careful technical descriptive details of structure for all the known stages These are printed in rather smaller type than the rest of the book, a fact which will considerably facilitate reference. Then follows a general description, giving any interesting features in the distribution and habits of the perfect insect and larva, the food plant, variations and enemies, and lastly a list of the points upon which further information is needed

On page 127 appears the first of a series of essays, of which there are to be over 70 distributed throughout the work, and to which the author has applied the somewhat inelegant title of " Excursuses " These discuss separately all the interesting problems which arise in the study of butterflies (whether of distribution, structure, history, or relation to the outer world), in themselves forming a complete treatise on the life of these insects These will be a charming feature of the work by means of which a book, which must necessarily contain a large amount of technical scientific description, will be made attractive to many who will subscribe to it merely to possess the most extensive and beautiful book which has ever appeared on the diurnal Lepidoptera of North America. The scope of these may be inferred from the titles of those which occur in the first part.

1. The White Mountains of New Hampshire as a home for butterflies.
2 The clothing of caterpillars
3. The general changes in a butterfly's life and form
4 The eggs of butterflies.
5 The modes of suspension of caterpillars

The species described in the first part are *Œneis semidea* and *Œ. jutta, Cercyonis alope* and *C nephele, Enodia portlandia, Satyrodes eurydice, Neonympha phocion* and the beginning of the description of the genus *Cissia*

The nomenclature, we are told in the prospectus, follows the rules of the American Ornithologists' Union   As is well known Mr. Scudder's views upon some points with regard to nomenclature are very extreme, and it must be conceded that he has so far few followers   This state of affairs, however, we anticipate will be changed.   After many years of close study upon a special subject by so able a student, the writer, at any rate, is prepared to weigh carefully, without previously condemning them, his views as expressed in this his greatest work

The illustrations are, as above stated, most profuse, superbly executed, and each is accompanied by copious explanatory text, which will be bound opposite each plate.

The eight plates in Part I. are as follows   No 1 is a beautifully coloured chromo-lithograph of butterflies, showing in most instances both the upper and lower sides   The complete work will contain about twelve of these plates.   The second plate, No. 14, is uncoloured, but is exquisitely engraved, and by some may possibly be preferred to the last   It shows seventeen figures of butterflies artistically grouped   There are to be five plates similar to this.   The next plate, No 18, comprises eight small maps, showing separately the distribution of the different species treated of in Part I   There will be fifteen of these sets of maps.   No. 46 shows scales of butterflies, and there will be six of this nature   No. 52 gives the heads of butterflies.   The work on this plate, drawn by J H. Emerton, is very beautiful   There are to be eight others like it. No 67 is the first of three plates showing the micropyles of eggs magnified highly   No 70 is devoted to magnified figures of young larvæ just after leaving the eggs, and there will be three others like it   No 93 is a physical map of New England, prepared specially for this work by John H. Klemroth, under the supervision of the Geographer of the U. S. Survey   These, however, do not by any mean exhaust the styles of plates which will appear, for in subsequent numbers new sorts of subjects will come forward, all of which will be fully illustrated whenever figures can make the text more intelligible.   Special articles upon hymenopterous and dipterous parasites are to be prepared by the able specialists, Messrs. L. O. Howard, of Washington, and Dr Williston   In fact all the phases of life passed by the insects treated of as well as the important circumstances connected therewith, will be presented to the reader in the most complete manner possible.   There will be about two thousand figures on ninety-six plates, of which over forty will be coloured   The small inconvenience of not always having all the plates referred to in the text issued at the same time with it, cannot of course possibly be obviated in a systematic work, where everything is treated fully in its proper place under each species, and in which the number of subjects needing illustration in each part is greater than can be shown on the quotum of plates for that part.   The whole will be issued in a year, in 12 parts, each to contain 8 plates and about 150 pages of text.

JAMES FLETCHER

The Canadian Entomologist.

VOL. XX.   LONDON, DECEMBER, 1888.   No. 12.

THE CLASSIFICATION OF THE BOMBYCIDÆ.

(Fourth and Last Paper.)

BY A. R. GROTE, A. M., BREMEN, GERMANY.

Sub-family *Attacinæ*.

The subfulcate primaries ally this group to the *Platypteryginæ*, and a certain vague resemblance to the *Geometridæ* may be found in the tendency which the upper surfaces of the wings show to display the same pattern on both wings. The ocelli are absent, the oral structure undeveloped, the hind wings are without frenulum. The species form mostly large cocoons, and the characteristics of the family are pronounced in this sub-family of silk-spinners. The male antennæ are feathered to the tips, each joint bearing a double pectination. The antennæ are comparatively short ; in the female the pectinations are shorter. On the fore wings, vein 5 is much closer to 6, than to 4, arising from the upper corner of the cell. The caterpillars are thick and short rather than long, the segments tending to become centrally elevated, with prominent incisions. In the early stages they are bristled ; in the later stages of *Platysamia* and *Saturnia*, for instance, characteristic colored warts appear. They are almost polyphagous. Long lists have been given by Mr. Beutenmuller, of the food plants of our common North American forms. Our beautiful *Actias luna* has an Asiatic ally in *A. selene*, and, I conclude, that the genus *Actias* in our fauna must be regarded as a relic of a former Arctic, circumpolar fauna, the more so as it is seen to be absent south of the equator in the New World. Leach's genus *Actias* is older than *Tropæa* of Hübner, which Dr. Packard used, hence I retain it in my Check Lists. We have in California, and again in Texas, species of the European genus *Saturnia ;* I have elsewhere drawn attention to the fact that there exists a certain resemblance between the two faunæ, of which this is an instance.

Sub-family *Hemileucinæ*

Whereas the *Attacinæ* spin thick cocoons above the surface, and have subfalcate primaries, in this group, so far as I have studied them, the fore wings are blunt or rounded, and the cocoon is made at the surface of the ground mixed with *debris*. The caterpillars in their last stage are bristled. and resemble those of *Platysamia* in their earlier stage. This group, represented by the typical genus *Hemileuca*, prepares us for the following *Ceratocampinæ*, in the gradual modification of its characters. In its closely allied species and tendency to local modification it recalls such lower genera as *Clisiocampa* Perhaps the genus *Quadrina* belongs here , of this I have had only a single specimen to examine. When both sexes are known and nearer comparisons are made it may be that we have to do with a distinct sub-family type Mr Smith, after seeing the type, referred it to the *Cossinæ*. I do not believe this, or that we have to do with an internal feeder. Later, he appears to have reverted to my original idea that the genus was related to *Gloveria*, referred by Dr. Packard to the *Lachneinæ*, perhaps from its resemblance to the European *Otus*. The eggs of *Hemileuca* are laid like those of the *Lachneinæ*, in ring form, and the abdomen is likewise tufted at the extremity.

Sub-family *Ceratocampinæ*

In this group, defined by Harris, a cocoon is rarely made and the transformation is subterranean The female antennæ are sub-simple or simple, and the male antennæ are not pectinate at the tip The abdomen is longer, the squamation smoother, and, while the main Attacid characters are still retained, there is an evident departure in a fresh direction The ocellate marks on the secondaries are here and there apparent, but the ornamentation has become simpler, and the lowest form, *Dryocampa rubicunda*, has a resemblance in all stages to the ensuing *Lachneinæ*. The caterpillars are often bizarre in appearance from the spines and horns with which they are ornamented, especially in the genus *Citheronia*, where they probably serve as a defence by frightening their different enemies There seem to be two groups of larval types, the extremes of which are displayed by *Eacles* and *Citheronia;* the larvæ of the *Eacles* type, approaching the preceding Attacid type, those of the *Citheronia* type approaching gradually the *Lachneinæ* The distribution of this sub-family is somewhat limited It appears to be American, and to be confined to the plains east of the rocky backbone of the continent from north to south In our fauna it seems to be a southern element Hubner calls this group *Communiformes* Perhaps he intended thereby to indicate a return to the more usual moth form, the fore wings tending to become narrower, the secondaries subordinating, the abdomen lengthening I have in my " Hawk Moths" alluded to the probability that the Hawk Moths may be a further offshoot from the Lepidopterous stem in a parallel direction with the *Ceratocampinæ*.

Sub-family *Lachneinæ*.

In this group there is a return to the normal moth form with a tendency to the lengthening of the abdomen noticeable in the caterpillars. This lengthening of the abdomen and a certain weakness in structure dependent upon this lengthening, seems to be indicative of lower rank in insects generally and in the several suborders. The moths of the *Lachneinæ* resemble preceding groups in the absence of ocelli and frenulum The hind wings are subordinate to the primaries, the colors mostly of shades of brown and gray, with oblique transverse bands, more or less broken. The palpi are more prominent than in the preceding groups the tongue remaining weak The ornamentation of the long-bodied caterpillars consists of tufts of hair Our North American fauna is poor in species. We have two genera derived from a former circumpolar fauna, also found in Europe. *Clisiocampa* and *Gastropacha* We have, then, two genera which seem to me of South American extraction, *Tolype* and *Artace* The species of *Clisiocampa* are very closely allied. They offer ground for the correctness of the view which I have expressed that in North America, species tend to vary, to throw off local, perhaps, what Walsh called phytophagic varieties or species The wide extent of country, with its differing climate and flora, inhabited by *Clisiocampa*, has led to the throwing off of specifically appearing forms, which may have hardened in most cases into true species, separable in nearly all stages by external characters An instance is offered also by *Datana*, which I regard as an offshoot from *Phalera ;* while there are only two species of *Phalera*, there seem many closely allied species of *Datana* The eggs are laid in a ring-form on twigs, and the caterpillars of *Clisiocampa* are well-known as enemies by the orchardist.

Sub-family *Cossinæ*

The larva and moth are long-bodied, and this group is characterized by the former being internal feeders They are brown and livid in color and coleopterous-looking, as are internal feeders generally, belonging to whatever order of insects.   They have this habit in common with *Castnia,* and *Sesia,* but this has probably survived, while the other characters have differentiated so that we cannot consider the habit as uniting them in a modern family. The female *Cossus* has an external ovipositor, which is an index for the habit of the caterpillar. The ocelli are wanting and the tongue is quite rudimentary The male antennæ are pectinate, the wings are somewhat narrow and the habitus is sphingiform.   I have watched the exclusion of *Cossus* from the cocoon, the very active and moveable chrysalis being forced out into the air before the shell is broken Dr. Bailey gives a good account of the transformations of Bailey's Goat Moth, *Cossus centerensis* of Lintner. We have representatives of the European genera *Cossus* and *Hypopta,* while *Prionoxystus robiniæ,* the Locust Goat Moth, seems to me decidedly a distinct form of North American origin

Sub-family *Hepialinæ.*

In this group we have, without a doubt, the lowest Spinners.   The long thorax, with its subequal metathorax, draws the insertion of primary and secondary wings apart.   The subequal wings with pointed tips and the 12-veined secondaries, the short antennæ, spurless tibiæ are suggestive of the Neuroptera The distribution of the group is very general throughout the world , and this fact, together with the striking structural resemblance of its members, leads us to believe we have to do with an old and long preserved type of moth.   The caterpillars are root feeders, like those of the *Cossinæ,* sixteen footed, naked, yellowish.   The eggs are remarkable for their fineness, looking like gunpowder.   The cocoon is subterranean, a cell lined with silk.   We have very fine species in North America, referred by Dr. Packard to *Sthenopis,* but which, notwithstanding their size, seem to me congeneric with the European *Hepialus humuli.* The limits of the genus may be reached with the beautiful *H auratus,* which has a structural ally figured by Herrich-Schæffer from Brazil The species are generally rare , the moths fly in the dusk of evening and are an object of interest with most collectors

So far we have gone over the principal features of the *Bombycidæ*, more in explanation of the sequence adopted by me in the Check Lists, and which is that of Dr Packard's Synopsis of 1864, than in any attempt to re-classify the family But Dr Packard gives no definitions of the higher groups, and the diagnoses of the new genera do not include certain structural characters, as, for instance, the neuration I cannot here attempt to limit the genera, and I only give the characters which render the higher groups more or less recognizable The neuration must be comparatively studied As a whole it seems to me to show characters of simplicity The cells are generally open , there is an absence of accessory cells and crowding of veins, such as we see in some other familes of moths We can believe that the *Sphingidæ* may have been thrown off from the same stem when we compare the neuration Other characters, such as the absence of ocelli, may be additional indices. In the *Noctuidæ* the ocelli are quite rarely absent, in the Geometridæ quite rarely present But they appear in some sub-families of *Bombycidæ*, though not in the lower ones and in the more typical Spinners, such as, I think, stand nearer to the Hawk Moths The *Bombycidæ* are, as we find them now, detached groups with very diverse resemblances to other now distinct families of Moths In this diverse resemblance lies the proof of the synthesis which the Spinner Moths present To detach the different sub-families which we have here discussed is to lose sight of some of those finer questions of relationship which a close study of these insects calls up No family of Moths is more interesting to the student on this account than the *Bombycidæ*, with its great diversity of structure, appearance and habit. To the collector the beauty of the moths, their bright colors, the soft shading, the size of most of the species is equally tempting, while to the practical mind, the fact that the silk-worm, *Bombyx mori*, and other silk-producers, belong to the *Bombycidæ*, must render the pursuit of these insects sufficiently attractive They live short lives, the incomplete mouth parts render food-taking to many kinds an impossibility, they live so long as caterpillars or chrysalids, and lay their eggs and die But the human mind seizes upon the many considerations, which it has evolved from a study of the facts presented by these creatures, and turns them to its profit or its pleasure.

NOTES ON DANAIS ARCHIPPUS, Fabr.

BY MISS EMILY M MORTON, NEW WINDSOR, N. Y.

Having been requested by my friend, Mr. Wm H Edwards, to make observations on *Danais Archippus* during the seasons of 1887 and 1888, and subsequently having written to him the result of such observations, he requested me to publish in the CANADIAN ENTOMOLOGIST the substance of what I had already written him in my letter   I wrote out a paper about July 5th, which, however, was lost in the mails, and the paper now sent is a partial copy of the original, though somewhat altered, as the first was over four months old.

All my observations were made in New Windsor, N Y, which town is situated on the banks of the Hudson, directly opposite the hills which bound the northwestern borders of Connecticut.

Archippus is not more rare with us than many of our hybernating butterflies, and seems to me in no way abnormal.

It has always appeared when a certain Persian-lilac bush blooms, flying over and alighting on the blossoms.

Last summer (1887), the first hybernators came, as has already been stated by Mr Edwards, May 3rd and 4th, this season everything being later with cold rains and high winds, the lilacs did not blossom out until May 10th, when *Danais Archippus*, (how I love the dear old familar names!) allured by the first warm sunny day, and the perfume of the opening blossoms came forth to drink of the nectar, and having refreshed herself, hastened away to deposit her eggs before her few remaining days are gone, and she is gathered to her forefathers.   This butterfly could not have been a " colonist," for nothing so frail could have flown any distance in the high wind and beating rain of the preceding day, and it was not later than 9 30 a. m , the flowers and leaves still heavy with rain, so she must have come from a very short distance—possibly from the ruins of an old shed a hundred yards or so from the bush.

Has any one ever found a hybernating Archippus ?   Yet, we all know they do hybernate.

In the earlier days of my collecting, many and many a stump has been peeled of its bark, and even split to satisfy the craving for something new, yet never an Archippus has rewarded the most untiring search in that direction, though once, and in early May too, a *Vanessa Antiopa*, torpid, though still alive, was revealed in the very centre of a stump cosily mixed up with the damp saw-dust left by the ants and other borers

An egg of Archippus is a very tiny thing, and not easily found, even when sought for, and as Mr Edwards says, "there are thousands of Asclepias plants to one Archippus butterfly," cspccially a successfully hybernated butterfly, as probably not one in ten of the hosts of September and October flies live to leave their hybernacula in the spring.

How many people have found eggs of *Hemaris Thysbe?* Yet in most places Thysbe is as common as blackberries, and the larvæ are often to be found on the snow-ball bushes, though not one in a dozen ever reaches maturity. Once I spent an hour looking for the egg which I saw Thysbe deposit on a tiny bush which might have been covered by a three quart pail, yet had to depart without it in the end.

Mr Marsh, though an unusually intelligent and original observer, only succeeded in finding one egg, which goes to prove that Archippus eggs are harder to find than the larvæ or butterflies.

Mr. Fritz Senff, another very intelligent and accurate observer, though a recent acquisition to our small band of students and collectors, tells me he saw two perfectly fresh examples of Archippus, July 3rd and 6th, one flying in the veranda of his home in New Windsor, the other, which he caught, in a field not far distant , these were, doubtless, the first brood from the eggs of the hybernators ; besides these, we saw while driving June 19th, 1888, five or six examples, none of which were broken or faded, though we were not near enough—that is we had none in our hands, so as to be able to distinguish that rich plum-like bloom so dear to the collector of cabinet specimens, but which no butterfly ever carries having once flown even "for a few short hours."

Every collector or exchanger well knows how perishable is that same bloom, and how utterly different is any hand-raised specimen, from a poor wind-blown, grass-scratched passé imago, or even one who has dragged its undeveloped wing through the sharp blades of grass to find a resting place whereon to expand them

Surely *Archippus* is one of the most perishable species, for the "bloom" is as ephemeral as the dew of a summer morning, or the purple down of all the Hemaris tribe , one slight breath and it is gone forever !

As to any species laying " for a month or so," what collector or breeder of any lepidopterous insect has ever known any species to live and deposit eggs for two weeks—to say nothing of "a month or so?"

In most of the Heterocera five days is the usual period of life after the ♀ has paired. Every collector of course knows that most species will live longer if kept from their mates, which is a provision of nature to prevent the extermination of species   A *Phobetron pithecium* accidentally kept from her mate lived eight days, mating the fifth , another mating the first day from pupa deposits her eggs and dies the fourth day

I am no friend to the theory of colonization, though of course, I know eggs and pupa are often brought to and from distant countries in the commerce of nations , but that anything so fragile as a butterfly or moth should fly hundreds of miles, and not only that but entirely change its habits on its arrival, even though that country should be nearly identical with its own in climatic properties, becoming from a double or three brooded species a single one, seems out of all reason

That a hybernating Archippus should be more or less shabby, according to its hybernacula, is of course, highly probable ; and, I agree with Mr. Edwards, in judging that a freshly hatched butterfly, finding a cold dry place wherein to hybernate should appear in the late spring, less faded and unstained than another in a wet and exposed situation , but that any should appear after the wear and tear of a northern winter, or a flight of an hundred miles with the glorious hues of an imago fresh from chrysalis, is utterly beyond belief

This season, after an unparalleled winter, the first " western blizzard " ever experienced in the State of New York, we have had swarms of hybernated *P. Atalanta,* one would not suppose there were enough nettles in the whole of New Windsor to afford nourishment to the hundreds which have appeared during the month of May.   Did they fly from the Gulf of Mexico ? *Quien sabe ?*

A curious variety of *Papilio turnus* was found here in New Windsor, closely resembling fig 3 in plate 5 of Mr Edwards's Butterflies of North America.   She was taken in the grass July 8th, but could not fly as her wings were crippled on one side   She is darker than Mr Edwards's specimen, looking like a *Glaucus,* but with a powdering of yellow scales covering the inner surface of all the wings   Could the blizzard of the 12th of March have produced this variety ?

October 29th, 1888.

THE CHALCID GENUS RILEYA

BY WM H. ASHMEAD, PHILADELPHIA.

My good friend Mr. Howard, in his article entitled " The Chalcid Genus Rileya," published in the October Can. Ent., p. 191, makes several inaccurate statements , and, in the lines "An interesting interference in the adoption of the generic name Rileya has recently taken place between Mr. Ashmead and myself," implies that I knowingly appropriated this name for a genus in the *Eurytominæ,* after he had decided to use it for one in the *Encyrtinæ*, when I had no such knowledge, thereby placing me in an unenviable position before my colleagues

For the guidance of those who will have to settle this question, I must state that my description of the *Eurytomid* genus Rileya was drawn up and forwarded to Prof. E. A. Popenoe for publication about the last of November, 1887, and a synoptic characterization of the genus appeared in the *Entomologica Americana* for June 1888, although the full description of the genus was not published, as stated by Mr Howard, until afterwards—about July 5th, one month later, still, both of these descriptions were published three or four months ahead of Mr Howard's.

The opinion, expressed by Mr. Howard, that because the name Rileya is given in my synopsis of the Eurytominæ, " *not as a new genus, but as one already described and the few words given to it in the table fail to sufficiently characterize it,*" is a matter of surprise to me, for the characters given definitely separate it from all other Eurytomids, the characters are too unique among the *Eurytominæ* to be mistaken, and as to whether it was indicated as a new genus " has nothing to do with the case." I might have indicated the genus without my name, or in the usual way—nov. gen , mihi , *et cetera*, yet the genus would hold

As I have before stated, I had no knowledge of Mr. Howard's intention to dedicate a genus to Dr. Riley, and I regret that such knowledge was withheld from me, so that a controversy of this kind could have been avoided. The first intimation that I had of his intention to do so was on receipt of my July number of the *Entomologica Americana,* received, I think, about July 12th, and several months after my description of the genus had been forwarded to Prof. Popenoe , and just one month after the publication of my " Revised Generic Synopsis of the Eurytominæ."

Mr. Howard's paper on Rileya n g . was not read before the Entomological Society of Washington until June 7th, 1888, and not 1887, as stated in the CANADIAN ENTOMOLOGIST , while my synopsis was at that time already published   If there is any " interference " in the adoption of the generic name Rileya, it is on the part of Mr Howard.

Besides the above " facts," I would state that the types of my genus *Rileya* were shown to both Dr. C. V Riley and Mr H G. Hubbard, at my home in Jacksonville last winter, and at that time Dr Riley made no mention of Mr Howard's genus *Rileya*, although he did desire, for reasons of his own, that if it were possible, the name of the genus should be changed.

It is unfortunate that Mr. Howard, in describing his new genus *Rileya*, failed to go over the European literature on the subject. for, both from his figure and description, it seems to be identical with Dahlbom's genus *Lonchocerus*, described in 1857, Ofversigt af Kongl Vetenskaps-Akademiens Forhandlungar, vol. xiv , p. 293. Mr. C. G. Thomson, Hymenoptera Scandinaviæ, Tom iv , Fasc. I , p 116, in speaking of this genus, says —" Abdomen globosum Pronotum magnum   *Antennæ scapo et flagellum valde compressis,*" and on p 130, in speaking of the scutellum —" Scutellum *dense holocericeo-pubescens* " These characters seem to be the essential characters of Mr Howard's genus *Rileya*, the only real difference being in the shape of the head ; but whether or not Mr. Howard's genus is identical is immaterial, my Eurytomid genus of the same name having the priority.

In seeking to suppress the genus Mr. Howard has violated all the well established rules of zoological nomenclature.

JOHN ABBOT, THE AURELIAN.

BY W F KIRBY, BRITISH MUSEUM, LONDON, ENGLAND.

In the August part of the CANADIAN ENTOMOLOGIST, pp 149–154, I notice an article on this subject by my friend, Mr Scudder, and I may, perhaps, be able to add some additional remarks

The volume on Exotic Moths, published by Duncan in Jardine's " Naturalist's Library," contains (pp. 69–71) a short account of Abbot's life and works, and incorporates the notice by Swainson, to which Mr. Scudder refers. Swainson remarks, respecting the plates, " M. Francillon possessed many hundreds, but we know not into whose hands they have

as every volume bears the book-plate of 'John Francillon " There are
passed." I may say that this is evidently the set in the British Museum,
17 volumes (not 16); the first 15 bear the date 1792 on the printed title
pages, and the two last volumes 1804 (not 1809). The contents are as
follows :—

Vols. 1–4. Coleoptera
"   5 Orthoptera, Hemiptera, Homoptera and Heteroptera.
"   6. Lepidoptera Rhopalocera
"   7–11. Lepidoptera Heterocera.
"   12. Neuroptera, Hymenoptera
"   13. Diptera.
"   14. Arachnida
"   15. Myriopoda, Mallophaga, Acarina, Crustacea, Lepidoptera
           (transformations), &c.
"   16 Portrait, Orthoptera, Coleoptera (transformations), Lepidop-
           tera (transformations)
"   17 Lepidoptera (transformations).

The drawings of transformations of *Lepidoptera* are rarely, if ever,
duplicates of those published by Smith, sometimes representing a different
variety of the larva of the same species , and they are nearly three times
as numerous   There are only about a dozen drawings of transformations
of *Coleoptera*   Among the lesser-known orders, there is little doubt that
many species figured are still undescribed

I fully expect that some of Abbot's correspondence will be discovered
(of course, including his autograph), perhaps at the Antipodes, for
Swainson left England towards the close of his life, and died, according
to Hagen, in New Zealand, in 1856.

I am surprised that Mr. Scudder has not mentioned the volume of
Abbot's Drawings presented by Edward Doubleday to Dr T W.
Harris (Harris, Entomological Correspondence, p 123). If this volume
is the same as that said by Mr. Scudder to have been presented by Dr
J F. Gray to Dr Asa Gray, some error must have arisen   Possibly it
came into Dr Asa Gray's hands directly, or indirectly, from Dr Harris,
with an erroneous impression respecting the original English donor

There are a number of specimens originally collected by Abbot in the
British Museum, and probably in other collections. The Museum of the
Royal Dublin Society (now known as the Dublin Museum of Science and

Art) contains a large series of bleached specimens of insects of various orders (*Lepidoptera, Neuroptera,* &c,) which were not improbably collected by Abbot (Cf some notes by Mr McLachlan, Ent. M. Mag x., pp 227, 228).

NOTE BY MR. SCUDDER —The small volume of paintings referred to by Mr Kirby is in the library of the Boston Society of Natural History, and was not mentioned by me because the less said about it the better.   It was picked up at a book shop, bears the date 1830, and though Doubleday paid seven guineas for it, it is certainly not the work of Abbot, but of a very inferior copyist—some of the paintings being the merest daubs. It has scarcely the least value   The notice by Duncan I had not seen, but I find that it adds nothing to the facts of Abbot's life   Either I have never seen the seventeenth volume of Abbot's drawings at the British Museum referred to by Mr Kirby, or, if it concerns the moths only, may for that reason have taken no note of it   My memorandum of the dates must have been incorrectly copied.

ANNUAL MEETING OF THE ENTOMOLOGICAL CLUB OF THE AMERICAN ASSOCIATION FOR THE ADVANCEMENT OF SCIENCE

(Continued from page 198.)

Thursday, Aug. 16th —The Club reassembled at 3 30 p. m.   Papers by Mr. Clarence M. Weed on " The Parasites of the honey-suckle Sphinx, *Hemaris diffinis,* Boisd ," and on " The Hymenopterous Parasites of the Strawberry Leaf-roller, *Phoxopteris comptana,* Frol ," were read by the Secretary in his absence   Mr. H Osborn read an interesting paper on " The Food-habits of the Thripidæ '   Mr Smith gave an account of the collection of Mr D. Bruce, of Rockport, N. Y., which was chiefly made in Colorado ; it is especially remarkable for the long series of specimens of many species of Lepidoptera.   Among others he has *Chionobas bore* in great numbers from the Rocky Mountains, proving it to be distinct from *C. Semidea* of the White Mountains , also an immense series of *Colias eurytheme* in all its varieties, and numbers also of many species of Noctuidæ.

Friday, Aug. 17th —The Club met at 9 o'clock a. m.   A paper was read by Dr D S Kellicott, on *Hepialus argenteo maculatus,* which he succeeded in raising from larvæ obtained in Oswego County, N Y., it bred in the roots and stems of *Alnus incana* Mr Schwarz stated that he had taken the moth, near Marquette Lake Superior, on July 29th, this year Mr Smith considered it to be quite generally distributed, breeding in oak, willow and poplar. Mr H Osborn read a note on the occurrence of *Cicada rimosa* Say., in Iowa

Prof O. S Westcott, related the occurrence of a large gathering of butterflies about the carcass of a dead dog at Port Arthur, in June last , one hundred and ten specimens were counted, chiefly consisting of *D archippus* and some *L arthemis, Colias* and *Melitœa* In the same locality he captured, July 20 to 23 nineteen examples of *Melitœa* , of these one was *Nycteis*, and seventeen *Tharos*—eight of the form *Marcia*, and nine *Morpheus* He next gave an interesting account of the numbers of *Lachnosterna fusca* and *gibbosa* taken at Maywood, Ill., by means of a trap attached to a street-lamp, during the months of May and June, 1887 and 1888. He also gave a list of 1192 specimens belonging to 65 species captured in his trap on the night of June 13th, 1888 , of these 730 were *Agonoderus comma* and 204 *Lachnosterna gibbosa.*

Mr. Howard gave an account of some recent experiments made under Dr. Riley's direction at Washington, with kerosene emulsion as a remedy for white grubs, the larvæ of *Allorhina nitida* He stated that the grass had died over large areas of the affected lawn, and the soil was full of the grubs. The affected portion was treated with kerosene emulsion diluted fifteen times with water and applied with an ordinary watering-pot , the ground was then kept saturated for some days with ordinary water from a hose A month afterwards, on digging into the part treated, the grubs were found to have descended sixteen inches into the soil, and all had died. In the untreated parts the larvæ were all alive and only two or three inches below the surface There was no injurious effect upon the grass, even when the emulsion was only diluted half as much He considered that the experiment was entirely successful In the discussion that followed, it was evident that this remedy is much too expensive for adoption on a large scale, and could only be of practical use on a lawn or plot of land of special value Dr Peabody stated that Prof. Forbes had found the kerosene emulsion entirely successful against the common white-grub *(Lachnosterna)*, but as its application cost at the rate of about $100 per acre, it was far too expensive for ordinary purposes.

The Club met again at 3 p m   Mr Fletcher gave an account of his expeditions to Nepigon, Lake Superior, in search of the eggs of butterflies Very little is known, he stated, regarding the early stages of many of our diurnals , of even so common a species as *Pamphila cernes* they were unknown.   In 1885, Prof Macoun, of the Geological Survey of Canada, collected specimens at Nepigon of a new butterfly, which was named after him by Mr. W H. Edwards as *Chionobas Macounii*.   In 1886 and 1887, Mr Fletcher went to Nepigon in search of this insect, travelling about 1,500 miles on each occasion, but without success.   This year he went again, early in July, accompanied by Mr. S. H. Scudder, of Cambridge, Mass ; on the first day after their arrival they caught five males , the next day nine females were caught and caged ; from these they obtained about 250 eggs   The egg is larger than and quite different from that of *C. Jutta*, which has been found near Quebec, and bred by Mr Fyles.   Mr. Fletcher also obtained eggs of *Jutta* at Ottawa, and reared the larvæ from them ; the eggs were laid on July 1st, and hatched on the 16th , those of *Macounii* were laid on the 12th and hatched on the 27th   At Nepigon, he and Mr. Scudder obtained the eggs of 14 species out of 16 that they caged   He then gave a full and most interesting account of the methods of capturing, caging and treating butterflies in order to obtain their eggs, and mentioned that he had received very valuable information and aid from Mr. Scudder in the matter.   The simplicity of the apparatus employed deserves mention :   " Cages for all small species can be made in a few minutes by cutting off the top and bottom of a tomato can, and then fastening a piece of netting over one end, either by slipping an elastic band over it, or tying it with a piece of string   The female is then placed in this over a growing plant of the species that the larvæ are known to feed upon   These cages had answered well for all the skippers which feed on grass, and the small Argynnides.   For such species as lay their eggs on the foliage of shrubs or trees bags had to be tied over living branches, care being taken that the leaves were not crowded up, but that they should stand out freely, so that the female could lay, if such were her habit, upon either the upper or lower side, or on the edge of the leaves.   In this way eggs were obtained of *Nisoniades icelus* and *Papilio turnus*.   Another cage for insects which lay upon low plants, and which is easily constructed, is made by cutting two flexible twigs and bending them into the shape of two arches which are put one over the other at right angles with the ends pushed into the ground , over the pent-house thus formed a piece of gauze is placed, and the edges are kept down either with pegs or earth laid upon them   This kind was useful for larger insects than could be placed in the tomato cans. In these eggs of *C. Macounii, Colias eurytheme*, etc , had been secured." *(Entom · Americana* iv , 159) Mr. Fletcher then described the habits of a number of the species collected, referring especially to those already mentioned, and to *Pyrameis huntera, Pamphila hobomok, Mystic*, and *Cernes, Carterocephalus mandan, Colias interior, Argynnis Vialis, Myrina* and *Bellona, Nisoniades Persius, Fenesica Tarquinins*, etc   He also exhibited living larvæ of *C Mandan, P. hobomok* and *Mystic*, and living imagines of *C. eurytheme*, which had emerged since his arrival in Cleveland.   At the close of his address, Mr. Smith expressed the gratifica tion all present felt in listening to so lucid and interesting an account from which everyone would carry away many practical and valuable hints

The next paper was read by Mr. E A. Schwarz, of Washington, on " The Geographical Distribution of the Semi-tropical Floridian Coleopterous Fauna." It was followed by a discussion, in which nearly all present took part, as to what should be considered the limits of the North American Fauna, and what species should be included in the fauna of a particular region, reference being especially made to semi-tropical species that are from time to time found in the north.

The Club next proceeded to the election of officers for the ensuing year, and unanimously selected the following   President. James Fletcher, Ottawa, Ont ; Vice-President, L O. Howard, Washington, D C , Secretary-Treasurer, Dr D. S. Kellicott, Buffalo, N Y

Saturday, Aug. 18th —A most enjoyable excursion was made to Put-in-Bay by steamer on Lake Erie   There was a very large attendance of the members of the Association, including the Entomologists.   This pleasant feature of the proceedings gave the members a much better opportunity of becoming acquainted with each other than would otherwise have been the case   Arrangements were made for the excursionists to stay on shore for about an hour, and this time was made good use of by the members of the Club.   The insect of most interest was secured by Mr Westcott, who collected in large numbers by beating a small spruce-tree, a remarkable Hemipteron, identified by Prof Osborn as *Emisa longipes*. Many galls and parasitic fungi were also collected.   Among the butterflies noted were *Colias philodice, Pieris rapæ*, and what appeared strange to Canadian eyes at this time of the year, *Papilio turnus , P. asterias* and

Pyrameis cardui were also observed, and a few specimens of *Utetheisa bella* were captured. The party returned to Cleveland much delighted with their day's outing, and separated to meet next year in Toronto.

ARCTIIDÆ vs. NOCTUIDÆ.

BY JOHN B. SMITH, WASHINGTON, D. C.

Mr. Grote takes occasion in CAN. ENT. vol. xx., p. 168, to criticise my reference of *Cerathosia* to the *Arctiidæ*, contending that it is a *Noctuid*. He complains that I do not give " the reason *why* it belongs to the family." This I hasten to supply, and must beg Mr. Grote's pardon for having presumed him conversant with the characters separating the two families. All authorities give for the *Noctuidæ* a furcate dorsal or internal vein of primaries, while the costal vein of secondaries is from the root, sometimes united with the sub-costal a short distance from base.

In the *Arctiidæ* on the contrary, the dorsal vein of the primaries is simple, while the costal of secondaries is not free, but springs from the sub-costal, a variable distance from base.

In these essential characters, used in all systematic works, my genus is *Arctiid* and *Lithosiid*. The only difference between the *Arctiidæ* and *Lithosiidæ* is in the absence of ocelli in the latter family. Mr. Grote seems never to have seen an unspread specimen of *Cerathosia*, else the striking habital resemblance to *Lithosia* could not not have escaped him.

Mr. Grote has sent to Entom. Amer. a criticism of my genus in a different form, which I have answered more at length.

Some months since, I sent a paper on *Cydosia* and *Cerathosia*, which have considerable resemblance in clypeal structure, to the Proceedings U. S. Natl. Museum, and this when printed will show that my genus is not at all abnormal where I have placed it.

As I can hardly expect to convince Mr. Grote if the specimen itself failed, I have sent an example to Mr. H. B. Moeschler, of Germany, and requested his determination of family, for publicaiton.

It is scarcely worth while to deal with Mr. Grote's objections in detail. Not one or all of them, even were they *all* true, would militate against the *Arctiid* character of *Cerathosia*. I must confess that I consider the venation and habitus *Lithosiid* rather than *Arctiid*, and would prefer so to place it, even despite the presence of ocelli.

Lest Mr Grote consider me ignorant, I will say here that I am aware that there are some Noctuids which have the dorsal vein of primaries not distinctly furcate, and some where the costal of secondaries is united with the sub-costal a short distance from base, and thus appears to spring from it.

With this I leave *Cerathosia* to its fate. In my papers I have given *all* the characters, family and otherwise, and shall let each form his own judgment. It needs no more defence from me In fact, I feel as though I owed an apology for answering objections, not a single one of which is vital

Mr. Grote's characterizations in his series of papers on the *Bombycidæ* are thoroughly superficial, none of the essential characters being emphasized, while some of them are absolutely incorrect—his definition of the *Lithosiinæ* furnishes an example He says unqualifiedly, " No accessory cell on primaries." Now, Von Heineman shows that in some genera it is present, while as a matter of fact some species of *Lithosia* have the cell *(cephalica)*, while others have not. It is therefore not even a generic character in this group To point out all the misleading and inaccurate statements, would necessitate criticising almost every paragraph of Mr Grote's paper—a task I have neither time nor inclination for. In future I shall not reply to any criticisms Mr. Grote may make, save to admit their correctness where they are well founded.

Postcript.—Since sending in the above, I have heard from Mr. Moeschler in regard to the specimens sent him He writes me under date, Sept 28th. —"To-day I received the parcel containing the two moths I have examined them, and there is no doubt you are right. This species belongs to the *Arctiidæ*, as the costal nervule is not derived from the base of the hind wings, but from the discoidal cell; this characteristic separating the *Arctiidæ* and *Lithosiidæ* from the *Noctuidæ*, which have this nervule derived from the base of the wing, only a little connected with the fore edge of the cell. I do not doubt this species is an *Arctiid*, near allied to *Deiopeia* and *Emydia*."

Under date Sept. 30th, Mr. Moeschler again wrote me .—" I received *Entomologica Americana* No. 6 to-day, and it was of great interest to me to read yours and Mr. Grote's paper on *Cerathosia tricolor* Sm. If Mr. Grote had looked into Lederer's *Noctuinen Europa's* he could read, p. 2, ' sie (die *Noctuinen*) unterscheiden sich von den *Lithosiiden* (inclusive *Nola, Sarrothripa* u. *Nycteola,)* und *Arctiiden* durch die bei diesen aus der mitte oder zwei-drittel des vorderrandes der Mittelzelle entspringenden Rippe 8 der Hinterflügel.'

" Mr. Grote would have spared much pain to prove something not existing, by reasons which are not of any value, if he had remembered the only important characteristic separating the *Lithosiidæ* and *Arctiidæ* from the *Noctuidæ*. I am much surprised that so distinguished a writer as Mr. Grote can omit so important a characteristic ; but the systematic position of the genera of the so-called *Zygænidæ*, in his New Check List, is sufficient to prove that Mr. Grote's systematic views are sometimes more than singular.

" Seeing the specimens of *C. tricolor*, my first thought must be : that is a Genus very allied to *Deiopeia (Utetheisa)* and *Emydia*, and I should have been much surprised if an exact examination had given another result."

CORRESPONDENCE.

Dear Sir : In reference to my note on the use of Creolin, I found subsequently discolorations on the leaves which did not appear to be either rust or mildew, but possibly were the result of the Creolin mixture. It is, however, probable that in this disinfectant we have a useful aid against insects as it seems to be avoided by cockroaches and ants, and probably woodwork might be preserved by it in greenhouses. I wished merely to draw attention to Creolin, so that those interested might try it ; my own opportunities for doing so being very limited. The rose-bushes, of which I am very fond, seem on the whole no freer from insects in Europe than in America.　　　　　　　　　　A. R. GROTE.

ARZAMA OBLIQUATA.

Dear Sir : In regard to Mr. Brehme's query, I may mention that all the Arzama larvæ and chrysalids taken here have been found in similar situations, but in no instance has there been the slightest indication that they fed there. The impression made by my observations is :—That the caterpillars seek out their hibernacula in the fall, remain in that state during winter, and change to chrysalids with the first warm weather in spring   Caterpillars have been found yet imbedded in the winter's frost. In one instance I found one, in early spring, travelling about as if looking for a place to transform , it produced a *Diffusa*.   They have never been looked for here in the reeds ; as they grow almost entirely in the water, one would require the aid of a boat to make the investigation   When surveying the situation where I have found the Arzamas, I have often wondered how the caterpillars got from the reeds to the land.   The shallow part of our marsh where they might easily get ashore is invariably burned over in early spring by pike shooters for their own convenience.

J. ALSTON MOFFAT, Hamilton.

BOOK NOTICES.

AN INTRODUCTION TO ENTOMOLOGY, by PROFESSOR J. H. COMSTOCK, Cornell University, Ithaca, N.Y.   Published by the Author.   Part I —pp 234, 8 vo.   (Price $2.00).

The autumn of 1888 is certainly a notable one in the annals of North American Entomology, owing to the publication of so many important works   Last month we drew attention to Dr. Packard's excellent " Entomology for Beginners," and the issue of the first part of Mr. Scudder's grand work on the Butterflies of the Eastern States and Canada. We have now before us the first portion of another admirable work, which is intended to serve as a text-book for students, and to enable them " to acquire a thorough knowledge of the elementary principles of Entomology, and to classify insects by means of analytical keys similar to those used in Botany."   The first two chapters of the book treat of the characters and metamorphoses, and the anatomy of insects , the next discusses the Orders of the Hexapoda, to which the author very properly limits insects.   In this chapter he gives his reasons for [adopting *ten* orders, the number being made up of the seven generally accepted orders and the Thysanura, Pseudoneuroptera and Physopoda ; in adhering so closely to the old classification, he states that he has been greatly influenced by a desire to make his book as simple as possible, and " by the belief that an elementary text-book should follow rather than lead in matters of this kind," in which opinion we thoroughly concur.   The remainder of this part of the work treats of the Orders Thysanura, Pseudoneuroptera, Orthoptera, Physopoda, Hemiptera and Neuroptera. In each chapter is given a general account of the Order treated of, an analytical table of the Families, a descriptive account of each family with, in many cases, tabular keys of the genera, and illustrations of the commoner species. Future parts will complete the discussion of the Orders, and furnish chapters on the remedies for noxious insects, directions for collecting and preserving specimens, etc Judging from the portion before us, we have no hesitation in saying that the complete work will be a most valuable and admirable manual of Entomology , in clearness and simplicity of style, in excellence of illustration and in arrangement of matter, it leaves nothing to be desired. We must not omit to mention that the two hundred wood cuts are for the most part drawn and engraved by the author's wife, and are very good indeed; another excellent feature is the marking of the pronunciation of the accented syllables of technical words, which will no doubt in time help very much to a desirable uniformity in this respect.

C. J. S. B.

INSECT LIFE.—A monthly bulletin, published by the Entomologist and his Assistants in U. S. Department of Agriculture at Washington. Vol I.—Nos. 1 to 4 ; July to October, 1888.

This new periodical, " devoted to the economy and life-habits of insects, especially in their relations to agriculture," is a very welcome one indeed. The four parts, of thirty pages each, which have thus far appeared, are filled with matter of great interest to both the scientific and economic Entomologist. With so able and experienced a staff as that at Washington, presided over by Dr. Riley, and with Field Agents at widely distant points, this new magazine cannot fail to be most useful, and to do good work in the spread of valuable and timely information.

C. J. S. B

INSECTS FEIGNING DEATH.—We have received several more communications on this subject, but we do not think that any useful purpose can be served by their publication The question is purely one of opinion and definition, and cannot possibly be authoritatively settled in one point of view or another.

Mailed December 8th.

INDEX TO VOLUME XX.

Abbot, John, the Aurelian, 150, 230
Annual meeting Ent Club A. A A. S.,
    195, 232.
    "   "   Ent Soc , Ontario, 211.
Ants' nest beetles, 161.
Anthomyia raphani, parasite on, 133
Arachnida of Labrador, 141.
Arctiidæ vs Noctuidæ, 236.
Argynnis Atlantis, preparatory stages of, 1.
    "   Edwardsii,   "   "   3
    "   Hesperis,   "   "   67.
Arzama obliquata,   "   "   119,
    130, 180, 238.
Ashmead, W. H , articles by, 48, 55, 101,
    172, 202, 229.

Acolus borealis, n. sp., 50.
    " *Canadensis*, n. sp , 50.
Agrotis agilis, n sp., 128.
    " hospitalis, 129.
Allorhina nitida, 233.
Aneurhynchus mellipes, n sp., 52
Anozus siphonophoræ, n. sp , 104.
Anthocharis pima, n sp., 158.
Anthonomus quadrigibbus, 67
Aphodius rufipes, 9, 66.
Apion herculanum, 66, 120
Aprostocetus Americanus, n. sp., 106
    " *Canadensis*, n sp., 106
    " *granulatus*, n sp,, 105.
Asecodes albitarsis, n. sp., 103.
Astichus Arizonensis, n sp , 101

Bates, J. E , article by, 100
Bethune, C. J. S , articles by, 195, 211,
    217, 232, 239, 240
Beutenmuller, W., articles by, 15, 16, 57,
    134.
Bombycidæ, classification of, 166, 181, 221
Book notices, 60, 77, 117, 159, 217, 218,
    239, 240
Brehme, H. H., articles by 119, 180.
Butterflies of Ceylon, Moore, 117.
    "   Eastern U S and Canada,
    Scudder, 218.
    "   Japan, Pryer, 77
    "   Labrador, list of, 148.
    "   North America, Edwards, 60.
    "   rearing from eggs, 234.

Butterflies of South Africa, Trimen, 159.

Bembidium assimile, 61
    "   pusillus, 61
    "   undulatum, 61.
Bolina fasciolaris, 139
Botis erectalis, 15
    " magistralis, 15.
    " quinquelinealis, 179.
Brachycrepis, n. gen., 176
    " *tricarinatus*, n sp , 176
Brachynemurus, n gen , 34.
    " abdominalis, 57.
    " blandus, 73
    " *Carrizonus*, n. sp., 93.
    " longicaudus, 35
    " *longipalpis*, n. sp., 95.
    " nebulosus, 36.
    " *nigrilabris*, n sp , 72.
    " peregrinus, 59.
    " *Sackeni*, n. sp., 94.
    " versutus, 37.

Calverley's Sphingidæ, 80.
Can insects distinguish between red and
    yellow ? 176
Canmore, N. W. T., species collected at,
    90.
Captures in 1887, Moffat, 178
    " made between Winnipeg and Vic-
    toria, 89.
Catocala desperata, preparatory stages of, 28.
    " innubens,   "   " 170.
    " palæogama,   "   " 108.
    " relicta,   "   " 17.
Caulfield, F B., articles by, 79, 198.
Chalcid, a new species from Canada, 55.
    " genus Rileya, 191, 229.
Chalcideous tribe Chiropachides, 172.
Chalcididæ, new North American, 101.
Chionobas jutta, preparatory stages of, 131.
Citheronia, geographical distribution of, 76.
Clark, Howard L , article by, 17
Clover-root borer, 138
Cockerell, T. D. A., articles by, 86, 156,
    176, 178, 200, 201.
Coleoptera, catalogue of Myrmophilous,
    161.
    " natural history notes on, 61.

Coleoptera of Labrador, 142.
Colias Cæsonia, preparatory stages of, 21.
     "   extreme case of seasonal dimorph-
          ism in, 201.
     "   notes on the genus, 24.
Comstock's Introduction to Entomology,
          239.
Conopinæ, new South American genus of,
          10.
Cotton moth, the, 98.
Creolin, remedy for rose-aphis, 160, 238.

Callimorpha, 39, 79.
Caratomus leucophthalmus, n. sp., 55.
Celiptera bifasciata, 100.
Cerathosia tricolor, 168, 236.
Chiropachys colon, 175.
Chrysomela præcelsis, 66.
Closterocerus, cinctipennis, n. sp., 104.
Cucullia Hartmanni, n. sp., 69.

Danais archippus, observations on, 45, 84,
          136, 200, 226.
     "   "   parasite on, 133.
Datana Angusii, preparatory stages of, 135.
     "   contracta,   "   "   134.
     "   Drexelii,   "   "   57.
     "   integerrima, "   "   134.
     "   ministra,   "   "   16.
Death, knowledge of, in insects, 120, 179,
          199, 240.
Diadema misippus in Florida, 128.
Dimorphism in butterflies, 86, 201.

Dasyglenes n. gen , 174.
     "   *osmiæ*, n. sp., 174.
Dendrocharis flavicornis, 64.
Dendroleon obsoletum, 187.
     "   pantherinum, 185.
Dicerca asperata, 66.
     "   divaricata, 64.
     "   dubia, 64.
     "   lurida, 65.
     "   obscura, 65.
     "   prolongata, 64, 120, 178.
     "   spreta, 65.
Diludia brontes, 56, 112.
     "   leucophæata, 56.
Dinotus elongatus, n. sp., 175.

Edwards, Henry, articles by, 12, 111.
Edwards, W. H., articles by, 1, 3, 21, 41,
          67, 81, 84, 128, 140, 158.
Entomological Club, A. A. A. S., meeting
          of, 195, 232.

Entomological Society of Ontario meeting,
          211.
Entomology for beginners, Packard, 217.
Ectadius Canadensis, n. sp., 51.
Entedon albitarsis, n. sp., 102.
     "   *Arizonensis*, n. sp., 103.
     "   *Columbiana*, n. sp., 103.
Erebus odora, 56, 99, 113.
Euderus Columbiana, n. sp., 104.
Eumegaspilus Canadensis, n. sp., 49.
     "   *Ottawensis*, n. p., 49.

Fletcher J., article by, 218.
French, G. H., articles by, 28, 69, 108,
          170.
Fyles, T. W., article by, 131.

Gillette, C. P., article by, 133.
Grote, A. R., articles by, 38, 39, 74, 75,
          76, 79, 80, 98, 114, 120,
          128, 139, 154, 157, 160,
          166, 181, 221, 238.

Graphoderes cinereus, 62.
     "   fasciatocollis, 62.

Hagen, H. A., articles by, 34, 57, 72, 93,
          185, 204.
Hamilton, J., articles by, 6, 61, 120, 161,
          179.
Hemileuca, description of a new, 31.
Hessian fly an imported insect, 121.
Holland, W. J., articles by, 77, 89.
Howard, L. O., article by, 191.

Hadena Evelina, n. sp., 71.
     "   turbulenta, 136.
Harpalus caliginosus, 62.
     "   compar, 62.
     "   longicollis, 62.
     "   Pennsylvanicus, 62.
Hemileuca Californica, n. sp , 31.
Hepialus argenteo-maculatus, 232.
     "   auratus, 100.
Holcopelte Floridana, n. sp., 102.
     "   *Microgaster*, n. sp., 102.
     "   *Missouriensis*, n. sp., 101.
     "   *Popenoei*, n. sp., 101.
Hylastes trifolii, 138.
Hyperteles hylotomæ, n. sp., 105.

Insects feigning death, 120, 179, 199, 240.
Insect life, 240.

Introduction to Entomology, Comstock, 239
Ips, notes on, 198.

Ips, fasciatus, 198
" 4-signatus, 198

Japanese Butterflies, 77.

Kerosene emulsion for white-grubs, 233.
Kirby, W F., article by, 230.

Labrador, list of spiders, myriopods and insects of, 141.
Lepidoptera of Ceylon, Moore, 117
" Labrador, 145
Lepidopterous larvæ, description of, 15.
Lyman, H H., article by, 24.

Loxotropa, abrupta, 54
" *armata*, n sp , 53
" *Harringtoni*, n sp., 53
" *pezomachoides*, n sp , 53.
Lycæna piasus, 97

Marsh, W. D., article by, 45
Melitæas, two new species of, 81.
Moffat, J. A , articles by, 136, 139, 178, 238.
Morton, Miss E M , article by, 226
Moths new to our Fauna, 12, 56, 111.
Myrmeleonidæ, stray notes on, 34, 57, 72, 93, 185, 204.

Macrosila Hasdrubal, 13.
Megaspilidea minuta, n sp , 49
Megaspilus Harringtoni, n. sp., 48.
Melanophila longipes, 92
Melitæa Brucei, n. sp., 81.
" *Taylori*, n. sp., 82
" rubicunda, 83.
Meristhus cristatus, 64
Metaclisis erythropus, n sp , 51
Monelata hirticollis, n. sp , 54
Myrmeleon formicalynx, 206
" formicarius, 210
" immaculatus, 188
" mobilis, 204
" rusticus, 210.

Nanaimo, B C , Coleoptera, collected at, 91

Nathalis iole, orange spot in, 156
Nepigon, butterflies taken at, 212, 234
Noctuidæ, late papers on, 38
" some new, 69, 128
Notes, 40.

Neoclytus capræa, 66

Obituary, 140.
Orange spot in Nathalis iole, 156
Ornamentation, origin of, in Lepidoptera, 114
Orthesia, new species from California, 202

Omphale bicinctus, 103.
Orthesia Edwardsii, n. sp , 203
Orthosia hamifera, n sp , 130
Oxyporus 5-maculatus, 64

Packard, A S , article by, 141
" Entomology for beginners, 217
Paphia troglodyta, preparatory stages of 41
Phycitidæ, the diagnoses of N American, 74.
Proctotrupidæ, new genera and species of, 48
Protection and defence in insects, characters of, 154
Pryer, H , death of 140
Paphia glycerium, 43
Papilio turnus, 228
Paramesius clavipes, n sp , 53
Pentacantha Canadensis, n sp , 51
Philampelus typhon, 14, 56, 99, 112
Philhydrus fimbriatus, 63
Phurys vinculum, 100
Pleurotropis leucopus, n sp., 102
Prosacantha brachyptera, n sp , 50
Pseudosphinx obscurus, 13
" tetrio, 12, 56, 112.
Pteromalus archippi, 133

Rileya, the chalcid genus, 191 229
Riley, C V , article by, 121.
Rose-aphis remedy for, 160, 238
Ross s second voyage, German edition of, 157
Rileya splendens, 193

Scudder, S H., articles by, 117, 150, 159, 232
Smith, J. B , articles by, 56, 236

Sactogaster Howardii, n. sp., 52.
Saperda concolor, 8, 66.
    „   Fayi, 6.
Selenia kentaria, 75.
Stenosphenus notatus, 66.
Syntomeida epilaris, 14, 112.

Trimen's Butterflies of South Africa, 159.
Types, notes upon authors, 75, 197.

Thyreus Abbotii, 154.
Trichogramma acuminatum, n. sp., 107.
    „   *ceresarum*, n. sp., 107.
    „   nigrum, n. sp., 107.
Trogosita virescens, 92.
Tropidomyia, n. gen., 11.
    „   *bimaculata*, n. sp., 11.

Van Duzee, E. P., article by, 100.

Webster, F. M., article by, 199.
White, J., article by, 138.
Williston, S. W., article by, 10.
Wind-visiting moths, 98.
Wittfeld, Miss A. M., death of, 140.
Wright, W. G., articles by, 31, 97.

Xylomiges Fletcheri, n. sp., 130.

Yokohama naturalist, death of the, 140.

Zygota Americana, n. sp., 54.

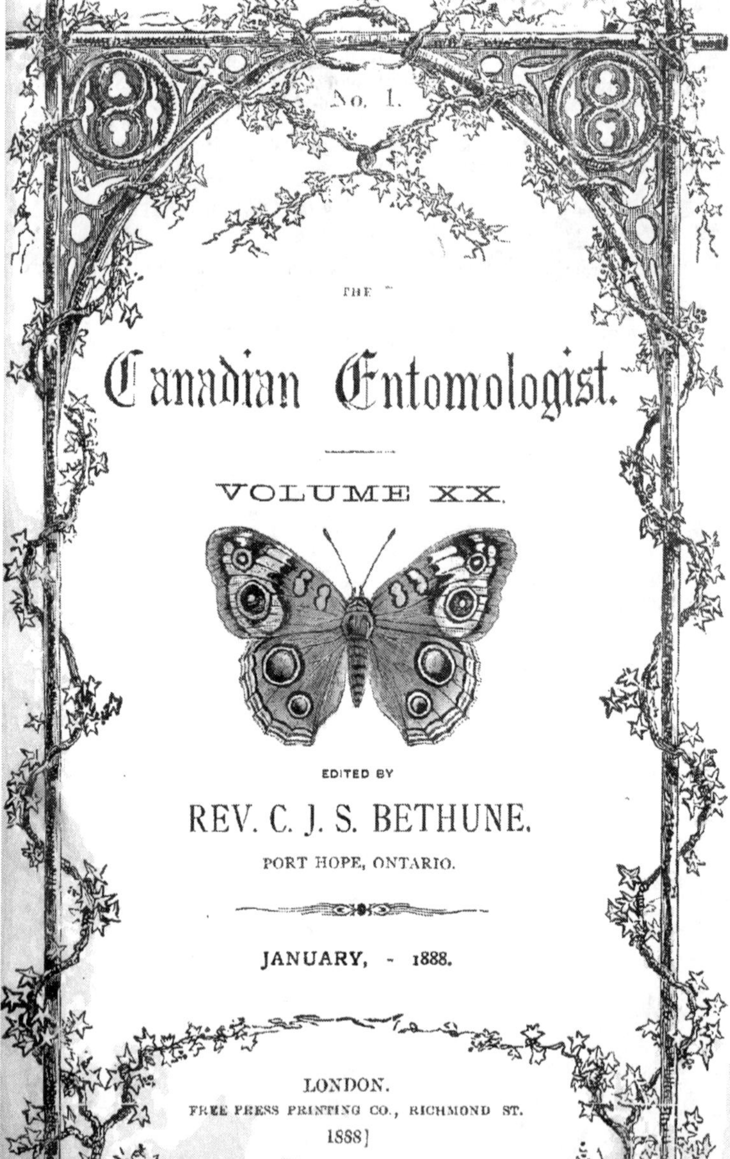

No. 1.

THE

Canadian Entomologist.

VOLUME XX.

EDITED BY

REV. C. J. S. BETHUNE.

PORT HOPE, ONTARIO.

JANUARY, - 1888.

LONDON.
FREE PRESS PRINTING CO., RICHMOND ST.
1888]

NOTICE TO SUBSCRIBERS.

Subscriptions to The Canadian Entomologist will be due Jan. 1.

FOR EXCHANGE.

Fine examples of J. B. SMITH'S new species, CERATHOSIA TRICOLOR, just described from Texas.

Send list of duplicates, and receive in return my list of desiderata, to

EDW. L. GRAEF,

40 Court St., Brooklyn, N. Y.

North American Lepidoptera.

THE HAWK MOTHS OF NORTH AMERICA: BY A. RADCLIFFE GROTE, A. M.

This work in pamphlet form will be sent on remitting price of One Dollar, by the publishers, Homeyer & Meyer, by the Author, Bremen, Germany; or address Rühle & Schlenker, Booksellers, Bremen.

BUTTERFLIES OF NORTH AMERICA.

Part 4, Vol. iii., will be ready for delivery 1st January.

Contents : COLIAS CHRYSOMELAS; ARGYNNIS NANSICA; COENONYMPHA CALIFORNIA.

Price $2.25.   3 plates.

Apply to HOUGHTON MIFFLIN & CO., Cambridge, Mass.

NOW READY.

A new and revised *List* of the *Coleoptera* of America north of Mexico, by Samuel Henshaw, assisted by Dr. George H. Horn.   Published by the American Entomological Society.   Edition limited.   **Price, $1.25.**   Price List of Entomological papers for sale, mailed on application.

E. T. CRESSON, TREASURER,

P. O. Box 1577, Philadelphia, Pa.

Published Fortnightly.   Annual Subscription, 6/6—Post free.

ENTOMOLOGISCHE NACHRICHTEN, Edited by Dr. F. KATTER.

A. DOSE, Putbus, Rügen, Germany.

The VI. year of Entomol. Nachr. gives, with the assistance of several illustrious Naturalists, a complete Review of Entomological Literature.

Back Volumes (1875 @ 2/, 1877 @ 3/, 1878 @ 5/, 1879 @ 6/6) may be had from the publisher post free; payment in advance.

THE AMERICAN NATURALIST.

A popular illustrated monthly magazine of Natural History, 8vo., 64 pages and illustrations in each number.   Subscription $4.00 a year.   Single numbers, 35 cents.

McCalla & Stavely, 237–9 Dock St., Phila., Pa.

North American Lepidoptera.

THE HAWK MOTHS OF NORTH AMERICA: By A. Radcliffe Grote, A. M.

This work in pamphlet form will be sent on remitting price of One Dollar, by the publishers, Homeyer & Meyer, or by the Author. Bremen, Germany.

FOR SALE.

A FINE COLLECTION OF INDIGENOUS AND EXOTIC BUTTERFLIES. Also, Handsome Walnut Cabinet.

For particulars address—

ROBT. BARTHOLOMEW, 1521 Poplar St., Philada., Pa.

Part 1, Volume 3. Butterflies of North America, will be ready for delivery Dec. 15th. Contents: Colias Eurydice, form Amorphæ, var. Bernardino ; Argynnis Nitocris, Argynnis Lais : 3 plates. Price $2.25. Apply to Houghton, Mifflin & Co., Cambridge, Mass.

SOUTH AMERICAN INSECTS.

Wishing to go to the Amazon Region in South America, to collect Lepidoptera and Coleoptera, but not having sufficient funds, I would like to get subscribers for Lepidoptera or Coleoptera in equal shares of $15.00 each. I intend to go first to Para, and after making collections in that vicinity, ascend the Amazon as far as Iquitos, making collections at towns on the River. Address,—

FRED. KNAB, P. O. Box 249, Chicopee, Mass.

References by permission : His Excellency, George D. Robinson, Governor Massachusetts ; Jos. E. Chase, Holyoke, Mass.

PATENTS

MUNN & CO., of the Scientific American, continue to act as Solicitors for Patents, Caveats, Trade Marks, Copyrights, for the United States, Canada, England, France, Germany, etc. Hand Book about Patents sent free. Thirty-seven years' experience.

Patents obtained through MUNN & CO. are noticed in the Scientific American, the largest, best, and most widely circulated scientific paper. $3.20 a year. Weekly. Splendid engravings and interesting information. Specimen copy of the Scientific American sent free. Address MUNN & CO., Scientific American Office, 261 Broadway, New York.

NOTICE TO ENTOMOLOGISTS.

Butterflies and Moths of North America.

Instructions for collecting, breeding, preparing, classifying, packing for shipment, etc.

A Complete Synonymical Catalogue of Macrolepidoptera, to which is added a FULL BIBLIOGRAPHY, a glossary of terms, a descriptive list of localities, and the food-plants of the larvæ. Diurnes. 8vo, pp. vi, 283. Sent by mail prepaid 1. receipt of $2.00 by

HERMAN STRECKER, Box 111 Reading P.O., Pennsylvania.

THE CANADIAN ENTOMOLOGIST.

Published by the Entomological Society of Ontario.

General Editor— REV. C. J. S. BETHUNE, Port Hope, Ont.

Editing Committee—WM. SAUNDERS, Ottawa; J. M. DENTON, E. BAYNES REED, London, Ont.; CAPT. GAMBLE GEDDES and DR. WHITE, Toronto.

ANNUAL FEES OF MEMBERSHIP.

For Ordinary Members $1 00
For Associate Members in the United States...................... 1 00
For Associate Members in England.............................4s. sterling
For Associate Members elsewhere................................$1 25

The Fees are payable in advance on the 1st of January in each year, and their payment entitles the members to a copy of all the Society's publications during the year, including the Illustrated Annual Report made to the Ontario Government.

Remittances and other business communications should be addressed to the Secretary-Treasurer of the Society, Mr. E. BAYNES REED, London, Ontario. All exchanges and articles for insertion, etc , to the General Editor.

Canadian Entomologist.—The back volumes 1 to 16 can be supplied at $1 each and cost of transportation.

Annual Reports.—Fifteen have been issued ; the back numbers can be supplied at 50c. each, excepting the three earlier ones, which are out of print.

ADVERTISING RATES.

For 1st insertion, per inch $1 00
For each subsequent insertion..... 50
No advertisement less than one inch.

SUPPLIES FOR SALE.

ENTOMOLOGICAL PINS.—Klaeger's, in packages of 500 each, $1 per 1000.
CORK —Double thickness, 30 cts. per square foot.
LIST OF CANADIAN COLEOPTERA.—Price 15 cts. each, embracing 55 families, 432 genera, and 1231 species (for labelling cabinets). Printed Numbers, in sheets, 1 to 2000, for labelling cabinets. Price 10 cts. each set.
These prices are exclusive of cost of transportation, and orders will please state whether the package is to be sent by mail or express.

Published Fortnightly. Annual Subscription, 6/6—Post free.

ENTOMOLOGISCHE NACHRICHTEN, Edited by Dr. F. KATTER
A. Dose, Putbus, Rügen, Germany.

The VI. year of Entomol. Nachr. gives, with the assistance of several illustrious Naturalists, a complete Review of Entomological Literature.

Back Volumes (1875 @ 2/, 1877 @ 3/, 1878 @ 5/, 1879 @ 6/6) may be had from the publisher post free; payment in advance.

THE AMERICAN NATURALIST.

A popular illustrated monthly magazine of Natural History, 8vo., 64 pages and illustrations in each number. Subscription $4.00 a year. Single numbers, 35 cents.

McCalla & Stavely, 237-9 Dock St., Phila., Pa.

Published Monthly, Price Sixpence.

THE ENTOMOLOGIST.
Edited by John T. Carrington, F. L. S.

AN ILLUSTRATED JOURNAL OF GENERAL ENTOMOLOGY.

SIMPKIN, MARSHALL & CO., Stationers' Hall Court,

No. 4.

THE

Canadian Entomologist.

VOLUME XX.

EDITED BY

REV. C. J. S. BETHUNE.

PORT HOPE, ONTARIO.

APRIL, - 1888.

LONDON.
FREE PRESS PRINTING CO., RICHMOND ST.
1888

JAPANESE LEPIDOPTERA.

Specimens of the Lepidoptera of Japan for sale.   Price, $10 (U. S. Currency, or Post Office Order) per hundred.   Cash with order.   Address—

REV. H. LOOMIS, Yokohama, Japan.

REV. W. J. HOLLAND, Ph. D., Pittsburgh, Pa., offers for sale or exchange a limited quantity of JAPANESE LEPIDOPTERA and COLEOPTERA of his own collecting.   Has also on hand a large mass of West African and Asiatic Lepidoptera, for sale or exchange.   Has been authorized to receive subscriptions in the United States and Canada for Mr. H. Pryer's magnificent work upon the Rhopalocera of Japan, to be issued in three parts, 4to., profusely illustrated with colored plates, at $4 a part.   Part I is now ready to deliver to subscribers.   3-12

CLASSIFICATION OF HYMENOPTERA.

The "Synopsis of the Families and Genera of the Hymenoptera of America north of Mexico," compiled by E. T. Cresson, and published by the American Entomological Society, containing synoptic tables of Families and Genera.   A full catalogue of the described species, and bibliography (350 pp. 8 vo.), is now ready **Price $3.00.**   Price List of Entomological Publications for sale, mailed on application.

Address,   E. T. CRESSON, Treasurer,

3-12   P. O. Box 1577, Philadelphia, Pa.

FOR EXCHANGE.

Fine examples of J. B. Smith's new species, Cerathosia tricolor, just described from Texas.

Send list of duplicates, and receive in return my list of desiderata, to

EDW. L. GRAEF,

40 Court St., Brooklyn, N. Y.

ENTOMOLOGICAL WORKS FOR SALE.

One complete set of Proceedings Entomological Society of Philadelphia, six volumes, almost new and substantially bound.   One set LeConte's Say, two volumes, colored plates.   Sets of Canadian Entomologist and American Naturalist.

Having received several letters, recently, inquiring if back numbers or full sets of FIELD and FOREST were still to be obtained, I will state that the undersigned has a few complete sets on hand, unsold, the three volumes of which will be furnished in paper, postpaid, at $3.25.   I have also a very few separate back numbers.   The Magazine contains considerable entomological matter and descriptions from Edwards and others   Address—

CHARLES RICHARDS DODGE, Box 1362, Boston, Mass.

EXCHANGE.

Under this heading two lines will be inserted for 25 cts.; additional matter, 10 cts. per line.

Duplicates for Exchange.—Cocoons and Pupæ of Eacles imperialis, Actias luna, Hyperchiria io, Callosamia angulifera (nec Cynthia), Smerinthus excæcatus, and many others, beside set specimens.   Lists exchanged.   Miss Emily L. Morton, Newburgh, New York, Box 228.

Orthoptera Wanted.—I am especially interested in the study of the Orthoptera, and wish to obtain, either by exchange or purchase, perfect specimens of these insects from all parts.   North American and West Indian material preferred.   Persons having specimens for sale or exchange will please correspond with me.   Lawrence Bruner, West Point, Cuming Co., Nebraska, U. S. A.

THE CANADIAN ENTOMOLOGIST.

Published by the Entomological Society of Ontario.

General Editor—REV. C. J. S. BETHUNE, Port Hope, Ont.
Editing Committee—J. FLETCHER, Ottawa ; H. H. LYMAN, Montreal ;
REV. T. W. FYLES, South Quebec ; J. H. BOWMAN, London.

ANNUAL FEES OF MEMBERSHIP.

For Ordinary Members $1 00
For Associate Members in the United States....................... 1 00
For Associate Members in England and elsewhere.... .... 1 25

The Fees are payable in advance on the 1st of January in each year, and their payment entitles the members to a copy of all the Society's publications during the year, including the Illustrated Annual Report made to the Ontario Government.

Remittances may be made in the form of Express Order, P. O. Order, Canadian, U. S. or English Stamps. Cheques on local banks not received, unless 25c. is added for collecting.

J. A. BALKWILL, Treasurer.

All remittances, business communications and exchanges should be addressed to
ENTOMOLOGICAL SOCIETY OF ONTARIO,
Victoria Hall, London, Ont.

All manuscript for publication, books for review, etc., should be sent to the General Editor, Port Hope, Ont.

ADVERTISING RATES.
Payable Strictly in Advance.

For each insertion, per inch ....$ 50
One inch per year...... .... 4 00
Half page,   '' 10 00
Whole ''   '' 15 00

Canadian Entomologist.—The back volumes 1 to 24 can be supplied at $1 each and cost of transportation (postage 3 cts. a volume to Canada and United States, and registration fee 5c. on each package of six volumes or less). Single copies, 10c. each.

Annual Reports.—1870 to 1872 inclusive are out of print ; later numbers can be supplied at 50 cents each, and 2 cts. postage to Canada and United States.

SUPPLIES FOR SALE.

ENTOMOLOGICAL PINS.—Nos. 00 to 5 inclusive, in packages of 500 each; Nos. 6, in packages of 250 $1 per 1000. Postage 3 cts. per 500, to Canada and United States, and registration fee 5c.

CORK.—¼ inch, 25 cts. per square foot; postage 5 cts ; ⅛ inch, 15 cts. per square foot ; postage 3 cts. a foot to Canada and United States, and registration fee 5c.

LIST OF LABELS FOR CANADIAN COLEOPTERA FOR CABINET USE.—This list is based upon Henshaw's List of 1885, and the supplement, 1887, and has a synonymical list connecting by number the names of the old list (after Crotch) to those of the new, in such cases as the change is too great to allow of the ready recognition of the new name. These lists will be supplied to members at 25c. per set of 26 sheets, post-paid.   Address,

ENTOMOLOGICAL SOCIETY OF ONTARIO,

No. 5.

THE

Canadian Entomologist.

VOLUME XX.

EDITED BY

REV. C. J. S. BETHUNE.

PORT HOPE, ONTARIO.

MAY, - 1888.

LONDON.
FREE PRESS PRINTING CO., RICHMOND ST.
1888

JAPANESE LEPIDOPTERA.

Specimens of the Lepidoptera of Japan for sale.   Price, $10 (U. S. Currency, or Post Office Order) per hundred.   Cash with order.   Address——

REV. H. LOOMIS, Yokohama, Japan.

REV. W. J. HOLLAND, Ph. D., Pittsburgh, Pa., offers for sale or exchange a limited quantity of JAPANESE LEPIDOPTERA and COLEOPTERA of his own collecting.   Has also on hand a large mass of West African and Asiatic Lepidoptera, for sale or exchange.   Has been authorized to receive subscriptions in the United States and Canada for Mr. H. Pryer's magnificent work upon the Rhopalocera of Japan, to be issued in three parts, 4to., profusely illustrated with colored plates, at $4 a part.   Part I is now ready to deliver to subscribers.   3-12

CLASSIFICATION OF HYMENOPTERA.

The "Synopsis of the Families and Genera of the Hymenoptera of America north of Mexico," compiled by E. T. Cresson, and published by the American Entomological Society, containing synoptic tables of Families and Genera.   A full catalogue of the described species, and bibliography (350 pp. 8 vo.), is now ready.   **Price $3.00.**   Price List of Entomological Publications for sale, mailed on application.

Address,   E. T. CRESSON, Treasurer,

3-12   P. O. Box 1577, Philadelphia, Pa.

FOR EXCHANGE.

Fine examples of J. B. Smith's new species, Cerathosia tricolor, just described from Texas.

Send list of duplicates, and receive in return my list of desiderata, to

EDW. L. GRAEF,

40 Court St., Brooklyn, N. Y.

COLLECTING BOTTLES WITHOUT A NECK.

Every Collecting Entomologist needs them.   Endorsed by prominent members of the Entomological Society of Ontario.   Set of 5 bottles witout Cyanide, 40c.; with Cyanide, 60c.   Send for a sample set by express.   Smallest size by mail as sample 12c., postage paid.

W. E. SAUNDERS & CO., London, Ontario.

EXCHANGE.

Under this heading two lines will be inserted for 25 cts.: additional matter, 10 cts. per line.

Orthoptera Wanted.—I am especially interested in the study of the Orthoptera, and wish to obtain, either by exchange or purchase, perfect specimens of these insects from all parts.   North American and West Indian material preferred.   Persons having specimens for sale or exchange will please correspond with me.   Lawrence Bruner, West Point, Cuming Co., Nebraska, U. S. A.

THE CANADIAN ENTOMOLOGIST.

Published by the Entomological Society of Ontario.

General Editor—REV. C. J. S. BETHUNE, Port Hope, Ont.
Editing Committee—WM. SAUNDERS, Ottawa ; J. M. DENTON, London ;
CAPT. GAMBLE GEDDES and DR. BRODIE, Toronto.

ANNUAL FEES OF MEMBERSHIP.

For Ordinary Members $1 00
For Associate Members in the United States........................ 1 00
For Associate Members in England..............................4s. sterling
For Associate Members elsewhere...............................$1 25

The Fees are payable in advance on the 1st of January in each year, and their payment entitles the members to a copy of all the Society's publications during the year, including the Illustrated Annual Report made to the Ontario Government.

Remittances may be made in the form of Express Order, Postal Note, Canadian, U. S. or English Stamps, P. O. Order or draft on New York, but cheques on local banks will not be received.

All remittances and other business communications should be addressed to the Secretary-Treasurer of the Society, W. E. SAUNDERS, 240 Central Ave, London, Ontario.   Send all manuscript for publication to the General Editor.

Canadian Entomologist.—The back volumes 1 to 19 can be supplied at $1 each and cost of transportation (postage 3 cts. a volume to Canada and United States).

Annual Reports.—1870 to 1873 inclusive are out of print ; later numbers can be supplied at 50 cents each, and 2 cts. postage to Canada and United States.

ADVERTISING RATES.
Payable Strictly in Advance.

For each insertion, per inch ....$ 50
One inch per year......   ....   4 00
Half page,   " 10 00
Whole "   " 15 00
Exchange notices of 2 lines, each insertion......................   25
Additional matter in exchange notices, per line..................   5

SUPPLIES FOR SALE.

ENTOMOLOGICAL PINS.—Nos. 00 to 5 inclusive, in packages of 500 each; Nos. 6, in packages of 250 $1 per 1000.   Postage 6 cts. per 1000, and every fraction of 1000, to Canada and United States.

CORK.—¼ inch, 30 cts. per square foot ; postage 6 cts ; ⅛ inch, 18 cts. per square foot ; postage 6 cts. for 20 inches, and every fraction of 20 inches, to Canada and United States.

LIST OF CANADIAN COLEOPTERA.—Price 15 cts. each, embracing 55 families, 432 genera, and 1231 species (for labelling cabinets). Printed Numbers, in sheets, 1 to 2000, for labelling cabinets. Price 10 cts. each set.   Postage extra.

No. 6.

THE

Canadian Entomologist.

VOLUME XX.

EDITED BY

REV. C. J. S. BETHUNE.

PORT HOPE, ONTARIO.

JUNE, - 1888.

LONDON.
FREE PRESS PRINTING CO., RICHMOND ST.
1888

JAPANESE LEPIDOPTERA.

Specimens of the Lepidoptera of Japan for sale.   Price, $10 (U. S. Currency, or Post Office Order) per hundred.   Cash with order.   Address——   .
REV. H. LOOMIS, Yokohama, Japan.

PAMPHILA and CATOCALA.
The undersigned will pay good price, either in cash or exchange, for perfect specimens of Pamphila and Catocala.

PHILIP LAURENT, 621 Marshall St., Philadelphia, Penn.

REV. W. J. HOLLAND, Ph. D., Pittsburgh, Pa., offers for sale or exchange a limited quantity of JAPANESE LEPIDOPTERA and COLEOPTERA of his own collecting.   Has also on hand a large mass of West African and Asiatic Lepidoptera, for sale or exchange.   Has been authorized to receive subscriptions in the United States and Canada for Mr. H. Pryer's magnificent work upon the Rhopalocera of Japan, to be issued in three parts, 4to., profusely illustrated with colored plates, at $4 a part.   Part I is now ready to deliver to subscribers.   3-12

CLASSIFICATION OF HYMENOPTERA.

The "Synopsis of the Families and Genera of the Hymenoptera of America north of Mexico," compiled by E. T. Cresson, and published by the American Entomological Society, containing synoptic tables of Families and Genera.   A full catalogue of the described species, and bibliography (350 pp. 8 vo.), is now ready. **Price $3.00.**   Price List of Entomological Publications for sale, mailed on application.

Address,   E. T. CRESSON, Treasurer,
3-12   P. O. Box 1577, Philadelphia, Pa.

FOR EXCHANGE.

Fine examples of J. B. Smith's new species, Cerathosia tricolor, just described from Texas.

Send list of duplicates, and receive in return my list of desiderata, to
EDW. L. GRAEF,

40 Court St., Brooklyn, N. Y.

BUTTERFLIES OF NORTH AMERICA.
Part 5, Vol. iii., will be ready for delivery 1st June.
Contents : Melitæa Rubicunda ; Debis Portlandia ; Erebia Magdalena, E. Haydenii. Price, $2.25 : 3 plates.
Vol. 1, bound, $35 ; Vol. 2, $40.

Apply to   HOUGHTON, MIFFLIN & CO.,

Cambridge, Mass

EXCHANGE.

Under this heading two lines will be inserted for 25 cts.; additional matter, 5 cts. per line.

ORTHOPTERA WANTED.—I am especially interested in the study of the Orthoptera, and wish to obtain, either by exchange or purchase, perfect specimens of these insects from all parts. North American and West Indian material preferred. Persons having specimens for sale or exchange will please correspond with me. LAWRENCE BRUNER, West Point, Cuming Co., Nebraska, U. S. A.

THE CANADIAN ENTOMOLOGIST.

Published by the Entomological Society of Ontario.

General Editor—REV. C. J. S. BETHUNE, Port Hope, Ont.
Editing Committee—WM. SAUNDERS, Ottawa ; J. M. DENTON, London ;
CAPT. GAMBLE GEDDES and DR. BRODIE, Toronto

ANNUAL FEES OF MEMBERSHIP.

For Ordinary Members $1 00
For Associate Members in the United States...................... 1 00
For Associate Members in England.........................4s. sterling
For Associate Members elsewhere.............................$1 25

The Fees are payable in advance on the 1st of January in each year, and their payment entitles the members to a copy of all the Society's publications during the year, including the Illustrated Annual Report made to the Ontario Government.

Remittances may be made in the form of Express Order, Postal Note, Canadian, U. S. or English Stamps, P. O. Order or draft on New York, but cheques on local banks will not be received.

All remittances and other business communications should be addressed to the Secretary-Treasurer of the Society, W. E. SAUNDERS, 240 Central Ave, London, Ontario. Send all manuscript for publication to the General Editor.

Canadian Entomologist.—The back volumes 1 to 19 can be supplied at $1 each and cost of transportation.

Annual Reports.—1870 to 1873 inclusive are out of print ; later numbers can be supplied at 50 cents each.

ADVERTISING RATES.
Payable Strictly in Advance.

For each insertion, per inch ....$ 50
One inch per year......   ....   4 00
Half page,   " 10 00
Whole "   " 15 00
Exchange notices of 2 lines, each insertion...   25
Additional matter in exchange notices, per line.....................   5

SUPPLIES FOR SALE.

ENTOMOLOGICAL PINS.—Nos. 00 to 4 inclusive, in packages of 500 each; Nos. 5 and 6, in packages of 250 each, $1 per 1000. Postage extra. (New lot just received ; in all sizes.)

CORK —Double thickness, 30 cts. per square foot. Postage extra.

LIST OF CANADIAN COLEOPTERA.—Price 15 cts. each, embracing 55 families, 432 genera, and 1231 species (for labelling cabinets). Printed Numbers, in sheets, 1 to 2000, for labelling cabinets.

No. 7.

THE

Canadian Entomologist.

VOLUME XX.

EDITED BY

REV. C. J. S. BETHUNE.

PORT HOPE, ONTARIO.

JULY, - 1888.

LONDON.
FREE PRESS PRINTING CO , RICHMOND ST.
1888

JAPANESE LEPIDOPTERA.

Specimens of the Lepidoptera of Japan for sale. Price, $10 (U. S. Currency, or Post Office Order) per hundred. Cash with order. Address—

REV. H. LOOMIS, Yokohama, Japan.

PAMPHILA and CATOCALA.

The undersigned will pay good price, either in cash or exchange, for perfect specimens of Pamphila and Catocala.

PHILIP LAURENT, 621 Marshall St., Philadelphia, Penn.

REV. W. J. HOLLAND, Ph. D., Pittsburgh, Pa., offers for sale or exchange a limited quantity of JAPANESE LEPIDOPTERA and COLEOPTERA of his own collecting. Has also on hand a large mass of West African and Asiatic Lepidoptera, for sale or exchange. Has been authorized to receive subscriptions in the United States and Canada for Mr. H. Pryer's magnificent work upon the Rhopalocera of Japan, to be issued in three parts, 4to., profusely illustrated with colored plates, at $4 a part. Part I is now ready to deliver to subscribers.   3-12

FOR SALE.

TRANSACTIONS OF THE AMERICAN ENTOMOLOGICAL SOCIETY.—Vols. i. to x.; the first three bound. Price, $40.00. The early volumes are scarce.

ENTOMOLOGISTS' MONTHLY MAGAZINE.—Vols. i. to xxiii., except ii. and iii.; up to xvi. bound. The early volumes of this magazine are not to be had, having long been out of print. Vol. i. was from Glover's library. Price, $50.00.

BOISDUVAL AND GUENEE'S SPECIES GENERALE, ETC.—Eight Vols., half mor., in good condition. Price, $40.00.   WM. H. EDWARDS, Coalburgh, W. Va.

FOR EXCHANGE.

Fine examples of J. B. SMITH'S new species, CERATHOSIA TRICOLOR, just described from Texas.

Send list of duplicates, and receive in return my list of desiderata, to

EDW. L. GRAEF,

40 Court St., Brooklyn, N. Y.

BUTTERFLIES OF NORTH AMERICA.

Part 5, Vol. iii., will be ready for delivery 1st June.

Contents : Melitæa Rubicunda ; Debis Portlandia ; Erebia Magdalena, E. Haydenii. Price, $2.25 : 3 plates.

Vol. 1, bound, $35 ; Vol. 2, $40.

Apply to   HOUGHTON, MIFFLIN & CO.,

Cambridge, Mass

EXCHANGE.

Under this heading two lines will be inserted for 25 cts.; additional matter, 5 cts. per line.

ORTHOPTERA WANTED.—I am especially interested in the study of the Orthoptera, and wish to obtain, either by exchange or purchase, perfect specimens of these insects from all parts. North American and West Indian material preferred. Persons having specimens for sale or exchange will please correspond with me. LAWRENCE BRUNER, West Point, Cuming Co., Nebraska, U. S. A.

THE

Canadian Entomologist.

VOLUME XX.

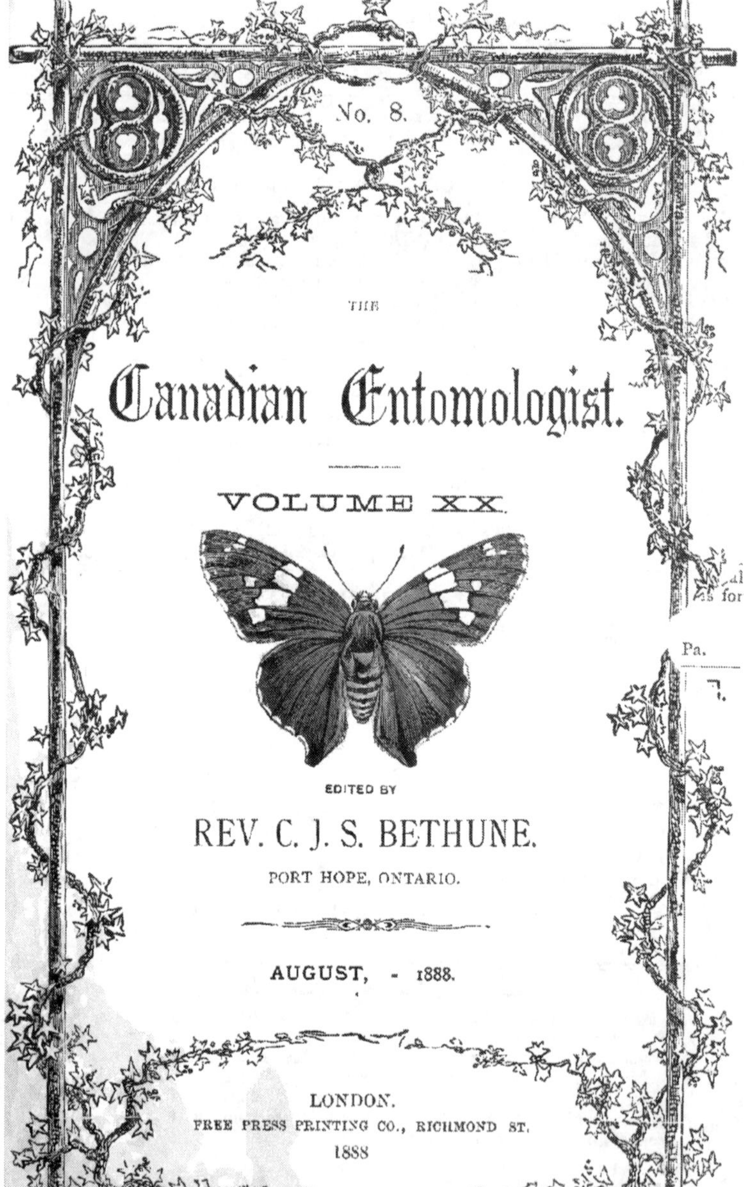

EDITED BY

REV. C. J. S. BETHUNE.

PORT HOPE, ONTARIO.

AUGUST, - 1888.

LONDON.
FREE PRESS PRINTING CO., RICHMOND ST.
1888

JAPANESE LEPIDOPTERA.

Specimens of the Lepidoptera of Japan for sale.   Price, $10 (U. S. Currency, or Post Office Order) per hundred.   Cash with order.   Address—

REV. H. LOOMIS, Yokohama, Japan.

PAMPHILA and CATOCALA.

The undersigned will pay good price, either in cash or exchange, for perfect specimens of Pamphila and Catocala.

PHILIP LAURENT, 621 Marshall St., Philadelphia, Penn.

REV. W. J. HOLLAND, Ph. D., Pittsburgh, Pa., offers for sale or exchange a limited quantity of JAPANESE LEPIDOPTERA and COLEOPTERA of his own collecting. Has also on hand a large mass of West African and Asiatic Lepidoptera, for sale or exchange. Has been authorized to receive subscriptions in the United States and Canada for Mr. H. Pryer's magnificent work upon the Rhopalocera of Japan, to be issued in three parts, 4to., profusely illustrated with colored plates, at $4 a part.   Part I is now ready to deliver to subscribers.   3-12

FOR SALE.

Transactions of the American Entomological Society.—Vols. i. to x.; the first three bound.   Price, $40.00.   The early volumes are scarce.

Entomologists' Monthly Magazine.—Vols. i. to xxiii., except ii. and iii.; up xvi. bound.   The early volumes of this magazine are not to be had, having long been in good print.   Vol. i. was from Glover's library.   Price, $50.00.

Isduval and Guenee's Species Generale, Etc.—Eight Vols., half mor., condition.   Price, $40.00.   WM. H. EDWARDS, Coalburgh, W. Va.

BUTTERFLIES OF NORTH AMERICA.

Part 5, Vol. iii., will be ready for delivery 1st June.

Contents: Melitæa Rubicunda ; Debis Portlandia ; Erebia Magdalena, E. Haydenii.   Price, $2.25 : 3 plates.

Vol. 1, bound, $35 ;   Vol. 2, $40.

Apply to   HOUGHTON, MIFFLIN & CO.,

Cambridge, Mass

EXCHANGE.

Under this heading two lines will be inserted for 25 cts.; additional matter, 5 cts. per line.

Orthoptera Wanted.—I am especially interested in the study of the Orthoptera, and wish to obtain, either by exchange or purchase, perfect specimens of these insects from all parts.   North American and West Indian material preferred.   Persons having specimens for sale or exchange will please correspond with me. Lawrence Bruner, West Point, Cuming Co., Nebraska, U. S. A.

THE CANADIAN ENTOMOLOGIST.

Published by the Entomological Society of Ontario.

General Editor—REV. C. J. S. BETHUNE, Port Hope, Ont.
Editing Committee—WM. SAUNDERS, Ottawa ; J. M. DENTON, London ;
CAPT. GAMBLE GEDDES and DR. BRODIE. Toronto.

ANNUAL FEES OF MEMBERSHIP.

For Ordinary Members...$1 oo
For Associate Members in the United States.........................1 oo
For Associate Members in England............................4s. sterling
For Associate Members elsewhere...............................$1 25

The Fees are payable in advance on the 1st of January in each year, and their payment entitles the members to a copy of all the Society's publications during the year, including the Illustrated Annual Report made to the Ontario Government.

Remittances may be made in the form of Express Order, Postal Note, Canadian, U. S. or English Stamps, P. O. Order or draft on New York, but cheques on local banks will not be received.

All remittances and other business communications should be addressed to the Secretary-Treasurer of the Society, W. E. SAUNDERS, 240 Central Ave, London, Ontario. Send all manuscript for publication to the General Editor.

Canadian Entomologist.—The back volumes 1 to 19 can be supplied at $1 each and cost of transportation (postage 3 cts. a volume to Canada and United States).

Annual Reports.—1870 to 1873 inclusive are out of print ; later numbers can be supplied at 50 cents each, and 2 cts. postage to Canada and United States.

ADVERTISING RATES.
Payable Strictly in Advance.

For each insertion, per inch ....$ 50
One inch per year......... .... 4 oo
Half page,   "   .... 10 oo
Whole "   "   .... 15 oo
Exchange notices of 2 lines, each insertion...   25
Additional matter in exchange notices, per line........................   5

SUPPLIES FOR SALE.

ENTOMOLOGICAL PINS.—Nos. oo to 5 inclusive, in packages of 500 each; Nos. 6, in packages of 250 $1 per 1000. Postage 6 cts. per 1000, and every fraction of 1000, to Canada and United States.

CORK.—¼ inch, 30 cts. per square foot ; postage 6 cts ; ⅛ inch, 18 cts. per square foot ; postage 6 cts. for 20 inches, and every fraction of 20 inches, to Canada and United States.

LIST OF CANADIAN COLEOPTERA.—Price 15 cts. each, embracing 55 families, 432 genera, and 1231 species (for labelling cabinets). Printed Numbers, in sheets, 1 to 2000, for labelling cabinets.

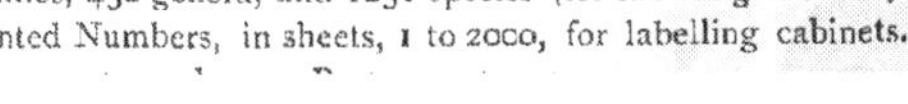

THE

Canadian Entomologist.

VOLUME XX.

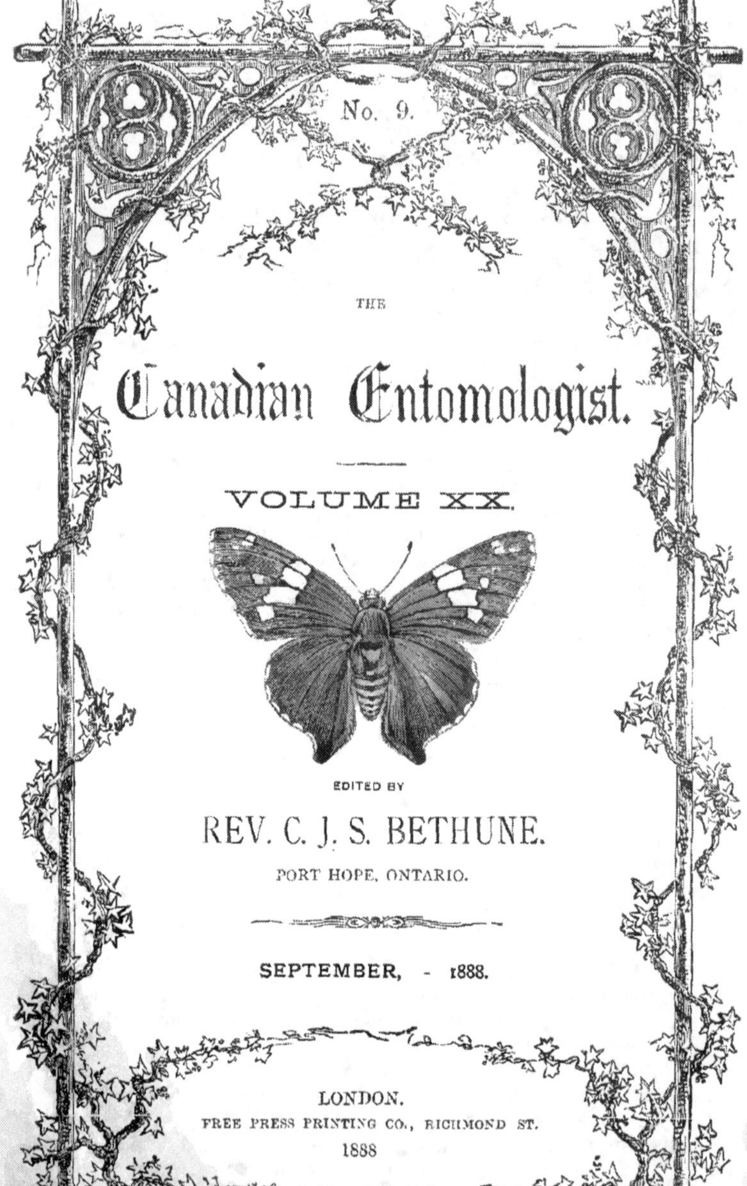

EDITED BY

REV. C. J. S. BETHUNE.

PORT HOPE, ONTARIO.

SEPTEMBER, - 1888.

LONDON.
FREE PRESS PRINTING CO., RICHMOND ST.
1888

JAPANESE LEPIDOPTERA.

Specimens of the Lepidoptera of Japan for sale.   Price, $10 (U. S. Currency, or Post Office Order) per hundred.   Cash with order.   Address—

REV. H. LOOMIS, Yokohama, Japan.

PAMPHILA and CATOCALA.

The undersigned will pay good price, either in cash or exchange, for perfect specimens of Pamphila and Catocala.

PHILIP LAURENT, 621 Marshall St., Philadelphia, Penn.

REV. W. J. HOLLAND, Ph. D., Pittsburgh, Pa., offers for sale or exchange a limited quantity of JAPANESE LEPIDOPTERA and COLEOPTERA of his own collecting.   Has also on hand a large mass of West African and Asiatic Lepidoptera, for sale or exchange.   Has been authorized to receive subscriptions in the United States and Canada for Mr. H. Pryer's magnificent work upon the Rhopalocera of Japan, to be issued in three parts, 4to., profusely illustrated with colored plates, at $4 a part.   Part I is now ready to deliver to subscribers.   3-12

FOR SALE.

TRANSACTIONS OF THE AMERICAN ENTOMOLOGICAL SOCIETY.—Vols. i. to x.; the first three bound.   Price, $40.co.   The early volumes are scarce.

ENTOMOLOGISTS' MONTHLY MAGAZINE.—Vols. i. to xxiii., except ii. and iii.; up to xvi. bound.   The early volumes of this magazine are not to be had, having long been out of print.   Vol. i. was from Glover's library.   Price, $50.00.

BOISDUVAL AND GUENEE'S SPECIES GENERALE, ETC.—Eight Vols., half mor., in good condition.   Price, $40.00.   WM. H. EDWARDS, Coalburgh, W. Va.

BUTTERFLIES OF NORTH AMERICA.

Part 5, Vol. iii., will be ready for delivery 1st June.

Contents :   Melitæa Rubicunda ; Debis Portlandia ; Erebia Magdalena, E. Haydenii.   Price, $2.25 : 3 plates.

Vol. 1, bound, $35 ;   Vol. 2, $40.

Apply to   HOUGHTON, MIFFLIN & CO.,

Cambridge, Mass

EXCHANGE.

Under this heading two lines will be inserted for 25 cts.; additional matter, 5 cts. per line.

ORTHOPTERA WANTED.—I am especially interested in the study of the Orthoptera, and wish to obtain, either by exchange or purchase, perfect specimens of these insects from all parts.   North American and West Indian material preferred.   Persons having specimens for sale or exchange will please correspond with me.   LAWRENCE BRUNER, West Point, Cuming Co., Nebraska, U. S. A.

THE CANADIAN ENTOMOLOGIST.

Published by the Entomological Society of Ontario.

General Editor—REV. C. J. S. BETHUNE, Port Hope, Ont.
Editing Committee—J. FLETCHER, Ottawa; H. H. LYMAN, Montreal;
REV. T. W. FYLES, South Quebec; J. H. BOWMAN, London.

ANNUAL FEES OF MEMBERSHIP.

For Ordinary Members $1 00
For Associate Members in the United States...................... 1 00
For Associate Members in England and elsewhere.................. 1 25

The Fees are payable in advance on the 1st of January in each year, and their payment entitles the members to a copy of all the Society's publications during the year, including the Illustrated Annual Report made to the Ontario Government.

Remittances may be made in the form of Express Order, P. O. Order, Canadian, U. S. or English Stamps. Cheques on local banks not received, unless 25c. is added for collecting.

J. A. BALKWILL, Treasurer.

All remittances, business communications and exchanges should be addressed to

ENTOMOLOGICAL SOCIETY OF ONTARIO,
Victoria Hall, London, Ont.

All manuscript for publication, books for review, etc., should be sent to the General Editor, Port Hope, Ont.

ADVERTISING RATES.
Payable Strictly in Advance.

For each insertion, per inch ....$ 50
One inch per year...................   .... 4 00
Half page,   " 10 00
Whole "   " 15 00

Canadian Entomologist.—The back volumes 1 to 24 can be supplied at $1 each and cost of transportation (postage 3 cts. a volume to Canada and United States, and registration fee 5c. on each package of six volumes or less). Single copies, 10c. each.

Annual Reports.—1870 to 1872 inclusive are out of print; later numbers can be supplied at 50 cents each, and 2 cts. postage to Canada and United States.

SUPPLIES FOR SALE.

ENTOMOLOGICAL PINS.—Nos. 00 to 5 inclusive, in packages of 500 each; Nos. 6, in packages of 250 $1 per 1000. Postage 3 cts. per 500, to Canada and United States, and registration fee 5c.

CORK.—¼ inch, 25 cts. per square foot; postage 5 cts; ⅛ inch, 15 cts. per square foot; postage 3 cts. a foot to Canada and United States, and registration fee 5c.

LIST OF LABELS FOR CANADIAN COLEOPTERA FOR CABINET USE.—This list is based upon Henshaw's List of 1885, and the supplement, 1887, and has a synonymical list connecting by number the names of the old list (after Crotch) to those of the new, in such cases as the change is too great to allow of the ready recognition of the new name. These lists will be supplied to members at 25c. per set of 26 sheets, post-paid. Address,

ENTOMOLOGICAL SOCIETY OF ONTARIO,

No. 10.

THE

Canadian Entomologist.

VOLUME XX.

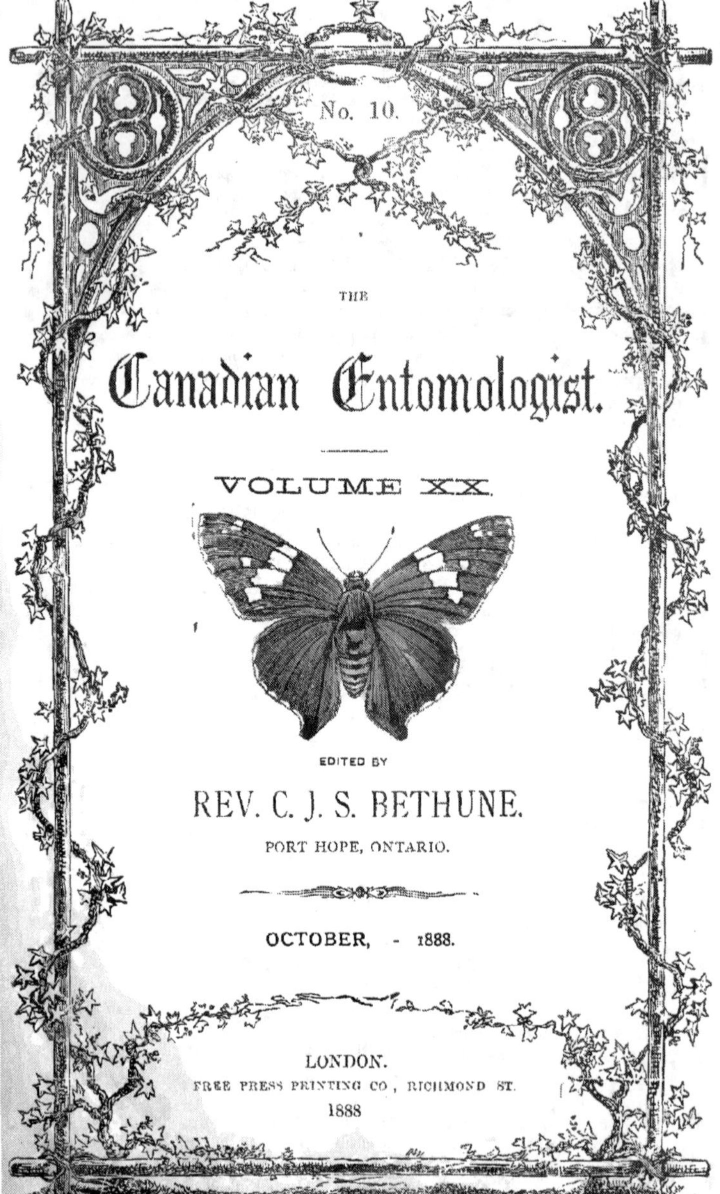

EDITED BY

REV. C. J. S. BETHUNE.

PORT HOPE, ONTARIO.

OCTOBER, - 1888.

LONDON.
FREE PRESS PRINTING CO., RICHMOND ST.
1888

JAPANESE LEPIDOPTERA.

Specimens of the Lepidoptera of Japan for sale.   Price, $10 (U. S. Currency, or Post Office Order) per hundred.   Cash with order.   Address—

REV. H. LOOMIS, Yokohama. Japan.

PAMPHILA and CATOCALA.

The undersigned will pay good price, either in cash or exchange, for perfect specimens of Pamphila and Catocala.

PHILIP LAURENT, 621 Marshall St., Philadelphia, Penn.

REV. W. J. HOLLAND, Ph. D., Pittsburgh, Pa., offers for sale or exchange a limited quantity of JAPANESE LEPIDOPTERA and COLEOPTERA of his own collecting.   Has also on hand a large mass of West African and Asiatic Lepidoptera, for sale or exchange.   Has been authorized to receive subscriptions in the United States and Canada for Mr. H. Pryer's magnificent work upon the Rhopalocera of Japan, to be issued in three parts, 4to., profusely illustrated with colored plates, at $4 a part.   Part I is now ready to deliver to subscribers.   3-12

FOR SALE.

TRANSACTIONS OF THE AMERICAN ENTOMOLOGICAL SOCIETY.—Vols. i. to x ; the first three bound.   Price, $40.00.   The early volumes are scarce.

ENTOMOLOGISTS' MONTHLY MAGAZINE.—Vols. i. to xxiii., except ii. and iii.; up to xvi. bound.   The early volumes of this magazine are not to be had, having long been out of print.   Vol. i. was from Glover's library.   Price, $50.00.

BOISDUVAL AND GUENEE'S SPECIES GENERALE, ETC.—Eight Vols., half mor., in good condition.   Price, $40.00.   WM. H. EDWARDS, Coalburgh, W. Va.

BUTTERFLIES OF NORTH AMERICA.

Part 5, Vol. iii., will be ready for delivery 1st June.

Contents :   Melitæa Rubicunda ; Debis Portlandia ; Erebia Magdalena, E. Haydenii.   Price, $2.25 : 3 plates.

Vol. 1, bound, $35 ;   Vol. 2, $40.

Apply to   HOUGHTON, MIFFLIN & CO.,

Cambridge, Mass

EXCHANGE.

Under this heading two lines will be inserted for 25 cts.; additional matter, 5 cts. per line.

ORTHOPTERA WANTED.—I am especially interested in the study of the Orthoptera, and wish to obtain, either by exchange or purchase, perfect specimens of these insects from all parts.   North American and West Indian material preferred.   Persons having specimens for sale or exchange will please correspond with me.   LAWRENCE BRUNER, West Point, Cuming Co., Nebraska, U. S. A.

THE CANADIAN ENTOMOLOGIST.

Published by the Entomological Society of Ontario.

General Editor—REV. C. J. S. BETHUNE, Port Hope, Ont.
Editing Committee—WM. SAUNDERS, Ottawa ; J. M. DENTON, London ;
CAPT. GAMBLE GEDDES and DR. BRODIE, Toronto.

ANNUAL FEES OF MEMBERSHIP.

For Ordinary Members $1 00
For Associate Members in the United States....................... 1 00
For Associate Members in England............................4s. sterling
For Associate Members elsewhere................................$1 25

The Fees are payable in advance on the 1st of January in each year, and their payment entitles the members to a copy of all the Society's publications during the year, including the Illustrated Annual Report made to the Ontario Government.

Remittances may be made in the form of Express Order, Postal Note, Canadian, U. S. or English Stamps, P. O. Order or draft on New York, but cheques on local banks will not be received.

All remittances and other business communications should be addressed to the Secretary-Treasurer of the Society, W. E. SAUNDERS, 240 Central Ave, London, Ontario.   Send all manuscript for publication to the General Editor.

Canadian Entomologist.—The back volumes 1 to 19 can be supplied at $1 each and cost of transportation (postage 3 cts. a volume to Canada and United States).

Annual Reports.—1870 to 1873 inclusive are out of print ; later numbers can be supplied at 50 cents each, and 2 cts. postage to Canada and United States.

ADVERTISING RATES.
Payable Strictly in Advance.

For each insertion, per inch ....$ 50
One inch per year...... .... 4 00
Half page,   " 10 00
Whole "   " 15 00
Exchange notices of 2 lines, each insertion............ 25
Additional matter in exchange notices, per line....................... 5

SUPPLIES FOR SALE.

ENTOMOLOGICAL PINS.—Nos. 00 to 5 inclusive, in packages of 500 each;
Nos. 6, in packages of 250 $1 per 1000.   Postage 6 cts. per 1000, and every
fraction of 1000, to Canada and United States.

CORK.—¼ inch, 30 cts. per square foot ; postage 6 cts ; ⅛ inch, 18 cts. per
square foot ; postage 6 cts. for 20 inches, and every fraction of 20 inches, to
Canada and United States.

LIST OF CANADIAN COLEOPTERA.—Price 15 cts. each, embracing 55
families, 432 genera, and 1231 species (for labelling cabinets).
Printed Numbers, in sheets, 1 to 2000, for labelling cabinets.

No. 11.

THE

Canadian Entomologist.

VOLUME XX.

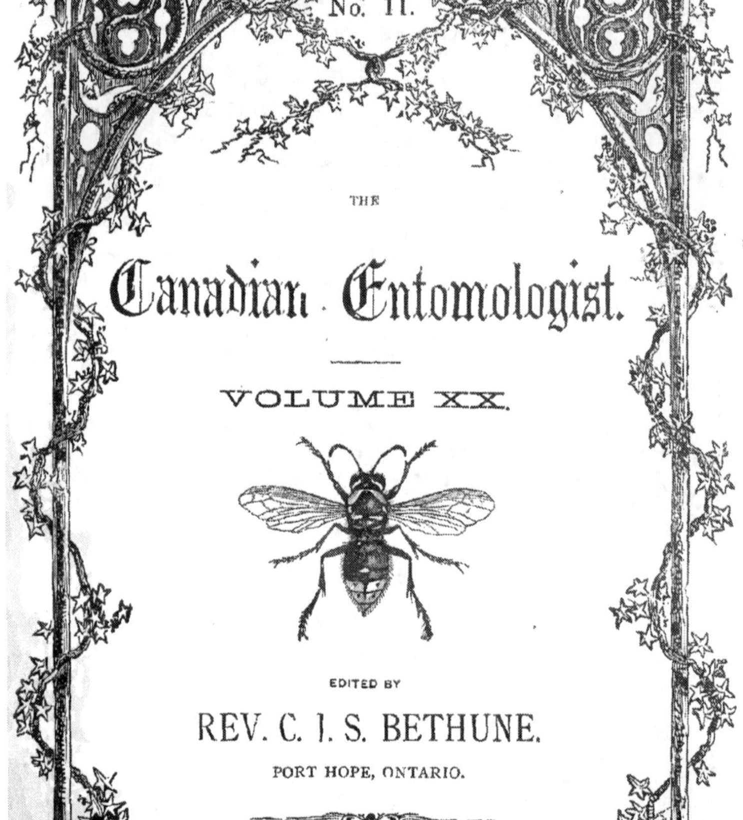

EDITED BY

REV. C. J. S. BETHUNE.

PORT HOPE, ONTARIO.

NOVEMBER, - 1888.

LONDON:
FREE PRESS PRINTING CO., RICHMOND ST.
1888.

The Butterflies of the Eastern United States and Canada

—WITH SPECIAL REFERENCE TO—

NEW ENGLAND.

Their structure in all stages of life, their variation, habits, manners, life histories and their enemies, accompanied by frequent discussions of problems suggested by their study, by Samuel Hubbard Scudder. Issued in twelve monthly parts, beginning November, 1888, of eight plates (colored and plain), and about 144 pages of text. Price $5.00 per part, payable on issue; or $50 for the entire work, if paid during 1888.

Address, SAMUEL H. SCUDDER, Cambridge, Mass.

PAMPHILA and CATOCALA.

The undersigned will pay good price, either in cash or exchange, for perfect specimens of Pamphila and Catocala.

PHILIP LAURENT, 621 Marshall St., Philadelphia, Penn.

North American Lepidoptera.

THE HAWK MOTHS OF NORTH AMERICA: By A. Radcliffe Grote, A. M.

This work in pamphlet form will be sent on remitting price of One Dollar, by the publishers, Homeyer & Meyer, by the Author, Bremen, Germany; or address Rühle & Schlenker, Booksellers, Bremen.

REV. W. J. HOLLAND, Ph. D., Pittsburgh, Pa., offers for sale or exchange a limited quantity of JAPANESE LEPIDOPTERA and COLEOPTERA of his own collecting. Has also on hand a large mass of West African and Asiatic Lepidoptera, for sale or exchange. Has been authorized to receive subscriptions in the United States and Canada for Mr. H. Pryer's magnificent work upon the Rhopalocera of Japan, to be issued in three parts, 4to., profusely illustrated with colored plates, at $4 a part. Part I is now ready to deliver to subscribers.   3-12

NOW READY.

A new and revised *List* of the *Coleoptera* of America north of Mexico, by Samuel Henshaw, assisted by Dr. George H. Horn. Published by the American Entomological Society. Edition limited. **Price, $1.25.** Price List of Entomological papers for sale, mailed on application.

E. T. CRESSON, Treasurer.
P. O. Box 1577, Philadelphia, Pa.

EXCHANGE.

Under this heading two lines will be inserted for 25 cts.; additional matter, 5 cts. per line.

ORTHOPTERA WANTED.—I am especially interested in the study of the Orthoptera, and wish to obtain, either by exchange or purchase, perfect specimens of these insects from all parts. North American and West Indian material preferred. Persons having specimens for sale or exchange will please correspond with me. LAWRENCE BRUNER, West Point, Cuming Co., Nebraska, U. S. A.

THE CANADIAN ENTOMOLOGIST.

Published by the Entomological Society of Ontario.

General Editor—REV. C. J. S. BETHUNE, Port Hope, Ont.
Editing Committee—WM. SAUNDERS, Ottawa ; J. M. DENTON, London ;
CAPT. GAMBLE GEDDES and DR. BRODIE, Toronto.

ANNUAL FEES OF MEMBERSHIP.

For Ordinary Members $1 00
For Associate Members in the United States....................... 1 00
For Associate Members in England................................4s. sterling
For Associate Members elsewhere................................$1 25

The Fees are payable in advance on the 1st of January in each year, and their payment entitles the members to a copy of all the Society's publications during the year, including the Illustrated Annual Report made to the Ontario Government.

Remittances may be made in the form of Express Order, Postal Note, Canadian, U. S. or English Stamps, P. O. Order or draft on New York, but cheques on local banks will not be received.

All remittances and other business communications should be addressed to the Secretary-Treasurer of the Society, W. E. SAUNDERS, 240 Central Ave, London, Ontario. Send all manuscript for publication to the General Editor.

Canadian Entomologist.—The back volumes 1 to 19 can be supplied at $1 each and cost of transportation (postage 3 cts. a volume to Canada and United States).

Annual Reports.—1870 to 1873 inclusive are out of print ; later numbers can be supplied at 50 cents each, and 2 cts. postage to Canada and United States.

ADVERTISING RATES.
Payable Strictly in Advance.

For each insertion, per inch ....$ 50
One inch per year..................... .... 4 00
Half page,   " 10 00
Whole "   " 15 00
Exchange notices of 2 lines, each insertion............. 25
Additional matter in exchange notices, per line........................ 5

SUPPLIES FOR SALE.

ENTOMOLOGICAL PINS.—Nos. 00 to 5 inclusive, in packages of 500 each; Nos. 6, in packages of 250 $1 per 1000. Postage 6 cts. per 1000, and every fraction of 1000, to Canada and United States.

CORK.—¼ inch, 30 cts. per square foot ; postage 6 cts ; ⅛ inch, 18 cts. per square foot ; postage 6 cts. for 20 inches, and every fraction of 20 inches, to Canada and United States.

LIST OF CANADIAN COLEOPTERA.—Price 15 cts. each, embracing 55 families, 432 genera, and 1231 species (for labelling cabinets). Printed Numbers, in sheets, 1 to 2000, for labelling cabinets.

THE

Canadian Entomologist.

VOLUME XX.

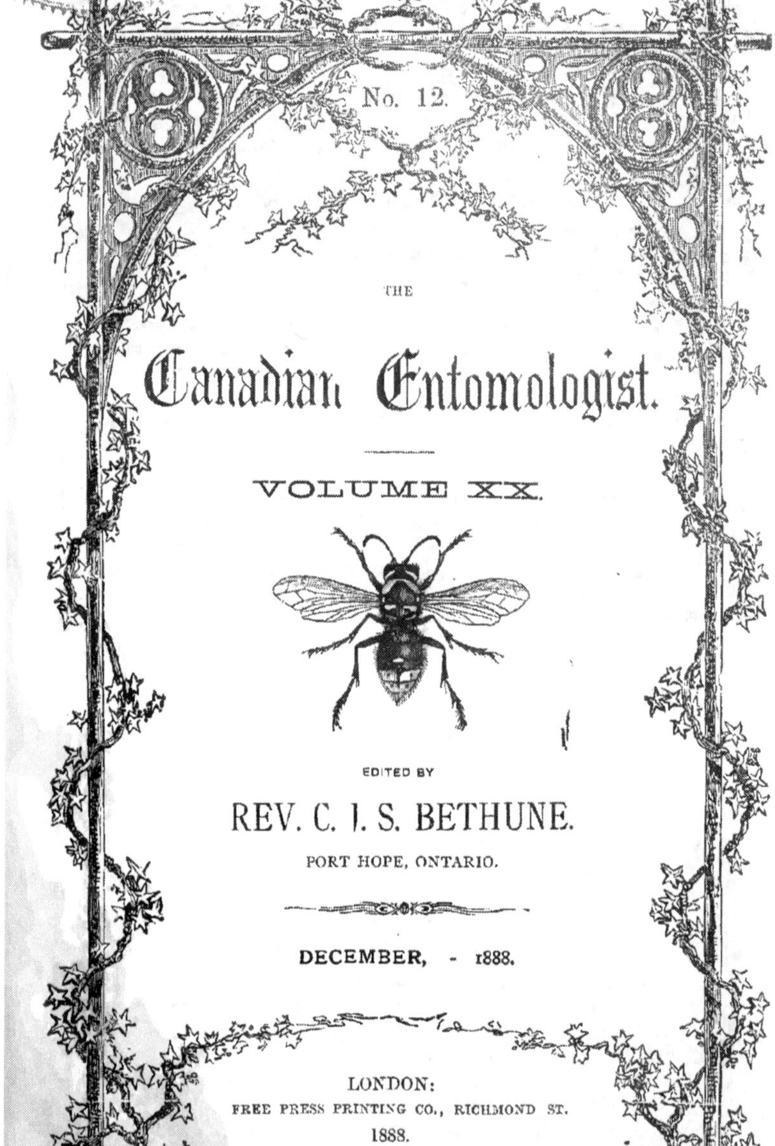

EDITED BY

REV. C. J. S. BETHUNE.

PORT HOPE, ONTARIO.

DECEMBER, - 1888.

LONDON:
FREE PRESS PRINTING CO., RICHMOND ST.
1888.

ENTOMOLOGY for BEGINNERS

For the use of Young Folks, Fruit Growers, Farmers, and Gardeners. By A. S.
PACKARD, M. D:, Ph. D., 12 mo., $1.75.

"It is the best thing of the kind in English, or any other language. There is no
work that I would recommend to the young student so heartily." S. W. WILLISTON,
Professor in Yale University, NEW HAVEN, Conn. U. S. HENRY HOLT & Co.,
Publishers, New York.

THE AMERICAN NATURALIST

Was commenced twenty-two years ago, by an association of the sudents of Professor
Agassiz, at Cambridge. While it has followed the fortunes of its founders from comparative youth to a vigorous maturity, it has gathered to its support most of the biologists and
geologists of North America.

Its constituency of authors includes a majority of the men of this class in the country.

The proprietors have associated with Professors Cope and Kingsley, its principal
editors, a number of leading scientists, whose names are a guarantee of editorial ability.

Dr. C. O. Whitman, of Milwaukee, one of our ablest histologists, directs the department of Microscopic technique.

Prof. W. T. Sedgwick, late of John Hopkins University, now of the School of
Technology, Boston, has charge of the Physiology.

Prof. C. E. Bessey, of the University of Nebraska, edits the Botanical departments.

The division of Anthropology is under direction of Mr. Thos. Wilson, whose connection with the Smithsonian Institution, Washington, D. C., gives him exceptional facilities.

Prof. J. H. Comstock, the able Professor of Entomology of Cornell University,
sustains both pure and economic Entomology.

Prof. W. S. Bayley, of the University of Wisconsin, has charge of Mineralogy.

Mr. W. N. Lockington, naturalist and man of letters, of Philadelphia, furnishes the
best, and indeed the only abstract of the results of Geographical Explorations of the
World that is published on this Continent.

Prof. J. A. Ryder, of the University of Pennsylvania, edits the department of Embry-
ology, a subject in which he is a well-known master.

It has been the aim of the NATURALIST to preserve its well-known national character,
which is illustrated in the wide distribution of its editorial responsibilities.

It appears to be the most favored medium of publication of the naturalists and
biologists in the United States, when they wish to bring the results of their investigation
before the general public in a more or less popular form. *It is the only magazine in the
world to-day which keeps its readers en rapport with the work of Americans in the field
of the Natural Sciences.* The NATURALIST publishes 96 large octavo pages per month,
with numerous illustrations. TERMS : $4 PER YEAR ; 40c. PER NUMBER.

LEONARD SCOTT PUBLICATION CO.,

501 Chestnut Street, PHILADELPHIA.

NORTH AMERICAN DIPTERA.

Synopsis of the Families and Genera of North American Diptera (exclusive of
the Genera of the Nematocera and Muscidæ sens. lat.), with Bibliography and New
Species, 1878-88. By S. W WILLISTON ; 82 pages ; price, $1.00.

Address the publisher,

JAMES T. HATHAWAY, New Haven, Conn

PAMPHILA and CATOCALA.

The undersigned will pay good price, either in cash or exchange, for perfect
specimens of Pamphila and Catocala.

PHILIP LAURENT, 621 Marshall St., Philadelphia, Penn.

THE CANADIAN ENTOMOLOGIST.

Published by the Entomological Society of Ontario.

General Editor—REV. C. J. S. BETHUNE, Port Hope, Ont.
Editing Committee—WM. SAUNDERS, Ottawa; J. M. DENTON, London;
CAPT. GAMBLE GEDDES and DR. BRODIE, Toronto.

ANNUAL FEES OF MEMBERSHIP.

For Ordinary Members $1 00
For Associate Members in the United States...................... 1 00
For Associate Members in England...........................4s. sterling
For Associate Members elsewhere.................................$1 25

The Fees are payable in advance on the 1st of January in each year, and their payment entitles the members to a copy of all the Society's publications during the year, including the Illustrated Annual Report made to the Ontario Government.

Remittances may be made in the form of Express Order, Postal Note, Canadian, U. S. or English Stamps, P. O. Order or draft on New York, but cheques on local banks will not be received.

All remittances and other business communications should be addressed to the Secretary-Treasurer of the Society, W. E. SAUNDERS, 240 Central Ave, London, Ontario.   Send all manuscript for publication to the General Editor.

Canadian Entomologist.—The back volumes 1 to 19 can be supplied at $1 each and cost of transportation (postage 3 cts. a volume to Canada and United States).

Annual Reports.—1870 to 1873 inclusive are out of print; later numbers can be supplied at 50 cents each, and 2 cts. postage to Canada and United States.

ADVERTISING RATES.
Payable Strictly in Advance.

For each insertion, per inch ....$ 50
One inch per year.. 4 00
Half page,   " 10 00
Whole "   " 15 00
Exchange notices of 2 lines, each insertion..........................   25
Additional matter in exchange notices, per line......................   5

SUPPLIES FOR SALE.

ENTOMOLOGICAL PINS.—Nos. 00 to 5 inclusive, in packages of 500 each; Nos. 6, in packages of 250 $1 per 1000.   Postage 6 cts. per 1000, and every fraction of 1000, to Canada and United States.

CORK.—¼ inch, 30 cts. per square foot; postage 6 cts; ⅛ inch, 18 cts. per square foot; postage 6 cts. for 20 inches, and every fraction of 20 inches, to Canada and United States.

LIST OF CANADIAN COLEOPTERA.—Price 15 cts. each, embracing 55 families, 432 genera, and 1231 species (for labelling cabinets). Printed Numbers, in sheets, 1 to 2000, for labelling cabinets.